Miracles
of
Christmas

Miracles
of
Christmas

Santa
Miracles

and

Christmas
Miracles

by

Brad Steiger &
Sherry Hansen Steiger

Avon, Massachusetts

Santa
Miracles

Santa
Miracles

50 True Stories That Celebrate the Most
Magical Time of the Year

Brad Steiger &
Sherry Hansen Steiger

Avon, Massachusetts

Published by
Adams Media, a division of F+W Media, Inc.
57 Littlefield Street, Avon, MA 02322 U.S.A.

ISBN 13: 978-1-59869-612-7
Printed in the United States of America.

Interior photo © Martin Valigursky / istockphoto.com

Introduction

When our daughter Melissa was teaching English in Japan, we were surprised when she told us that Santa Claus was extremely popular in all the department stores and served the same role as the jolly iconic representative of the December holiday that he did in North America.

Apparently, Santa's popularity in Japan has not diminished in the years after Melissa returned to the States. Recently, a diver dressed as Santa Claus swam with a dolphin at Sea Paradise in Yokohoma, Kanagawa, Japan.

Nearly every city in the United States has its own Santa Claus parade, and even small rural villages have Santa arriving by fire engine or some other vehicle to greet the kids with bags of candy. There is hardly a mall or department store that doesn't have Santa and his elves visit for at least a few days during the festive season between Thanksgiving and Christmas Eve.

In 1937, Charles W. Howard established a Santa Claus School that still thrives today. Located in Midland, Michigan, the mission of the school is to uphold the traditions and preserve the history of Santa Claus.

This is not a book about who Santa Claus is, but, rather, a collection of stories about the miracles of happiness, love, and joy that his spirit can bring to individuals of all ages.

There are numerous histories of the evolution of Santa, the best-known and best-loved of all mysterious gift-givers in the world. Numerous scholars agree that there were many Pagans who worshipped a red-clad hearth god who would come down the chimney to bless those he deemed worthy of his favor.

Others have traced the origins of Santa's supernatural powers to Norse legends of Odin, who flew across the night skies and cured those who sought his powers as a god to heal them of illnesses contracted during the long winters. Some researchers suggest that traditions about Odin became combined with those of his fellow Norse god Thor, who rode a chariot drawn by two goats named Cracker and Cruncher. And some scholars claim that Santa is simply a modernized version of the tribal shaman, who dressed in brightly colored robes and who may have worn a set of antlers as a symbol of his mystical powers.

Christmas as a time to honor the birth of Jesus probably began about the year 336 when Roman Christians combined their observance of their savior's nativity with Saturnalia, the popular Pagan celebration of the festival of lights that coincided with the Winter Solstice on December 25.

To find a precise date for the advent of a Santa Claus figure in Christian Europe is more difficult. We know that the popular bishop Nicholas of Myra, who died in Lycia, Anatolia (present day Turkey) on December 6 in about 350, had a reputation as being a generous person who was even capable of producing miracles. Credited as the "Worker of Wonders" both before and after his death, Nicholas was recognized as a saint by the Eastern Catholic Church in the Eleventh century. By that time, he had become the third most beloved figure in Christendom, after Jesus and Mary. He became the patron saint of Greece and Russia, as well as many cities throughout Europe.

But the question remains: When did St. Nicholas become associated with the idea that his spirit could mysteriously visit good children on Christmas Eve—or December 6, depending upon the family's location?

We believe the tradition began in a French village on December 6 sometime during the twelfth century. Honoring their patron saint, St. Nicholas, local nuns decided to bring candy to all the children in the village who had been good during the past year. The nuns entered some homes when the families were away and left candy in the shoes of the good children and switches in those of the naughty children. Because the energetic nuns managed to cover so much territory, some parents thought it had to have been St. Nicholas himself who had brought the gifts. From this French village and the efforts of the generous nuns, the Christmas visits of St. Nick spread slowly across all of Europe.

The evolution of gifts from candy to larger items may have been a result of the blending of traditions regarding the three Magi, the three wise men from the Orient, who brought gifts to the manger where the baby Jesus lay, and the giving of gifts by the Romans who celebrated Saturnalia. The belief that St. Nicholas enters a home through its chimney survives as a tradition established by the Pagan hearth god's means of entry.

St. Nicholas was often named according to the spirit that he represented. In France, he was known as "Pere Noel" and in Spain as "Papa Noel," Father Christmas. In Denmark and Germany, his title became

"Christmas Man." In northern Germany, interestingly enough, he was named after the Christian holiday—"Christkindle" or "Kris Kringle," the latter of which has become an alternate name for Santa Claus in our contemporary culture. During the 1500s, the English dropped St. Nicholas after the nation became Protestant and favored naming the miraculous gift-giver "Father Christmas," a much thinner and austere individual in contrast to plump old St. Nick. In the 1600s, when the Dutch began immigrating to the British colonies in America, they brought with them their "Sinterklaus" or "Sinte Klaus," who, in their colony of New Amsterdam (presently New York City), became Santa Claus.

The Dutch colonists viewed Santa Claus or "Santy" as a very tall, slender, dignified, and somewhat stately individual, as befitted a benevolent saintly spirit. Washington Irving, famous for his tale of the eerie spook, the Headless Horseman in "The Legend of Sleepy Hollow," reinvented the traditional image of the somewhat aloof Santa Claus and in his *A History of New York*, recast Santy as a good-natured, jolly guardian spirit who soared above the treetops in a wagon and dropped presents down the chimneys of good children.

In 1822, Clement C. Moore wrote the classic poem, "A Visit from St. Nicholas," which described Santa

Claus driving a sleigh drawn by eight tiny reindeer. Moore also spoke of Santa as being a jolly, plump elf, thus linking him to the ancient Pagan traditions of the generous shaman surrounded by his supernatural entities, the elves, the same beings who observed humans throughout the year to see if they merited being blessed or gifted during the Yule season.

Thomas Nast, a political cartoonist, famous for popularizing the image of the Democratic Party's donkey, began in 1863 to create images of Santa Claus for the Christmas covers of *Harper's Weekly*. In 1866, inspired by Moore's poem, Nast created the famous drawing of Santa Claus in his North Pole workshop, reviewing the list of good and bad children. Santa is depicted as definitely plump and jolly, a cheery gift-giver who rides off into the night on a sleigh pulled by reindeer to deliver gifts around the world.

Nast captured the image of Santa Claus that remained virtually unchanged until slight modifications were made in 1931 in the advertisements featured on the back covers of popular magazines. Coca Cola, the popular soft drink, commissioned artist Haddon Sundblom to paint a new Santa in their print ads from 1931 to 1964. Building upon Nast's famous drawings, Sundblom polished the image of Santa Claus that is most well known today—a plump, jolly, red-cheeked, white-bearded man attired in a bright red suit trimmed with white fur, a black belt, and leather boots.

The depictions of Santa Claus in the popular media—especially, perhaps in motion pictures—remain very flexible. In the warmhearted classic, *A Miracle on 34th Street* (1947), a department store Santa might really be the kindly old elf himself. In *The Santa Clause* (1994), a man commits the unthinkable when he accidentally kills Santa and magically begins transforming into Santa Claus and assuming his duties. The 2007 film, *Fred Claus* reveals two startling bits of information: St. Nicholas has an older brother who has always been jealous of Nick's selfless acts of generosity; and once an individual is canonized, his entire family remains frozen in time. Because of Nicholas's status as a beloved saint, Fred, a ne'er-do-well still alive today, is given the chance to redeem himself by helping his brother, Santa Claus, at the North Pole. The trapped-in-time destiny of a saint's family no doubt came as news to the Vatican.

As we declared at the beginning of this Introduction, this is not a book about Santa or the many traditions that surround him. The Santa Miracles experienced by the individuals who have contacted us throughout the years really occur in a magical space and time that may well be separate from the normal three-dimensional world that we all share. Indeed, some of the miracles described in this book may have taken place within a timeless magical kingdom that contains the essence of the true meaning of Christmas.

It is our firm hope that all readers, young and old, will experience the "deep magic" and true wonder of this collection of Santa Miracles.

—Brad Steiger and Sherry Hansen Steiger

As is true of many of us, David Oester learned about Santa's miracles as a youth. This is his story:

Let me give you some background. I attended the first six years of school in a two-room building; the first room held the first through fourth grades and the second room was for the fifth and sixth graders. The schoolhouse was located at Deer Island, Oregon, a campsite used by Lewis and Clark on their journey to the Oregon coast on November 5, 1805. In the 1950s, it was a wide spot on Highway 30 that followed the Columbia River to Astoria.

It was during this time that my dad, Raleigh Oester, got a job as a rural mail carrier for the Deer Island area. These were hard times for many people. I remember one of my classmates would not come to school one day a week, and it was always the same day each week. It turns out that that particular day was washday at his home and he only had one shirt and trousers to wear.

Another friend never wore shoes during the summer, as he had to save them for the school year.

I didn't realize while growing up that an economic depression had caused severe poverty. I had food to eat and a shelter over my head and never gave it another thought. I never knew that it was hard on my mom and dad who struggled to keep us clothed and fed. Recently, my mom told me that a few days before Christmas she would hide some of our old toys and then wrap them up so we would have something under the Christmas tree to open.

My most vivid childhood memory is when my brothers and I would accompany my parents on Christmas Eve to spread some holiday cheer. Dad would put on his red Santa suit, complete with padding and a fake white beard, load up the car with presents, and deliver gifts to some of the children on his mail route who he knew would not have a Christmas because money was too tight.

I did not realize at the time that many of the homes we visited were not much more than shacks. Dad knew the names of everyone in each household.

He knew the hardships they suffered, as he too experienced them in the past. He would park the family car away from the driveway so the occupants would not recognize it as the mailman's car. Then, my dad would call out the names to my brothers, mother, and I, and we would retrieve the presents and stuff them into his white bag.

When the family answered his knock on the door, he would greet the parents and children by name. They had no idea how this man dressed in a red Santa suit and a white beard could possibly know their names. The children's eyes would shine with a brightness that is hard to explain, and the parents' mouths would drop open in shock.

I remember the last stop we made. Dad walked up to the dairy farm, passing the main house, and stopped at the hired hands' cabin. He knocked on the door, and when the children opened it, he greeted them with a "Merry Christmas" and handed out the wrapped gifts.

While Dad was delivering the presents, I asked my mom why he gave away all the presents. I was thinking of how nice they would have been for our own Christmas.

Mom looked at me and said, "Those children will not have a Christmas; their parents are too poor to buy their children anything. You will have a Christmas, and now so will they."

"But why does Dad dress up as Santa," I asked. My mother told me it was so not to embarrass the families. They must not think it is charity, but a miracle on Christmas Eve.

I never forgot the kindness that my parents showed for those who were less fortunate than we were. My dad never attended church, but he lived the higher spiritual law of "love thy fellow man," a lesson that has stuck with me.

Years later, as a husband and father, when my oldest son was working on his Eagle Scout badge, he chose a "sub-for-Santa" project. He collected newspapers and soda cans, held car washes, and created other money-making projects to raise money for a family with two children who could not afford Christmas presents.

My son bought gifts for each of the children and cooked a turkey, potatoes, and all of the other trimmings for a nice Christmas dinner. A local merchant donated a Christmas tree and he built a tree stand, wrapped the presents, and together we hauled the dinner, presents, and tree to the family's home.

When my son told the woman who answered the door what he was doing there, she was shocked—especially when she saw the tree, dinner, and gifts my son brought into the house.

Even after he set up the tree and delivered all the gifts, the family had no idea who this young man was or why he performed a miracle for them on Christmas Eve.

I was so proud of my son for carrying on the tradition begun by his grandfather.

J acob White is completely convinced that he saw Santa Claus when he was eight-years-old. No one will ever convince him otherwise. Here is Jacob's story:

I grew up in a small town in Idaho, not terribly far from Boise City, and every Christmas the entire White family would drive to the old home place outside of Nampa where Grandma and Grandpa White still lived. Everyone—my mom and dad, my two uncles, my aunts, and us five cousins—would try to arrive two or three days before Christmas Eve. We'd attend Christmas Eve services at the little country church that my father and his two brothers had attended as kids, and then we'd head back to our grandparents' big, old farm-house for a fantastic dinner.

Grandpa White always had a Christmas tree set up in the living room, and on the first day that all of us cousins would arrive, we would have the honor of decorating the branches with the same lights, colored balls, and streamers that had served the White family for at least thirty years. I remember that some of the wires for the lights had electrician's tape wrapped around the worn spots.

On Christmas Eve, after Grandma White read "The Night Before Christmas," the kids were sent up to bed. Since it was a large house, there was plenty of room for everyone. My brother John and I got one room with a double bed, and our three cousins—Grace, Judy, and Margie—got another with two single beds. Since Grace, at eleven, was the oldest, she claimed a bed all to herself, while Judy and Margie had to snuggle up in the other bed. John and I could hear the girls whis-pering and giggling, and we lay there talking about what we were going to get from Santa on Christmas morning.

Grace, who thought she was so smart and grown-up, had tried to spread doubt earlier that evening when she said that she didn't believe that there really was a Santa. She got shushed pretty quickly by her parents, because she was upsetting Judy and Margie, who were both five years old and firm believers in Santa Claus.

I had heard rumors myself from some kids at school who no longer believed in Santa, but Mom said that they were certain to get lumps of coal in their stockings on Christmas morning. I didn't repeat the negative whispers to John, who, at six, had no doubts about the reality of the big guy in the bright red suit.

Grandma White had replaced the usual night light in the hallway with one shaped like an angel in honor of the season. Both the bedrooms where we cousins lay trying to fall asleep faced the hallway, and as I was lying in bed looking at the light, my eyelids grew heavier. Johnny was just drifting off. At least two of the girls were still whispering.

Suddenly, the night light was blocked by the shadow of a very big man. The adult men in the White family were all tall and quite thin. This man was extremely rotund. I shook Johnny awake, and I could hear the girls beginning to talk out loudly.

From above his head, a reddish light shone on the man. We could all clearly see the image of Santa Claus. He wore a red suit, black boots, and his white beard came down to the middle of his chest. He stood there for about ten seconds or so, smiling and waving at us. Then he disappeared.

All five of us kids ran screaming down the stairs. It was a wonder that one of us didn't trip and break a body part or two. We scampered into the living room, shouting at the top of our lungs that we had seen Santa Claus. Grace—the scoffer, the disbeliever—was screaming the loudest.

It took a long time for the adults to get us kids quieted down. We had all seen the same thing: A fat, jolly, bearded man in a bright red suit. Of course, all the grownups laughed at us. Grandpa wondered if we had sneaked down the stairs and sampled some of the cider from the big glass bowl while they weren't looking.

Since Grace and I were the oldest, we were singled out for false accusations of having told the younger kids ghost stories and having managed to scare them—and ourselves—with our spooky tales.

All of us kids knew what we had seen, and when we get together now, we still talk about the night we saw Santa Claus. It didn't matter how much our parents and Grandpa and Grandma teased us; we knew that for some unknown reason we were blessed—singled out, if you will—to have seen Santa.

I have thought long and hard about our vision over the many Christmas Eves since that very special one. Santa Claus is a supernatural being, and maybe as a spirit, he really can project his image to thousands, maybe millions, of kids who truly believe in the idea of a kind, benevolent gift bearer. Or perhaps the spirit of Christmas itself can manifest to the hearts and minds of young children however they may best receive the message of love and sharing.

Bruce Shayne Nelson told us a remarkable story of a true Santa miracle his cousin Tom had related to him that occurred during Tom's service in Vietnam:

One Christmas a few years back, we sat around the dining room table in Grandma's apartment: uncles, cousins, grandchildren, nieces and nephews, most of us stuffed with too much Christmas food and drink, listening to the shouts of the kids playing in the back room, to the voice of an uncle on the phone exchanging Christmas greetings with a relative in another state, and to the sound of the football game on TV mixed with carols from a little radio somewhere. In the air was the pleasant confusion of a late evening Christmas family gathering. Outside there was hardly any snow, but enough of a nip for it to feel *Christmassy*. Inside, we were moving to that mellow state which comes toward the end of a nice family holiday gathering.

"'I'll be Home for Christmas.' I love that song," Tom said as he toyed with a piece of pumpkin pie. "I've *always* loved it."

"Sure. It's a wonderful song." I concurred.

"For me," Tom went on, "it goes all the way back to 'Nam. That's where that song really meant something. In a jungle full of guys who wanted to kill you and in heat that had you sweating day and night."

"I'll bet." I said.

"That year, all of the guys in the outfit decided we were going to have a Midnight Mass on Christmas. I mean, guys of all religions, you understand. It was somehow just understood and agreed on. So we ordered up a chaplain."

"You *ordered* one?"

"Yeah, you know the Army," said Tom. "And it wasn't easy, either. Nothing's easy in the Army, particularly in 'Nam. Headquarters came back and said that maybe we *could* get a chaplain for Christmas Eve, but only if we had an 'appropriate space' for him. You know, such and such enclosed space, with so many places to sit, an altar, lighting . . . I forget all the details, but there were plenty. You know how the Army is."

"Sure, I guess I do."

"Well, what was really nice, I think, was the way everyone really pitched in. It was a lot of work getting that space together in time for Headquarters to approve it. And I think every guy in the outfit put in plenty of extra effort to make it happen. It was great!"

"But how did the idea get started?"

"Oh, jeez, sometime in October or something . . . I don't remember just who came up with the idea first, but before you know it, it was like *everyone's* idea. We scrounged, and swapped, and built, and dug and . . . and remember, we were doing this in the middle of a war. And in between the times we were trying to deal with Charlie. I mean, we weren't just sitting out there in the bush, we had a war going on. Like a lot of little guys hiding in the foliage a thousand yards away, or so—armed with pretty nasty weapons. Just try to level a terrain in those conditions, and then somehow come up with a hundred folding chairs or benches out in the bush like our outfit was. That stuff doesn't come in on the choppers . . . not usually."

"So you improvise."

"Yeah, or build it, or scrounge, as I said, but we were motivated. We were gonna have that Midnight Mass, period."

"And you did."

"Oh yeah, and how!"

"We even managed to cobble together a Santa costume for the big night," Tom chuckled. "You can imagine how tough that was, rounding up three or four yards of red material in the middle of a Southeast Asian jungle, and getting it sewn together into something resembling the Old Fellow's traditional outfit. You won't find many tailors in a company of infantrymen . . . but we still pulled it off. The mess sergeant, affectionately known as 'Tubby,' had the right figure for the job, and he agreed to be our Saint Nick on the big evening. The suit, which two of the boys eventually stitched together, fit him surprisingly well.

"An even tougher feature of Santa was the beard. One of the lads went as far as risking his neck by heading outside the perimeter and combing some nearby villages, trying to get something that would serve as a respectable beard. He claimed he had even offered to buy the beards off several of the old Viet grandpas in the region, but without any luck.

"'It didn't matter how much I offered, those old dudes just kept shaking their heads,' he said.

"So, our two volunteer tailors finally tore the Major's pet pillow apart and somehow got that sewn into a beard that almost looked like the real thing. With the whole outfit in place, Tubby looked a heck of a lot better than he ever did in his combat fatigues.

And seeing him there, blazing red and sweating like a horse in the boiling sun of Nam, practicing his 'Ho ho ho!' we all suddenly knew the rest was going to fall into place.

"And just the space was something. We had two huge hospital tents sewn together. It was beautiful. It didn't look like any church I'd ever seen, but considering where we were, it was quite a creation."

"And the chaplain came?"

"Oh yeah, we did our part, so they finally sent in a chaplain by chopper. Just in time for Christmas Eve."

"A great moment, huh?"

"Sure, here we are a thousand miles from anywhere, having Midnight Mass, just like we were home. And we're all singing. This chaplain had a nice strong voice and he's leading us in all the Christmas songs."

"Like, 'I'll Be Home for Christmas'?"

"Lots of them. And right in the middle of singing that one, Charlie opens up and we start getting rained on. Incoming mortars."

"Wow!"

"But this chaplain was something, you know. We got us a good one. He just kind of raised his voice a bit, sang louder, you know, and kept on singing, and we all stayed there singing with him. And not just that song, either. On he goes to the next, and the next."

"And the rounds are still coming in?"

"Cripes, I'll say. But at that point, no one was going to give up, not if the chaplain didn't. Normally, you'd run for the sand-bags and the shelters, but we just went on singing. It was something."

"You were *all* crazy!"

"It was Christmas! And hey, I told you, we were decided we were gonna have that Midnight Mass."

"Hell or high water . . . or mortars."

"Exactly. And the best thing was, about the time that service was over, Charlie finally let up. Ran out of mortar shells, maybe. And we came out of the tent and the place was flattened."

"The tent?"

"No, everything *but* the tent! I'm telling you that those incoming rounds had leveled everything above ground. But not a single guy in the outfit got hurt."

"Because you were all in the tent."

"Yeah. Normally, an attack like that, you'd have at least have a couple of casualties. Even with everyone dug in. Maybe more. Like, *right* next to the chapel we had put up the mess hall. Made of corrugated iron and stuff like that. It was *flattened*, gone, like just about everything else in the camp. If we'd been in *there*, there wouldn't have been many of us left in one piece."

"But no one got a scratch!?"

"I'm telling you, we could hardly believe it ourselves. Not even any shrapnel coming through the walls. And the funny thing was, all the rest of camp had been in the pitch dark, the only thing lit up at all was our tent chapel. Lit up like the proverbial Christmas tree."

"A miracle?"

"Call it what you want. It was great!"

"I can understand a little better now why you like that song so much!"

"Yeah," said Tom, a far-away look in his eye. "It always takes me back, you know what I mean?"

"Sure, but it's twenty-five years later, Tom, and this time you are home for Christmas."

"Yeah," said Tom. "Except when I hear that song. And then I'm back in 'Nam. At the Midnight Mass of my life and a real Santa miracle."

Bill did not hesitate to admit that growing up in a medium-sized city in Arkansas, he had been a troubled teenager. He quickly added that he had never done any kind of drugs or physically harmed anyone, but he had expressed his teenaged angst in acts of vandalism against people's property. And once, he admitted, he did do something that could have resulted in someone getting badly hurt—if he hadn't been arrested before his prank went too far.

At thirteen, Bill had begun his career of minor crimes by perpetuating an age-old tradition of flushing a cherry bomb down a toilet in the boy's bathroom at Thomas Jefferson Junior High School. He had made certain that he had been alone in the bathroom before dropping the depth bomb into the toilet, so he got away with that serious prank without being caught. Unfortunately for the school's budget, the cherry bomb managed to spring severe leaks in some outdated plumbing and flooded several class-rooms on the floor below.

The fact that Bill's nasty deed remained cloaked in anonymity encouraged him to continue his minor reign of terror. He consistently egged his math's teach-er's car until she finally had to get a new paint job. He threw a rock through the picture window of a grocer who had caught him stealing some candy bars and who had threatened to call the police if he ever again caught Bill shoplifting.

Bill's life of crime came to an end one Halloween night, however, when at the age of seventeen, he was caught dropping ripe tomatoes on cars passing under the Twelfth Street bridge. Bill was laughing so hard as the rotten tomatoes spattered on the hoods, roofs, and windshields of unsuspecting motorists that he didn't even hear the two police officers who came up behind him and grabbed him by the arms.

"What's the matter with you, kid?" one of the offi-cers growled. "You could cause someone to have an accident!"

"C'mon, officers," Bill laughed. "It's Halloween night. You know, trick or treat."

The shorter, stouter of the two officers shook his head and looked at Bill as if he had discovered a new species of idiot. "Well, punk, this little trick of yours is going to earn you a real treat in the slammer."

Bill was incredulous. The police officers were actually going to arrest him for such a harmless prank as dropping rotten tomatoes on cars. Unbelievable. Where was their Halloween spirit?

By the time the judge had finished lecturing Bill, he had a clearer idea of the terrible consequences that his "harmless" Halloween prank could have worked on unsuspecting motorists who suddenly had one of his tomato bombs splatter across their windshields, thus startling them, possibly blinding them, and causing them to crash or to career into oncoming traffic.

The desk sergeant had called his parents, and Bill could hear his mother crying throughout the judge's harsh scolding.

"I felt terrible hearing Mom crying," Bill said, "but the fact that Dad was standing there so quiet and grim-faced bothered me even more. I didn't fear a whipping when I got home. Neither of my parents every laid a hand on me. But I really looked up to Dad and I knew I had disappointed him."

Bill's parents would have to pay a fine for his act of public vandalism and possible crime of reckless endangerment. He was sentenced to sixty days of community service. Bill was also ordered to return to the court on December 15.

Bill said that he put on his best "tough guy" act when some of the neighborhood boys would come by the areas where he was picking up trash in public restrooms or raking leaves in the parks. He had never before smoked cigarettes, but whenever he saw any kids he knew approaching him, he would shake one out of a pack and light up. Sometimes he would cough or his eyes would tear up from the smoke, but he always managed to have a butt dangling on his lips when his friends came around.

He took a lot of teasing about getting caught and being a punk from some of the actual tough guys in his school, but Bill had a ready lingo all set to spiel off that would put down the police and ridicule the judge. In his opinion, Bill gave the impression of the perfect social rebel, hostile and defiant against all authority figures.

On December 15, Bill stood once again before the judge and heard him pronounce his final act of community service.

"I couldn't believe my ears," Bill said. "He ordered me to put on a Santa suit and distribute gifts at the local orphanage on December 23. Two police officers—the same two who arrested me—would officially escort me to and from the place."

As he left the courtroom, Bill was handed a Santa suit, complete with cap and broad black belt. The desk sergeant, a man of at least 260 pounds, chuckled and advised Bill to tuck in lots of pillows to fill out the suit. That was the suit that he always wore when he played Santa for the department Christmas party.

Word soon got around at the high school about Bill's unusual sentence, and because at that time he weighed about 145 pounds, he was constantly teased about having to put on some weight before his debut of Santa.

"I still played the tough guy," Bill said. "I told everyone that I was going to put Tabasco sauce and red peppers in the little kids' candy, that I would put dead mice in some of the packages, that I would smoke a cigarette and try to have Santa's beard catch fire."

On the afternoon of December 23, while his mother was helping him adjust the pillows in the over-sized Santa suit, she asked Bill to treat the little orphans with kindness. Bill grunted.

"I'm serious," his mother said, her eyes misting. "Those little children are so desperate for love and affection, hoping so much that some family, someone who will be their mommy and daddy will come to the orphanage and say, 'Oh, you sweet little girl, we want you for our daughter.'"

Bill remembered being puzzled by his mother's display of emotion. Suddenly she sat down on the edge of his bed and began to cry. Bill sat down beside her and awkwardly placed an arm around her shoulders. He had never before seen his mother cry, and he felt helpless.

She wiped her eyes with a handkerchief and took a few deep breaths, trying to compose herself.

What she said next, Bill remembered, truly rocked his teenaged world. "I was an orphan," she said. "I know the pain of living with dozens of other kids, hoping the next couple through the orphanage will pick you and allow you to have a home life. I . . . I was never chosen. I never had a family life like your father and I have tried to give you."

Bill protested. She had always told him that Grandpa and Grandma Meyers had died in an automobile accident when she was a little girl and she had gone to live with her aunt Sara.

His mother nodded. Her parents had been killed in an car accident—when she was twenty months old. The administrator of the orphanage in which she lived until she was eighteen was such a kind lady that all the children called her "Aunt Sara." She had won a scholarship to college. The second year that she was teaching elementary school, she had met Bill's father and they were married soon afterward.

"I did not have any time to absorb this incredible revelation from my mother," Bill said. "She had barely completed her story when the doorbell rang, announcing the arrival of my two escorts to the orphanage." All the way to the orphanage, the two officers warned Bill to be on his best behavior. Finally, one of them turned to him in the backseat and said that he actually looked pretty good in the Santa suit.

"I had none of my usual repertoire of wisecracks with which to snap back at the officers," Bill said. "All I could think about was the terrible time that my mother had to go through as an orphan, being rejected time and time again by prospective parents. How she must have hoped this or that couple would be her mom and dad, then being left, rejected with the other little boys and girls who no one wanted. For the first time in my life, I really, really appreciated Mom. How could she be so kind, so understanding, so well-adjusted, so resourceful, after all she had been through?"

And then Bill thought of what a disappointment he must be to both his mother and his father. Here he was a troublemaker, a juvenile delinquent, almost a criminal—and they still loved him and treated him with respect. They had stood by him in court and had never once brought up his arrest or his having to do community service. They had been supportive of everything that he had ever done. How could he be such a misfit when he had such wonderful parents?

Against every ounce of his will, Bill suddenly found himself crying in shame and humiliation.

"Hey, kid, what's the matter?" the stout officer asked, looking over his shoulder.

"I have a cold," Bill said. "I have to blow my nose."

Bill dug in the pockets of the Santa suit, looking for something with which to blow his nose and wipe away his tears.

The officer sighed and handed him a couple sheets of tissue. "Santa should always be prepared for any emergency," he scolded Bill.

"Talk about being unprepared," Bill said. "I was completely unprepared for the faces of those little boys and girls at the orphanage. I guessed the oldest kid was about nine and their ages ranged all the way down to some who were barely toddlers. But every single one of them was excited at seeing Santa. I was completely unprepared for the rush of emotion that I felt when I felt their joy.

"And in every little girl's face," Bill went on, "I saw my mother's. Whenever I gave a toy to one of the girls and saw the expression of gratitude, I saw my own mother as she must have looked at that age, grateful for any small act of kindness."

Bill knows that a skinny teenager couldn't have made a very convincing Santa Claus, but he also recalls that every child there forgave his awkwardness and his lack of experience at being a jolly dispenser of gifts. When Bill had given the last gift from Santa's bag of presents, he joined the children and two of the orphanage's employees in singing a rousing chorus of "Jingle Bells."

As he walked with the police officers back to the squad car, both of the men gave him hearty slaps of approval across his back.

"You did all right in there, kid," one of the men said. "The little guys and gals really seemed to like you."

The stout officer grumbled, "We were afraid you were going to be a wise guy, but you pulled off the assignment just fine. We'll put in a good word for you with the judge. We'll tell him that you must have had a personality adjustment."

"Either that," the other officer laughed, "or we just saw a miracle take place." As he crawled into the back-seat of the cruiser, Bill agreed with the officers that a kind of miracle had occurred.

"I suppose you can say that this was my Santa miracle," Bill concluded. "And I—not to mention my parents and teachers—were pleased that the effects of the miracle have lasted ever since."

Our old friend Jerry Twedt, a former television producer and director, currently a playwright and author, shared the following account of a Christmas crisis that had to have a little help from Santa:

My wife's will power held back the tears, but her eyes betrayed her fear.

"It will come," I assured her.

She nodded. The fear remained.

The trepidation she was feeling has been experienced by anyone who has planned a large dinner party and had the main course ruined or, much worse, not available.

It was mid-afternoon on Christmas Eve, and the *lefse* had not arrived. Barbara and I were tensely awaiting the arrival of the mailman, praying that he would have the *lefse* that my parents in Iowa had sent days before.

The tradition in my Norwegian-American family was, and is, to have fish and *lefse* on Christmas Eve. On this occasion, we had invited Barbara's parents and a number of neighbors and friends to join us. However, it is difficult to have a fish and *lefse* feast without the *lefse*.

There is not a doubt that some readers are scratching their heads and asking, "What is *lefse*?" For those of you who have been deprived the exquisite experience of devouring this Norwegian delicacy, *lefse* is an unleavened bread about fifteen inches in diameter, then cut in half. Think of a large potato cake, although the hard *lefse* we make has no potatoes in it. For the meal, *lefse* is combined with cod fish. Mid-westerners often serve *lutefisk*, which is cod soaked in a weak solution of lye water and then rinsed several times in fresh water. *Lutefisk* has a very distinctive smell. If you can get by the aroma, it is quite tasty.

The fun part of our *lefse* feast is making *betas*. To make a *beta*, you place a *lefse* on your plate; pile on boiled potatoes, fish, and cranberry relish; top it all with melted butter; roll it up like a burrito; and with melted butter oozing down your wrists, enjoy a meal fit for the Gods! Well, at least the Gods who dwell in Valhalla.

Back to Christmas Eve.

"I'll never go through this again!" I said to Barb. "I'll have my parents send down a *lefse* grill, and we'll make the *lefse* ourselves."

"Absolutely," she agreed.

Time crawled by as only time can when you are awaiting something important to happen. Finally, the harried mailman walked up to the door. No doubt he was surprised to be greeted by two frantic people who asked in unison, "Are there any packages?"

"No," he answered, in a manner that said he wished never to see another package as long as he lived. "Just the mail."

He handed me some flyers, credit card offers, and three Christmas cards from people we had sent cards to but had removed us from their list, and trotted off.

No *lefse*. Tears and terror replaced the fear in Barbara's eyes. "What are we going to do?"

"I don't know," came my unhelpful reply.

We stared at each other, then Barbara's Germanic heritage surfaced. She dried her eyes and ordered, "Go to the Post Office and check the packages!"

"They won't let me do that."

"They have to!" She answered and fled into the house. I did not argue. After rounding up our two small boys, ages four and three, I drove to the post office. I knew the last thing that Barbara needed was to deal with two squabbling children.

I approached the post office and saw that the gates to the loading dock were open. Fully aware this was a restricted area, I drove in anyway. The boys and I started for the dock, expecting at any moment to hear an employee yell to get myself and my kids off the premises. No such command was given.

I reached the dock and looked up at a kindly man of about fifty. I explained my dilemma and asked if I could please look through the packages for the *lefse*. Perhaps it was my pleading look or the presence of my boys, or something much more profound, but he sighed and pointed to a wall of boxes. We both knew he was breaking the number one rule in the postal rule book: *never let a non-employee touch unsorted mail.*

I thanked him profusely, and with the boys' help, began to sort through the stacks of undelivered boxes. It was obvious that a large number of people were going to receive late Christmas presents. *This is hopeless*, I thought. *It will take hours to go through this mess.*

My four year old, Christopher, held up a package. "Here's one, Daddy." Not to be outdone, Alexander, the three year old said, "Here's another one."

"Those aren't the ones I want," I replied impatiently. "Just stand back and don't touch *anything.*"

"Can't we help?" Alexander asked.

"I wish you could," I answered. "But neither of you can read."

I could tell from the look on his face that Alexander thought the fact that he could not read was no impediment to helping, but he and Chris stepped back while I pawed through the boxes. I was about to admit failure when I spied a familiar label partially hidden by another box. In a true "eureka" moment, I threw off the upper box and saw the unmistakable handwriting of my dear mother. "I found it!"

The boys cheered, the dock employees grinned, and I drove home the happiest man in the state of Florida. I presented the *lefse* to Barb with all the joy of the wise men presenting gifts to the Christ Child. I doubt if Barbara has ever received a Christmas present as desired as that box of *lefse*.

Now, as Santa miracles go, this was of the minor variety. I am sure you can argue that finding the *lefse* was no miracle at all, just dumb luck. However, I was allowed in a restricted area and then permitted to look through unsorted mail. I dare any of you to try duplicating that feat in a major city post office on any day other than December 24. That is why I call this a Santa Miracle.

The children were waiting excitedly for Santa to make an appearance at the Children's Center in Falmouth, Cornwall, United Kingdom. Word was that Santa was arriving by helicopter directly from the North Pole.

Actually, Santa was supposed to leave from Culdrose Airport, but his helicopter flight was grounded due to some very bad weather.

When the Falmouth fire brigade heard the news, they knew that dozens of kids were going to be very disappointed when Father Christmas did not appear as scheduled. Quickly agreeing that it was their job to help *anyone* who found himself in a difficult spot, the fire brigade decided to drive to Culdrose and rescue Santa.

Family support workers at the Children's Center said that the children's faces beamed with joy when they saw a fire engine pulling up with Santa sitting in the passenger seat. Perhaps it was not the dramatic aerial arrival that had been planned, but everyone agreed that the firefighters had performed a wonderful service, greatly in keeping with the unselfish spirit of Christmas. Besides, what could be more exciting than a shiny fire engine driving up with its siren blaring, announcing the visit of Father Christmas?

There is some precedent for Santa Claus as a superhero. In 2008, a film was released entitled *Santa Claus Conquers the Martians*, and in 1983, DC Comics published a special issue of *Superman* teaming the two champions of truth, justice, and true Christmas spirit called (what else?) *Superman and Santa Claus*.

Santa Claus impersonator Dieter Thurn, was holding court for the children in Santa's Grotto in a department store in Bremen, Germany, when he noted a couple of suspicious characters hanging out near the long line of kids waiting to see Santa.

Although the two young men thought they had escaped detection by all the surveillance cameras, they had not counted on the eagle-eyes of Santa in his grotto. Thurn was astonished as the two brazen thieves went about almost nonchalantly filling their rucksacks with expensive cosmetics from the nearby counters.

First, the children were frightened when Santa Claus suddenly shouted in a very loud voice that the two men should cease and desist.

The thieves, startled that their robbery had been detected, began to run with their loot.

Santa shot up from his throne, and with amazing speed for such a large man, grabbed the two men and held them down until the police arrived.

Daniel, a six-year-old who had watched wide-eyed as Santa sprang into crime fighter mode, told a journalist that Santa was "totally cool." Not only does Santa give away presents, but he also fights crime wherever he sees it. Daniel concluded that Santa was a superhero, like Superman, only better.

Caleb Parker had been a department store Santa for over eighteen years, but the child that he will always remember was a frail little girl named Alice.

It was a bitterly cold New Hampshire day in December when Caleb noticed a thin girl with a thread bare coat several sizes too large standing in line to sit on his lap. She was about three kids from the head of the line when she fainted.

"A couple of the children against whom she fell, felt that she was trying to push ahead in line," Caleb said. "When they saw her fall to the floor, they panicked and started trying to get back to their parents for safety." At that time, the department had a first aid room with an employee in attendance.

"Evelyn, the lady on duty in the first aid room when Alice was carried in, wasn't really a trained nurse," Caleb said, "but she had taken a couple weekend courses in health and safety that were conducted two or three times a year at the community college."

There was just something about the tiny child with the dark-rimmed eyes that cried out to Caleb. "She looked the classic waif or street kid in some old black-and-white film version of a Charles Dickens novel."

When there was a lull in the line of children waiting to crawl up on Santa's lap, Caleb put up the "Santa Has to Take a Nap" sign and headed for the first aid room.

"Evelyn had taken off the girl's coat and had her lying down on the couch," Caleb said. "She had on a nearly threadbare dress of very light weight, and you could almost see her ribs through the thin dress."

Evelyn was concerned that the child was severely malnourished. "No wonder the poor thing fainted," she told Caleb. "She looks as though she hasn't had a decent meal in weeks."

Caleb told Evelyn that he was on a break and that he would watch the girl while she went to get her something to eat from the cafeteria. Caleb handed her a couple of dollars, but Evelyn pushed his hand away and said that she would cover it.

"I've got to get home, Santa," the girl said, after she had told Caleb her name. "Can I just tell you want I want for Christmas and leave? Mommy will soon be coming home, and she will be worried if I'm not there looking after Daddy."

Caleb soon learned that Alice's father had been injured in a factory accident that summer, but they were still waiting for "'surance" to start paying some of the medical bills. In the meantime, Mom had taken a job at a grocery store where she helped people carry out their bags of groceries.

When Caleb inquired if Alice weren't a little young to care for her father, she sat up straight and announced that she was nine years old, certainly old enough to take care of Daddy.

Evelyn returned with a cup of chicken noodle soup from the cafeteria. At first Alice refused, saying that she wasn't hungry. But she soon dropped the facade. Within moments, in spite of her attempts at table manners, Alice had finished the cup of soup and was admitting that it had really tasted good.

Caleb listened as Alice told Santa what she wanted for Christmas.

"The dear unselfish child's requests were all for her parents and her two younger sisters," Caleb said.

Evelyn insisted on getting a cab for Alice in spite of all her protests.

As Caleb was leaving to assume his role as the jolly Santa on his mammoth snowdrift throne, he heard Alice give her full name and address to Evelyn. She was Alice Doyle, she said, and precisely gave her street address.

Caleb stopped in the doorway. "Would your father's name be Brian?" he asked.

Alice's eyes opened widely. "Yes, Santa. How did you know?"

Caleb smiled. "Because he was a good little boy."

Caleb had gone through all twelve years of school with Brian Doyle. At one time, they were the best of friends. They had lost touch after high school, but Caleb well remembered the times the tough Irish kid had kept him from taking a beating at the hands of bullies. He also knew that Brian Doyle was filled with pride.

After he had finished work that afternoon, he got the Doyle's address from Evelyn and told her what he planned to do.

"She helped me pick out the right size for a new winter coat for Alice and she made an intelligent guess for her two sisters," Caleb said. "On the way home, I stopped at a supermarket and loaded up with groceries. Quietly, I pulled my Pontiac up in front of the Doyle residence and put everything on the doorstep. I rang the doorbell, then ran for the car."

Caleb was just getting in behind the wheel when little Alice opened the door and saw all the packages of gifts and food. Then she got a good look at Caleb.

"Fortunately, I still had my Santa suit on," Caleb said. "Ho, ho, ho," he shouted in his best Santa voice. "Merry Christmas!"

As he drove away, he could hear Alice's voice excitedly calling to her family inside that Santa had just left something on their doorstep.

"I was not a well-paid executive," Caleb said, concluding his story," but I put fifty dollars in an envelope to Brian, with a note that read, 'You were always a good little boy. Take good care of your family and your very special daughter. Love, Santa.'"

Ed Lewis declared that he was still embarrassed to admit that he had only donned a Santa suit and visited The Good Servant nursing home because he lost a coin toss.

"I am ashamed to admit it," Ed says, "but I had an aversion to being around the elderly."

Ed had been extremely close to his maternal grandmother and when she became ill prior to her death, Ed had a difficult time dealing with the reality of aging.

"Nanna had been so full of life, so vivacious, so active," Ed recalled. "She took me to concerts in the park, to theater performances, and to the zoo. She had always been tireless, always ready to go on to the next attraction wherever it might be. She was youthful in appearance until she was in her mid-70s. Then it was if she became this little old lady overnight."

Nanna had enough money from her investments and her husband's life insurance to be able to afford a nurse to look in on her once a day. Ed will always remember the sound of her rasping cough, the smells of disinfectant, and a strong eucalyptus odor coming from the vaporizer.

"I was nineteen, a college student, a supposed grownup, and I had to psych myself up to hold my dear grandmother's hand when I came to visit her," Ed said. "I felt ashamed of myself, but I simply could not come to terms with the fact that this husk of a woman lying on the bed was really my dear Nanna. I offered thanks to God when Nanna passed, convinced that He had sent her a blessing so that she did not have to suffer the trials of growing old any longer than necessary."

Only once in the seven years since Nanna had died had Ed entered a nursing home. His wife's aunt Joyce had been placed in the Good Servant home, and Alexis insisted that she come along on a Sunday afternoon to bring Joyce some flowers.

"I was doing okay as we walked down the hallway to Aunt Joyce's room, until I caught the scent of various medicines, antiseptics, and other odors I did not attempt to identify," Ed said. "By the time we entered

Joyce's room, I could only stay long enough to wish her well and hand her the flowers. Then I had to excuse myself to find a restroom."

Ed never went back to Aunt Joyce's room that afternoon. He waited in the car until Alexis ended her visit. The angry look on his wife's face gave him advanced warning that all the way home he would receive a very pointed lecture on his rudeness to Aunt Joyce.

And so it was that on that December day, Ed looked at the back of his hand and saw that the quarter had landed heads-up. He had flipped with another member of the Junior Chamber of Commerce to see who would visit the Good Servant nursing home in the disguise of Santa Claus. Ed had called tails. There was no way out of it. He must don the Santa suit and spend an evening with several dozen elderly men and women.

The dinner hour at Good Servant was 5:30 to 7:00 P.M., so the administrators asked Ed to be there as soon after seven as possible. Some of the residents would already be getting sleepy and ready for bed.

Some of his fellow J-Cs helped him load his SUV with a bag of gifts for Ed to distribute. They had been informed there were fifty-six residents at the home, so Ed hoped that the committee had wrapped enough presents for everyone. There was a candy cane and a small plastic Santa figure in each package.

When Ed arrived at the home around 7:10, he was met at the front door by the administrator, a stout, pleasant man in his mid-fifties. He welcomed Santa to the Good Servant and rang a small bell to announce Santa's arrival.

"They're all waiting for you in the great room," the man smiled. "And they are all very excited for Santa to arrive with his sack of presents."

Ed's first impulse was to ask if the man was putting him on. How could a bunch of men and women in their seventies, eighties, and nineties be thrilled by the appearance of guy in a fake beard, a red suit stuffed with pillows, and a bag of meaningless gifts?

Ed received his answer when he stepped into the great room and was greeted by a rousing cheer from the residents and the staff members in attendance. Many of the residents were confined to wheelchairs, but a number of those who were not came forward on canes and walkers to accompany Santa as he walked toward the front of the room where a brightly decorated Christmas tree stood beside a piano. Upon a signal from the administrator, a nurse began playing, "Santa Claus Is Coming to Town."

"I could hear some of the men and women singing along with the piano," Ed said. "Nearly everyone in the room was either singing or laughing. Some were twirling around and dancing. And some were crying."

Ed admitted that those elderly men and women who were crying really got to him. "I suddenly felt like crying along with them," he said. "These were fathers and mothers, brothers and sisters—and they all had their memories of Christmases past. They all had their own precious memories of gathering with their families around Christmas trees in their own homes, surrounded by their children and parents, brothers and sisters. They were once vigorous men and women who worked hard, raised their families, and stood beside the hospital beds as their parents, their spouses, perhaps even their children, passed on to the other side. They were farmers, teachers, bankers, lawyers, factory workers, retail merchants—the complete width and breadth of community life. Some had been heroes, serving their nation. Others served by keeping the country running and the home lights burning. They were people!"

When he began to hand out the packages, Ed felt a strange warmth come over him. "Some people laugh when I say this, but I felt like something inside me suddenly started to glow," Ed said. "I think I had some kind of transformation experience or an epiphany of some sort."

Ed found himself laughing along with the residents as he began to hand out the packages. "I did a couple of Santa chuckles, some really deep-throated ho-ho-ho's."

The bag was soon nearly empty. "I had four packages left," he recalled. "We had been told by the administrator that there were fifty-six residents at Good Servant. I thought that maybe we had packed a few extra, and I was about to hand them to some of the nurses when one little lady came up to me and said that some friends of hers were too weak and sick to come out to the great room. She asked if Santa would please come to their rooms and give them their gifts."

Ed experienced a few unpleasant memories of the sick room that Nanna had occupied until her death and the manner in which he had rudely excused himself from Aunt Joyce's room. For a few moments the odors common to rooms in which old age and illness are claiming the vitality and life of once active and completely functional humans came back to cause him a few moments of hesitation.

Then, with a hearty Santa chortle, Ed said in a booming voice, "Lead me to the rooms of those boys and girls."

The lady who so cared about her friends took Ed by the hand and began to lead him down the hallway. A number of elderly men and women in their wheelchairs formed a train of laughing and giggling participants in the surprises that the residents forced to stay in their rooms were about to receive.

"I'll never forget one woman and the way that she smiled and whispered a 'thank you" when I gave her a brightly wrapped gift," Ed said. "Even then, as she lay on her pillow, her white hair billowing out around her head, I could tell that she had once been a beautiful woman. I held one of her hands until a nurse stepped into her room and told me that she had had enough excitement for one night."

As Ed drove home that night in the Santa suit, he said he spotted a shooting star streak across the cold December sky. He jokingly told himself that that was Santa's sleigh out for a trial run before the big night.

"I felt really good about myself for the first time in a long time," Ed concluded his story. "Before I had left the Good Servant nursing home that night, I told the administrator that he could count on my being Santa again next year."

Gary will always remember the miracle that Santa performed for him when he was in third grade.

"When I was a little kid, I had a real problem with my weight," Gary said. "I know the pain of being called "Fatty, Fatty, two-by-four," "Tubby," and "Fatso" on the playground during recess. And walking the five blocks home from school every day nearly always meant being teased. Kids would grab my lunch pail and pretend to find steaks, roasts, mashed potatoes, or whole pigs inside."

Gary said that nearly every night after school he would go up to his room and lie on his bed and cry. His older brother Ray was no comfort. He would listen outside the door and wonder aloud who the little girl was who was crying like a sissy in his room.

Ray was thirteen, much taller than Gary thought that he would ever be, and stout of build, but not fat. Gary's parents were a bit on the heavy side. His dad would sometimes comment that Mom was "pleasingly plump." Gary deemed himself to be disgustingly fat, doomed forever to be an object of ridicule and mockery.

Ever since first grade when Christmas rolled around and the teachers began to plan the holiday program for the parents, Gary was selected to play Santa Claus.

"I know the teachers thought that giving me the starring role would build my self-confidence," Gary said, "but I know that I was chosen because I was fat. The trouble was, I really had to work hard to act jolly like Santa, because my little heart was breaking inside that Santa suit."

"Although the third grade class was coupled with the fourth grade for the Christmas program and there were a lot of boys taller than I was, none were plumper, so once again I was fat old Santa," Gary recalled. "I felt it was my destiny to be Santa until I graduated from high school—and then probably the only career open to me would be as some department store Santa."

When he was in the third grade, Gary said that he was a firm believer in Santa, but he was not so true a believer that he accepted every fake-bearded guy in a red suit to be the real McCoy.

"One afternoon after school I made my way to a local department store that featured a Santa Claus," Gary said. "I wasn't going to tell him what I wanted for Christmas, but I was going to ask him for some advice."

The area of the department store that housed Santa's workshop was very nicely done. There were a number of animated elves tapping away with little hammers at a variety of toys. A large Christmas tree with beautiful decorations and lights stretched above the display, and Santa sat on a massive chair behind an icicle-covered arch to suggest the cold of the North Pole. Mrs. Santa Claus, a rather imposing woman with a large mane of snow white hair, stood outside the arch, limiting Santa's visitors to one at a time.

Gary stood in line, waiting his turn, summoning his courage. When, after what seemed hours, it was his turn to crawl up on Santa's lap, he nearly cried when Kris Kringle smiled through his fake beard and observed, "My, you're a heavy little boy, aren't you?"

After the traditional "ho-ho-ho" and the "what do you want for Christmas, little boy" had been uttered, Gary whispered that he hadn't come there to declare his wish for any presents.

Puzzled, Santa frowned, and attempting to maintain his jolly demeanor, asked Gary "Why, then, have you stood in line for so long? Why did you come to Santa's workshop?"

Feeling his face turning a fiery red of embarrassment, Gary said that he knew that the man wasn't the real Santa.

When Santa protested that, indeed, he was, Gary said, "I know that the real Santa is busy working with the elves making presents at the North Pole. But what I want to know is, why does Santa have to be so fat? Why do I have to be so fat? Every year at Christmas, I have to play Santa Claus at school. Do you have to be fat to be Santa?"

It all flowed out in a torrent of painful words of frustration and hurt.

"Don't you wonder why you are so fat, Mr. Pretend Santa?" Gary went on. "Doesn't it bother you to have people call you Fatty, just so you can be Santa at Christmas time?"

Santa sat in silence for a moment, and Mrs. Claus reminded him that other little boys and girls were waiting to tell him what they wanted for Christmas.

Just then, Gary started to cry. He tried so hard not to, but the hot tears stung his eyes, and he couldn't help himself.

"Kid, don't cry," Santa said in a voice very different from the jolly old elf, "look here, look here."

The man was pulling aside his suit and showing Gary the pillows and stuffing under the suit. "I'm not fat," he whispered. "I ain't skinny, but I ain't fat. It's not being fat that makes a Santa. I really love kids, and I really love this job, and I really like making kids feel good about maybe getting what they want for Christmas."

The man smiled and winked at Gary. "Look, the rest of the year I work on the loading dock of the store. All the guys know the way I love Christmas—the whole magilla: Santa, the elves, Rudolph, and the reindeer. So when the guy who used to play Santa got too old and cranky, the manager came to me and said, 'Murphy, you're the new Santa. We need someone playing Santa who loves Christmas and kids.'

"You just gotta fill yourself with love for life and other people," Murphy said, giving Gary's hand a squeeze. "You don't have to be fat. You don't have to be skinny. You just gotta be you. And never be afraid to be you."

Gary nodded his understanding, thanked Santa, and slid off his lap.

"Maybe I didn't really understand everything the man had said right at that minute," Gary said, "but the more I thought about what he said, the better I felt about myself."

That night at the elementary school's Christmas program, he was the absolute best Santa that he could be. "I gave an Academy Award-winning performance," Gary recalled fondly. "I gave it my all. My parents were proud; my teachers were complimentary; and even some of my harshest detractors gave me a couple 'good job, Fats.'"

Inspired by the pride he felt the night of the Christmas show, Gary cut down on snacks and junk food. He talked Ray into working out with him. When his father saw Gary's sudden interest in athletics, he bought the boys two sets of dumbbells.

At Christmastime in fourth grade, the teachers decided that Gary should play the part of one of three Wise Men who traveled to the manger of the Baby Jesus.

"Please," Gary pleaded, "I want to be Santa again this year, just like I have been every year."

Gary could tell by the look in the teachers' eyes that they were considering another boy, perhaps a bit heavier for the role.

"Just one more year," Gary said, stating his case. "I don't mean to brag, but you know what a great job I did last year. And believe me, a couple of pillows under the suit, and I'll be an even better Santa this year. I love being Santa."

Gary got the role for one more year, and everyone agreed that he had delivered another stellar performance as Santa. He was particularly pleased because he knew that he had won the role because of his ability, rather than his waist measurements.

"When it was time to cast for the Christmas program in fifth grade, I had lost so much weight that I gladly surrendered the role to another boy," Gary said, concluding his story. "However, I really hadn't grown much taller than when I was in third grade, so that year I played one of Santa's elves. I gave the audience the best elf that I could, and the boy who played Santa—who had wanted part so badly the year before—delivered a fantastic performance as St. Nick."

Until she was eleven-years-old, Julie carried a photo taken on the night that Santa Claus visited her when she was three. Whenever any schoolmate or friend would express doubt about Santa's existence, Julie would whip the wrinkled, crinkled photograph out of her purse and silence all the doubters.

"See for yourselves," she would challenge any who questioned the existence of Santa. "He came right into our house with a bag of gifts, and he held me on his lap so Mom could take a picture of us."

Triumphantly, she would smile at the "ooohs" and "aaahs" and "wows" of the once skeptical friends who now readily conceded all doubts in the face of absolute proof.

As an adult, Julie admits with a smile that she probably believed in Santa a bit longer than some of her friends because of that wonderful photograph. She also accepts the true identity of that particular Santa who visited her when her family lived in a suburb of Chicago.

"My dad had a Jewish actor friend who was big and stout and had a deep voice," she explained. "Steve loved to dress up like Santa and visit the homes of his Christian friends on Christmas Eve. He had purchased a very nice, authentic Santa suit, and as an actor, he really knew how to apply the false beard so it looked absolutely real. He also applied just enough makeup so his rosy cheeks looked like he had stepped off a sleigh that had come from the North Pole."

Although Julie had met Steve before, he was completely unrecognizable when he came through the front door on Christmas Eve. "Of course my mind was completely blown to see Santa coming into our home with a big sack of presents for my older sister, my two brothers, and me. He was Santa to perfection.I have never seen a department store Santa that could come anywhere near his magnificent presentation."

Julie remembered that she was in her long white nightgown and holding a new doll in the picture that she carried for so many years.

"It was our custom to open some gifts on Christmas Eve, then hang up our stockings for Santa to fill during the night while we slept," she said. "There hadn't been many gifts under the tree that year. Dad later admitted that things were tight financially, and we had the joy of each other. I was perfectly willing to accept that, but now I understand that he had wanted Santa's bag to be full of gifts for each of us kids. But I did have a new doll, just like the one I wanted."

Julie laughs now that she nearly squeezed the stuffing out of the doll when Santa arrived.

"And when he picked me up and held me on his lap, I knew it was the real Santa," she said. "Mom and Dad had taken me to see the Santa at Marshall Fields in downtown Chicago, and even I knew with the discerning eye of a three-year-old that he was not the real Santa. Based on my previous Santa encounter, I could speak for years with great authority that there, sitting in Dad's easy chair in our living room, was the real Santa."

Santa held little Julie in his lap all the time he was handing out gifts to the children. When all the presents were given out, he put a gloved hand to his ear and said that Rudolph was calling him back to the sleigh. "I have to move on to visit the homes of other good boys and girls."

With a hearty "ho-ho-ho, Merry Christmas, and good night," Santa walked out the door. But never out of Julie's sacred memories of that night.

Julie has always kept the photo of that glorious occasion. "My daughters are still young enough to accept it as awesome proof that Santa is real and that their mother was once chosen to meet the true Santa Claus."

When Ruth Butler's husband died, her nine-year-old son Kenneth was devastated. Her daughter, Janice, who was four, seemed unable to grasp fully the concept of death. She knew her father had been ill for quite some time and she kept asking when he would be coming home from the hospital.

"Ethan passed in November, shortly before Thanksgiving," Ruth told us. "I tried to divert Kenny's thoughts toward Christmas and Santa, but those words sounded meaningless and hollow to a nine-year-old who had just lost his beloved father. I became quite upset when I received word from his teacher that he had become disruptive in class when the children were given an assignment to write their letters to Santa. He had disturbed a number of his classmates when he had shouted that all he wanted was his father to come back to life and Santa couldn't do that."

Before his passing due to lymphatic cancer Ethan, Ruth, and their children spent as much of their remaining hours together as possible. Masking his pain with a broad grin, Ethan helped make his coming transition less traumatic for Kenny and Janice.

"In retrospect, we probably kept too much from Kenny, who was old enough to understand some of what was happening to his father," Ruth said. "Ethan tried to continue playing catch with Kenny and carrying Janice around on his back just as long as he could. Finally, he became too weak to play with the kids, but he continued to read them bedtime stories.

"One night as he sat in his easy chair reading to the children, his voice suddenly became no more than a rasping whisper," Ruth said. "He set the book aside, put his arms around the children, and asked me to come nearer. He told us all that he would always love us, then he smiled and closed his eyes."

The children thought that their father had fallen asleep while reading to them. Ruth held back her tears long enough to call an ambulance. Ethan never regained consciousness and died early the next morning.

Kenny had been very close to his father. He had always been an exceptionally healthy boy, very athletic and sports-minded, but now, after Ethan's death, it was all he could do to nibble at his food. He seemed to lose all interest in school, and he seldom bothered to return the telephone calls of his friends or respond to their invitation to come outside and play football. Kenny would sit for hours in front of the television set, but he wasn't really watching it. Although he had scarcely wept or shown any outward sign of grief, it was apparent that he had been devastated by his father's death.

"Ethan had always made a big deal out of Christmas," Ruth told us. "He had grown up in Minnesota, and although he missed the big snow banks and the white Christmases, he decorated the house with Santas and angels and set up his prized models of what he called his Christmas Village, miniatures of an old English village at Yule. This year, Kenny wanted nothing to do with any of it."

Ruth did buy a small artificial Christmas tree in spite of Kenny's indifference toward continuing his father's elaborate celebration of the coming of Santa and the onset of the holidays. Little Janice helped her mother decorate the tree and clapped her hands in glee when the lights were turned on.

Although Ethan had absolutely no culinary talents and freely admitted to his friends that he could barely boil water, he loved to make popcorn for the kids on special nights when the family would all watch a movie together. On Christmas Eve, he performed the ritual of making a special bowl of popcorn for Santa. Ethan made up stories of how Santa's favorite snack on his rounds of delivering gifts was to nibble on popcorn. Bah! Humbug to cookies and milk! Santa craved popcorn.

On Christmas Eve, Ruth tried her best to break through Kenny's wall of silence and sorrow by reminding him that it was time to make Santa's special bowl of popcorn. Kenny shook his head at his mother's suggestion. "Only Dad could make the Santa popcorn," he said. "Remember, he had the special recipe that his family had passed on for generations. Only Dad could make it."

At that very moment, little Janice lifted her head and sniffed the air above her. "Mmmm," she smiled. "I smell popcorn!"

Startled, Kenny inhaled the fragrant aroma of freshly popped and buttered popcorn. "Mom!" he shouted, wide-eyed with wonder at the miracle. "It's Daddy's special Santa popcorn for Santa's bowl. Smell it, Mommy! That's Daddy's famous popcorn, the family recipe."

"We all smelled it," Ruth said. "The aroma of freshly buttered popcorn was coming from the kitchen and filling the entire house. It was the unmistakable scent of Ethan's special popcorn for Santa Claus's snack. We all breathed its glorious smell as deeply as we could."

The aroma of popcorn lasted for about three or four minutes, then it was gone as quickly as it had come.

Kenny's eyes filled with tears. "Daddy wants us to make popcorn for Santa, doesn't he?" he asked his mother. "I used to watch Daddy real close. I think I can remember the special recipe."

Janice squealed her excitement. "We're going to make popcorn for Santa, just the way that Daddy did."

The memory of that wonderful contact with the loving spirit of Ethan Butler will stay with Ruth and her children until the day that they each, in their own time, rejoin him. In his own special way, Ethan had given them a communication that they could all share and understand—and he had allowed the Light of Santa to find a place in his children's hearts that would never dim.

When Robert Miller was teaching social studies and serving as wrestling coach at a medium-sized high school back in his home town in Connecticut, he was leaving a restaurant rather late at night when he saw some teenagers hassling a street person." Robert said, "so my wife was out of town visiting her sister in Ankeny," so rather than fixing something to eat at home, I decided just to grab a bite downtown after wrestling practice was finished. Now it seemed that I was at the right place at the right time."

Robert said that he recognized one of the four kids pushing the old man around, and he shouted at the gang to stop and to go home.

The teenagers started advancing menacingly toward Robert, but the student from the high school where Robert taught recognized him as a teacher. "Hey, that's that Mr. Miller, the wrestling coach," he warned the others in a hoarse whisper. "Let's get out of here."

One of the gang shouted a profanity at Robert, then asked him if he really wanted to take up for street trash. "These bums just make a mess in the alleys and stink up the neighborhood," said the bully, puffing his chest out to fill the jacket that denoted his gang's colors. "We're just going to teach this old creep not to loiter in the streets. Loitering is a crime, don't you know that, teach?"

Angered, Robert shot back at the boys. "He has a hard enough time surviving in this cold without you guys hassling him. Leave him alone. He's a human being. Maybe some day you could end up alone and homeless in the streets just like him."

Two of the boys cursed Robert for insulting them, calling them bums.

Another of the young tough guys grumbled that the four of them could take Robert, but the kid from his high school grabbed the arm of one of the more aggressive gang members and raised his voice: "Hey, you jerks! He knows who I am. Let's get out of here right now." Robert walked quickly to the poor man's side. He had fallen to the ground and Robert helped him to his feet.

"He didn't seem to be hurt too badly, but as I was helping him to his feet, one of the hoods jumped on my back," Robert said.

For someone who had wrestled all four years of high school, made the team in college, and now coached wrestling, it was a simple move for Robert to flip the kid over his back and toss him on the street.

"I told you idiots that he was the wrestling coach," Robert overheard as the rest of the gang helped their fallen warrior to his feet. Within the next few seconds, they were all running away.

The old man thanked Robert for coming to his rescue. "I'm not a street person," he said, brushing snow and mud off his coat. "I'm not homeless, and I am not a bum. I'm just old."

Robert insisted on taking the man inside the restaurant for a cup of hot coffee. At first, the man protested, but he at last allowed Robert to take him by the arm and lead him into the warmth of the restaurant.

"He was really quite a good-sized fellow when I saw him up close and he was leaning on me," Robert said. "He had a rather long beard, but he was nearly bald on top, and we had to find his stocking cap to cover his head before he would leave the street."

After he had taken a few sips of coffee, he extended his hand and introduced himself as Nicholas Christian. After Nicholas had warmed up, he became quite talkative, explaining that he had retired some years ago, and, after his wife had died, he rented a small apartment that suited his Social Security budget. His son had been killed in Vietnam, but he had a married daughter who lived in New Hampshire.

"It was when he was talking about the pleasure that he took in visiting with his daughter and grandchildren that his eyes seemed to light up, to twinkle, so to speak, and I recognized him," Robert said.

Placing an arm on the man's shoulders, Robert whispered so the counter waitress could not hear him, "You're Santa Claus."

Nicholas laughed heartily, and Robert said that the "ho-ho-ho" echoed clearly in his memory.

"Yes, I used to be," Nicholas admitted. "For 28 years I was the Santa at Chandler's department store. Loved every minute of it, too."

Robert shook his head in wonder and amusement. He must have sat on this man's lap and told him what he wanted for Christmas a dozen times.

"If I had known your name was actually Nicholas, it would have blown my young mind," Robert told him.

Nicholas chuckled a deep, Santa chuckle. "Yes, and Nicholas Christian is my real name. I thought of changing it to 'Nicholas Christmas,' but I figured my birth name was close enough."

After a hearty swallow of his coffee, Nicholas asked how Robert had recognized him after all these years. After all, he wasn't wearing his red Santa suit and cap.

"It was your eyes," Robert told him. "When you were talking about your grandchildren, you had that same old Santa twinkle in your eyes."

Those same twinkling eyes were now glistening with tears. "I really miss being Santa," Nicholas said, lowering his head. "When I was nearing seventy, the managers said that I was too old. They wanted a younger Santa."

Robert laughed at the irony. All the stories about Santa Claus claimed that he was hundreds of years old, but the managers wanted a younger appearing Santa than Nicholas to listen to the children's Christmas requests.

Robert suddenly had an idea. "Do you still have the red suit and hat?"

"In my closet," Nicholas said. "I couldn't bear to part with it."

Right then and there, Robert decided that Nicholas should play Santa as a guest at the school staff party.

"The rest of the staff was totally delighted," Robert said, "and Nicholas loved being Santa again and hearing what all the teachers wanted for Christmas. A couple of the more petite women even sat on Santa's lap! A number of my colleagues even recognized Nicholas from sitting on his lap at Chandler's department store.

"I was glad that Nicholas Christian got to be Santa one more time. I tried to keep in touch with him, but I heard that he left town to live with his daughter. Just before the Christmas holiday, she wrote to let me know that her father had died in September, but that his eyes had always twinkled when he remembered being Santa at our staff Christmas party."

Ilona Szabo wrote to tell us that growing up Jewish in a devoutly Catholic country like Hungary was not easy. But Santa Claus helped her through one particularly difficult time.

Here is Ilona Szabo's story:

I was only five. I had just arrived at our neighborhood park when Peter, who was seven, ordered me away. He said no one in our usual group would play with me because I had "killed Christ."

I had no idea what he was talking about, and I doubt he had a perfect sense of his words, given his age. I did realize he referred to some terrible event, and it seemed like I was being held personally responsible. When he insisted that I had to leave, I ran home in tears.

The clarity with which I still remember the painful incident is at least partially based on my relationship with this little boy, Peter. He was my first "boyfriend," a handsome child I loved with all my five-year-old heart. Our families lived in the same Budapest apartment building, a large 1920s house by the park from which he had banished me.

So that day, quickly reaching home, I recounted my sad tale to my grandmother who was essentially bringing me up since my mother worked. Grandma Ella was a small woman—everyone in my family is vertically challenged, including me. She was not quite five feet tall but with greater courage and a stiffer spine than almost anyone I've ever known; she had escaped from concentration camp during World War II. Now she sat me in her lap, the best place I knew, hugging me while repeating in a soft whisper: "Those naughty, naughty children; nobody listens to them." Then, in her characteristically practical fashion, she began to help erase the pain by having me prepare for a much happier occasion, the arrival of Santa Claus.

Santa comes to Hungarian children on the morning of December 6. Basically he looks like Santa in America, fat and jolly, wearing a red suit and red hat, traveling from the North Pole on a sled drawn by reindeer. He is the cheery personage everyone here knows from Christmas Day. And he brings lovely presents to good Hungarian children regardless of creed. He is an ecumenical figure, good to everyone. If you were well-behaved during the past twelve months, you could expect wonderful gifts even if you were Jewish. On the other hand, if you'd been naughty . . . well, more on that later in this story. The point is that hopes were fulfilled by behavior and never by religion.

Preparations for the big event began the day before, on December 5—as it happened, the day of my painful encounter in the park with Peter. In Hungary, the period of Advent, the four weeks before Christmas itself, is filled with both church services and superstitions. Shops carried branches of fruit trees for girls in their late teens and twenties; the branches were put into water and carefully tended until Christmas Eve. If they blossomed, it meant the girl would marry during the following year.

Children followed different beliefs. Regardless of religion, the first thing you had to do was clean and polish your best pair of shoes; I did mine twice to make sure of an extra shine. Then, as custom decreed, I carefully placed the footwear before our largest window so Santa wouldn't miss my shoes while his sled, laden with gifts, circled Budapest. Tradition called for the gifts to be put right by the shoes. And Santa knew exactly what to leave because a list of goodies was always put inside one of the pair of shoes. My grandma helped as holiday tradition called for this to be in writing. She knew my heart's desires; I had found it practical to share these in the weeks before Santa Day.

Basically, I wanted books. I had learned to read, to a degree anyway. And of course my grandmother often read to me. I can't recall the exact titles on that year's Santa list but they likely included classics: Hungarian translations of *Babar the Elephant, Polyanna, Tom Sawyer, Little Women, Pinocchio, The Wizard of Oz*. Of course I also wanted more dolls to add to an already humungous collection; a person could never have enough. And I yearned for yet another teddy bear—that would make three.

It wasn't easy to sleep that night. I ran to my shoes bright and early on the morning of December 6 thrilled to discover that Santa had done his job. He delivered everything on my list, all the books and toys I wanted.

The books were especially welcome! When it came to reading, this is what I learned very early on. Reading took you away from all sorts of misery; you could become lost in marvelous stories. While you read, you could be (you were) transported to other, better worlds. Even before I was five, Santa had made all these wonderful escapes possible.

And something else: Hungarian children who had misbehaved during the previous year could expect to find birch—a bunch of branches, usually painted gold but still useful for spanking—along with regular gifts. Of course even if you'd been a little monster, you would probably not be physically punished by loving parents. But the wooden sticks were there as reminders of what might happen as a result of misdeeds.

No stick for me. Didn't my grandmother always say I was a terrific little girl? Mind you, I had never doubted Santa's wisdom regarding such important matters. But now he fulfilled my deepest need for reassurance. Obviously, I didn't kill anyone. What relief! Who cared about Peter?

But on the morning of December 6 he returned to my life. Peter arrived at our apartment with his mother, looking spiffy, even if grim.

Now, I want to say that Peter's Mom was an exceptionally nice woman, a genuinely kind soul. Grandma Ella used to talk about how good she was during the war, how she shopped for Jews in places where they were forbidden to go. I'd been in her home for dinner where she was careful never to serve pork. She knew we were not particularly religious, my grandmother did not keep kosher. But she seemed to feel she was honoring Jewish tradition by cooking chicken or fish for me. Given their past relationship, Ella felt free to confide in her friend about what had happened to me in the park. And so this woman, a truly righteous Christian, brought her son to apologize to me, which he did with seemingly genuine regret.

But the romance was over. I never spoke to him again. And I never returned to the group of children who had stood silently by while Peter so cruelly barred me from their midst. I had books and new dolls, including yet another teddy, for loving company. And I had Grandma Ella—along with Santa Claus.

Jack Velayas, an actor friend of ours, remembers the Christmas Eve when the defroster was on high, yet the rear windows of the Oldsmobile were still fogged over, as his father, mother, and he drove to his brother Ron's house.

"I was seventeen years old that Christmas and looking forward to seeing my oldest brother, his wife, and my four-year-old nephew Shawn. I sat in the back seat as my father drove with my mother by his side. Fresh in our memory was the fall of Hanoi, the President resigning in disgrace, the stock market turning bearish, and unemployment rising higher than it had since the Great Depression. The world was a very uncertain place, and there were very few reasons to celebrate. Still it was

Christmas, and we had a sack of toys in the trunk of the car for Shawn, fully aware that a four- year-old does not care about the problems of the world."

As the Velayas family pulled into the driveway of Jack's brother's farm, a cold dense fog thickened making it hard to see more than 50 yards in any direction.

"As my father shut off the car, my mother and I opened our doors, Ron's voice could be heard as he welcomed us to his place," Jack said. "As he walked up the drive to where we had parked, we could see that Shawn was with him, following excitedly as a son does, wanting to be part of any happening around the home."

As soon as the greetings were over, Jack's father turned to Ron and asked him in his most concerned voice, "What's wrong with your neighbors?

"What do you mean, Dad?" Ron asked.

Shawn looked up at his grandpa, sensing his concern.

"Well we almost hit one of them as we drove in."

"You what?" Ron asked in mock alarm.

"Yeah," Grandpa Velayas said, "and just what is that old guy doing riding around in a sleigh pulled by deer?"

By now, Jack said, his brother knew what joke his father was pulling. Shawn's eyes opened wide as he took in all the adult talk about Grandpa almost hitting a man on a sleigh being pulled by deer.

Grandpa continued on about the foolish old man. "He was just sitting there in the middle of the road in a sleigh looking at a map. I think he must have been lost or something. We almost hit him!"

Shawn let out a little gasp.

"Who is that guy?" Grandpa asked. In a very serious tone Shawn answered, "Santa Claus."

"You know, I bet you're right," Grandpa agreed. We honked at him to get him to move out of the way. And he got all flustered and cracked his whip and those deer took off. You know with all this fog we couldn't see real good, but it looked like he might have flown away."

"You didn't scare him away did you?" Shawn asked, terrified by the very thought that Grandpa, Grandma, and Uncle Jack may have frightened away Santa before he had had a chance to deliver his toys to the little boy at the Velayas' residence.

"Well, he did leave in a big hurry," Grandpa said. "In fact, he was in such a hurry that a bag fell out of the back of his sleigh. He didn't even come back to pick it up."

"Where's the bag?" Shawn asked.

"We picked it up and tossed it in the trunk," Grandpa said, barely able to contain his laughter at Shawn's concern over Santa having left without leaving any toys for him.

Shawn hurried to the back of the car and watched as Grandpa opened the trunk. There he found the bag that Santa had dropped, filled with toys for Shawn.

"That was thirty-two years ago," Jack said. "Since then my father has passed away, and I have remained close with my nephew. Today, Shawn is married with two daughters of his own, ages four and five.

" Last Christmas, I made the drive to Sacramento where they live. It was a cold and foggy night, typical for the central valley of California in winter, the evening I pulled up in front of the house."

Shawn opened the door, flanked by Bridget and Bevin, his daughters, and welcomed him into his home. Jack immediately began to tell his nephew and grandnieces about the wild neighbor in the sleigh he had almost hit with his car.

Jack turned to the girls, "I wonder who it was."

They looked up and said in very serious tone, "Santa Claus."

"You know, I think you might be right. I hope he isn't too mad at me for honking at him to get out of the way."

"You honked at him?" Bridget asked, concerned that Uncle Jack had blown their chances for any presents from Santa Claus.

"Yeah, he got all flustered and flew off," Jack told the girls. "He didn't even stop to pick up the sack that fell out of his sleigh."

At just the right moment, Jack pulled the situation out of deep despair into joy and relief. "But I picked up the bag and put it in my trunk. Shall we go see what's in it?"

"It was a magical moment of continuity between the generations. Passing the story on to my grandnieces not only added to the miracle of their Christmas, but also to my nephew's, as he recalled the story from his own childhood. The miracle of Santa is the way he adds a touch of magic to the lives of children and to adults in different ways at the same time."

Clarisa Bernhardt, who has always been deeply interested in the mystical aspects of our culture, also has a deep fascination with the concept and image of Saint Nicholas.

"Once when I was a young girl of about eight-years-old, I was looking out at the night sky, and something that resembled a cloud moved into my view. The cloud opened up, and there was Saint Nicholas."

Clarisa said that the image of Saint Nick resembled a drawing that she had seen in a book at school. But some aspects of him were quite different.

"I recognized him mostly because of his snow-white beard," she said. "It was great fun to see him in that moment and to have a glimpse into another somewhere.

He was dressed in deep-red silken robes that had many sparkling jewels scattered over his costume. These jewels may have been snow crystals that shone in the radiance of his jolly light."

Clarisa remembered that Santa appeared to be moving quickly across a field of green flowing grass and that she could see mountains in the background.

"There were no mountains around where I was living on the North Texas plains," Clarisa emphasized.

"I was thrilled to see this remarkable vision of St. Nicolas, but it was only for a moment—and then he was gone. And so was the cloud."

Eight-year-old Clarisa continued to look up at the stars that had suddenly become more brilliant and dazzling.

"I have always remembered that moment, so I have no doubt that Saint Nicholas definitely exists, even if on a higher level of awareness."

Mary Benninghoff's Santa Miracle, occurred one Christmas Eve—just when she had given up on anything good coming from that year.

Mary explained her story to us in these words:

The year 2006 was a rough year for me. It seemed that from the first day of the bright new year, I was in trouble. Early January brought a serious eye infection that threatened the vision in my right eye. The treatment went well but it was long and my eye was in pain.

My one consolation was my three cats, Cookie, Sammy, and Grady. Cookie and Sammy were adopted from Pet Refuge in Mishawaka, Indiana, where I've volunteered for years. Grady came to me as a two-week-old bottle feeder kitten and by the time he reached five months, Grady kept eleven-year-old Cookie, and Sammy, five, on their toes. Sammy adored Grady and practically raised him when he became old enough to run around.

Grady was the first kitten I raised from a baby for Pet Refuge, a no-kill animal sanctuary in Mishawaka, Indiana. I'd volunteered in the office for about three years when I jokingly said one day at the shelter, "Gee, I think I'd like to raise a baby kitten." A few weeks later, I got a call from our President, Sandy, who said, "Mary, I've got something for you."

That something was a beautiful blue-eyed, long-haired kitten who weighed about 6 ounces and was all of 6 inches long. All the way home with the baby in a tub beside me, equipped with bottles, formula, towels, heating disc, and hurried instructions, I kept repeating to myself that I was a great-grandmother. I couldn't do this! On the other hand, I kept telling myself that I had always welcomed a challenge.

Grady and Sammy played all the time as matronly Cookie watched from her high perch. They raced, rolled, and then laid down to sleep together. They were so active and most of the time, Sammy was the one to wear out Grady.

One morning in 2006 (after my eye had healed), I called the kids for breakfast, and they didn't come as usual. I found Grady and Cookie in the bedroom sitting next to Sammy. He had gone to sleep and didn't wake up that morning.

The vet said Sammy had a heart defect from birth that had never been found in his exams because it would have taken an ultrasound machine to detect it. She could not believe he lived to be five years old with a valve that was almost totally closed. His heart finally gave out.

Again, 2006 had taken from me. My cats, now Cookie and Grady, were my salvation. Through the month of March, I functioned, but I felt so guilty about Sammy. It was my fault for letting him play so hard with Grady. It was silly, of course. I didn't know about his heart, but it was my way of grieving.

We survived March, and I thought maybe the rest of the year would be better. It wasn't.

In April, I was diagnosed with breast cancer. In June, my doctor removed my breast. By taking the breast, it took all the cancer and all my reports came back clean.

I had decided a long time ago that I would be very hesitant to undergo chemo as I had friends who had passed away from complications related to the treatment. I made my feelings clear to the doctor before the surgery. Fortunately, it wasn't necessary.

As the days passed and I felt better and better, I took in a young mother cat and two kittens, six weeks old. I named them Clarissa, Chloe, and Cleo. Clarissa, the mother, was only seven months old and had had her babies at five-and-a-half months old. The kittens were adopted, but Clarissa fit in so well with Cookie and Grady, she stayed with us.

I had a full house again, and things felt normal. Soon I took in a nine-day old kitten, a bottle-feeder, I named Grayci. She was about six weeks old and I was beginning to feel that the worst was over when I was diagnosed with uterine cancer.

My son took care of Grayci when I had the surgery in October. Again, the report came back as all clear. Grayci was adopted by a great family, and I was back with my three kids.

Then, in early December, a revised report said that retesting had found a cancer cell in one of the specimen nodes they had sent to the lab after the surgery. My doctor recommended I start chemo on December 14. I told him I wouldn't even consider chemo until after the holidays, if then. I would, however, have the PET scan he had ordered.

A week before the PET scan, I received a beautiful prayer from Brad and Sherry Steiger that began, "Great Spirit." It was so moving, I said it every night (and I still do) before I went to sleep, asking that my kids remained well and safe and I be allowed to stay with them.

It was my birthday, December 22, when I had the PET scan and was told the report would take about a month. The next day, I received a call from Pet Refuge Cat Coordinator, Karen, telling me that at Cat Adoption the night before, two ladies had brought three puppies to the shelter. Two were fine, and the ladies were going to keep them, but a third little one had a severely mangled leg. She and her siblings had been abandoned, along with the mother dog who was on a chain when the owners moved out of state. Two puppies died entangled in the chain and the little one was severely injured. The vet said it was the worst case of mangling she had ever seen and with the blood loss, it was touch and go.

The puppy had her surgery on my birthday as I was having my PET scan. Karen asked if I would care for the puppy as she recovered because my home was quieter than those of most dog volunteers who fostered dogs. Naturally, I said yes.

On Christmas Eve I picked up the puppy who had been named Merry by the Pet Refuge staff. She weighed only two-and-a-half pounds at five weeks old.

I couldn't help thinking of my own surgery as I looked at her open wound. The poor thing had lost her entire right shoulder and leg.

She lay on my lap, so trusting, with the most beautiful brown eyes I'd ever seen. She whimpered a bit as I moved her from my lap to the carrier that I would take her home in. That was the last complaint I ever heard from her. She spent the night on my lap as I sat in my lounge chair and dozed. I didn't want to let go of her for fear she wouldn't be there when I awoke.

On Christmas Day, my son, Frank, picked me up to go to my grandson's for Christmas dinner. He knew I had a new baby, but his expression was priceless when he saw it was a puppy, not a kitten. I worried a bit that the day might be hard on Merry, but my daughter-in-law, Kathy, spent most of the day with Merry on her lap. As the days with Merry unfolded, and I watched her grow more and more confident, I realized that she would be as hard to give up as the kittens I raised were.

I knew I couldn't have a dog. I already had three cats, but I cried at night, thinking that I would soon have to let her go. Her wound was healing so well and soon black fuzz was covering parts of it. She didn't realize she was supposed to have four legs so the loss never bothered her as she bounced all our over our home, playing with my cats and their toys.

When she was eight weeks old, I knew the Dog Coordinator would soon want to place her with a dog volunteer, so she could become accustomed to other dogs. Then my son, Frank, called to ask if he could take Merry home for a few days to see how she would work out with their cat. I knew my prayers for her were answered. I received permission from Pet Refuge and Frank picked Merry up that day.

Merry never came back to me. Frank and Kathy adopted Merry when she was about ten weeks old. I often think Merry was sent in answer to the prayer that Brad and Sherry had sent to me. She and I healed together, both physically and spiritually. She showed a bravery and strength that made me realize how fortunate I was and as her wound closed and grew over with fur, my own wounds healed.

Merry's future was insured—and sometime after the new year began, mine looked brighter, too. The PET scan showed no cancer and I was pronounced clear.

I know now that Merry was truly a Santa Miracle. My son brings Merry over almost every week. She has grown into a beautiful fifty pound Shepherd/Chow mix with a noble Shepherd head, shiny black fur, and a gorgeous Chow tail curved over her back. Just looking at her makes me smile. She hasn't forgotten her Grandma or her first real home and she still likes to play with our cat toys. The cats aren't too sure about playing with her now that she's gotten so big.

A happy note is that Pet Refuge also rescued Merry's mother, Josie, from Animal Control where she had been taken and found her a forever home, too.

I realize now that nothing has ever made me feel more complete than raising animals. Grady was only the start to the journey. Grady is now a 22-pound Russian Blue cat and still beautiful, and I have continued to raise kittens; more than fifty to date.

It was truly a Santa Miracle when he brought Merry to us and closed a year filled with sadness and pain—but also a year that, on Christmas Eve, brought great joy to my entire family.

Janice Gray Kolb, the author of such inspirational books as *Cherishing—Poetry for Pilgrims Journeying On*, recalled that in her memories of her childhood she esteemed Santa Claus as if he were like a gentle grandfather:

Year after year as a child, the magic of Christmas delighted my heart and my entire being. I truly felt that Christmas was another realm that brought softness and tenderness and love into my life, and it seemed to be protected and surrounded by mysteries. For a short period of time, it was almost as if I was encased in a delicate snow globe with my family, and nothing hurtful could touch us. I had many wonderful days when I felt loved, but Christmas somehow was always especially magical. I have happy memories of childhood Christmases, the lovely gifts of dolls and stuffed animals that I yearned for—and my exciting belief in Santa. I have all these wonderful memories of the holidays that I shared with Mother and Dad.

Christmas will always represent love and joy to me. Going to our fine Methodist Church not far from our row home on the outskirts of Philadelphia, being comforted by the precious story of the birth of Jesus, singing Christmas carols, and placing the little figures of the Nativity scene beneath our Christmas tree are all dear memories that have lived within me through all the years to the present. And also, this little girl, who still lives within me, believes in Santa Claus.

Jesus brought such spiritual joy and Santa such happiness and love, that they did not conflict in my young life.

Along with the Nativity scene, I also displayed a jovial figure of Santa that had been given to me by my parents.

Shortly before the war years of World War II, a family moved into the end house of our row of homes. We lived in the third house from the corner with one home between us.

The new family consisted of loving parents and six children, four of them older and grown up. There were four sons and two daughters, and one girl was my age. Her name was Eleanor, the same as our President Franklin Delano Roosevelt's wife's name. We soon became friends, and I grew to care deeply about her family.

It was so amazing to me to see such a large family in the same size row home that I lived in with only my parents and a little cat. I had joy there with Eleanor's family in their home. I had never known what it was like to have older brothers.

And, oh, how they all seemed to enjoy Christmas and appreciate Santa, as well as being faithful Christians and attending the Catholic Church two blocks from our homes. Though their spiritual lives were at the center of their existence, my friend also had a strong attachment to Santa. It was beyond what I had.

I surely believed in and loved Santa's mythical image in my growing up years. I was a true believer! But Eleanor's belief was stronger than anyone else I had ever known.

Santa appeared to be such an important part of her life year-round, and she was never discouraged from thinking differently by her parents or family members. I was in her home so often, and she was permitted to revere Santa as a symbol of goodness very much in keeping with their Christian beliefs. It seemed to me that this devotion to Santa was out of the ordinary. As we grew a little older, Eleanor's belief in Santa never waned and she was often teased by our other friends.

Even though some logical doubt about Santa was creeping into my beliefs, I could never mock Eleanor. I admired her strength in the face of the teasing she often took. I wanted to retain those beliefs, too, because Christmas with Jesus and Santa was the happiest and most blessed and normal time in the life of my family. So I tried to cling to the belief in Santa, and having Eleanor as my friend helped me to be stronger in this. I just never spoke of about Santa freely to other friends unless directly questioned. But I stood with Eleanor. I never let her down.

The war happened, and slowly one by one, her three older brothers went into the U. S. Armed Forces in three separate branches. They were really nice young men and handsome and fun loving and truly devoted to their family. All were still single.

The gray air raid box now situated on the side stone wall of Eleanor's end home on the block of row homes reminded us always of the war. She and I and other young friends often sat on this box side by side, telling happy stories and trying to deny why the box was there.

The air raid box was placed under Eleanor's windows and by her side basement door, filled with equipment to be used by Air Raid Wardens when the sirens went off in the times of suspected planes approaching. Perhaps we felt that by keeping the equipment intact it would some how keep the war away. Sadly, we did not keep the war from Eleanor's family. Soon one by one, all three of Eleanor's wonderful brothers were killed in the line of duty, fighting for their country.

I have tears even as I write this, for I remember so clearly hearing the tragic news about each of these sweet guys, Bill, Bob and Al. One by one, we all saw another gold star added to the service flag that hung in their front window. First the stars were in blue, declaring that three young men served their country. Then the blue stars became gold, signifying that they had been killed in action.

It was so overwhelmingly sad and crushing to my parents and others in our neighborhood. I remember the impact of it on me to this day when I realized that I would never see and talk with her brothers again. They were my friends!

I was not familiar personally with death in those years of my young life. Eleanor's family was depleted emotionally and physically, but amazingly strong, their personal faith in Christ and their love for each other the center of their lives.

But Santa remained in Eleanor's life too. He was like a gentle Grandfather, a man who looked over her and cared about her and her family. He was good Saint Nicholas, one of the loving saints of the Christian church, and she needed him.

Eleanor and her family moved away several years after her three brothers were killed. She did not move so far that we could not visit each other at times. But eventually we parted forever, and I do not know where she and her family settled.

Wherever they are, they carry within them their three sons. And Santa! Somehow I have always believed Santa remained strongly in Eleanor's life.

I never knew a teenager who protected a belief in Santa Claus as she did. Her undeniable belief in him, despite taunting, showed me her inner strength. Could it be that the simple joyful unrelenting friendship with Santa in her personal life even in the face of ridicule, was the clue to her strength in her unbearable loss?

Yes, she and her family were all one in God, but the joys of childhood too are often gifts given us by God for strength to carry on. Perhaps Santa was Eleanor's special gift, and, in turn, she provided strength to each of her family members, a sweet bond of love from an earlier, happier time in their lives.

People, animals, legends, and beliefs from our child-hood, as well as our religious backgrounds are often carried within us in never ending ways. Sometimes they are simply necessary, and there is no other explanation. I truly understand.

When we first met Wanda Sue Parrott some years ago, she was a feature writer and reporter for a major Los Angeles newspaper. Since that time, she has written a number of books of prose and poetry.

Wanda sent us her memories of "The Night Superman Saved Santa."

A muffled voice disturbed my culture-shocked Christmas Eve. My twelve-year-old mind strained to see through suburban darkness, but drapes on the bedroom windows blocked Southern California's moonlight.

That can't be Santa Claus, I thought to myself. *He doesn't exist!*

The sound of sobs prickled my spine. *That's Sister. Something's wrong!*

I waited for Daddy's comforting voice to tell seven-year-old Jan, as he'd reassured me back home in the city, "You didn't hear monsters here. You heard the house settling."

A waterpipe banged, but the hall floor didn't creak. Daddy wasn't coming. I panicked.

The heroic figure from the comic books that Mother made me give away before our move a month earlier flashed into mind. *Save Gotham!* Superman commanded.

"What?"

Trust in me! My hero vanished.

Other nights, we were allowed to turn on lights, open doors, explore our new house. Christmas Eve was an exception. Good children stayed in bed. Bad children scared Santa away. Disobedience wasn't worth the risk of finding no stocking or gifts on Christmas morning, even though I'd guiltily borne secret knowledge a schoolmate foisted on me at Jan's age: *There's no Santa Claus. Parents give us presents.*

Suddenly I heard a *thump!* coming from Jan's room.

Something powerful seized control, forcing my hand to open my door so smoothly that the hinges didn't even squeak. I boldly tiptoed across the hall and peeked into Jan's room. Shadow light through muslin curtains revealed tangled blankets beside the bed.

"Sister?"

Jan's head poked out from the pile. "I fell out . . . I had to tinkle. I tried to hold it, but . . . now Santa won't come."

I almost laughed aloud, nearly shouted: *Santa's not real!* But another voice whispered from my mouth. "We'll fix it before Santa arrives."

Jan's whimpers stopped.

"We'll blot your bottoms dry. I'll be right back."

I crept through the living room to the newspapers stacked behind Daddy's overstuffed armchair. Our scrawny scotch pine tree was silhouetted against still-uncurtained windows, lights off. Boxes that weren't at its base earlier proved that our parents had already played Santa. *But where are the Christmas stockings?*

Impulsively, defiantly, I flipped the switch. The tree lit up, its lights miraculously manifesting magic. Through the swirl of golds, reds, greens, blues that filled the hollow in my homesick heart, I spotted two red-net stockings hanging from the knobs on our old Stromberg-Carlson console radio. Impulsively, defiantly, I snatched the stockings and, with newspapers in tow, returned to my task without turning the Christmas tree off. I hung one stocking on Jan's doorknob, the other on mine. Then I reentered Jan's room.

"Did you see Santa?" My sister handed me her damp pajamas.

"No."

I rolled the garment in classified ad pages. "Step on 'em to blot 'em."

While she kneaded the wad with her feet, I pulled linens back onto Jan's new double bed. Until our move, she'd slept in a worn out, cramped crib. Now she had a new maple bedroom set in which to grow. The mattress was damp. I spread newspapers across it, stretched Jan's sheet over them, and pressed it dry, kicking wet papers beneath the bed like I used to stash Superman comic books under mine.

"What if Santa can't find us?" Jan whispered.

"Shhhh," I said. "He's here." I opened Jan's door a crack. "Look."

The glow of lights filtered through the wall heater, illuminating the hall. The pilot light created an illusion of bustling activity. I ushered Jan to bed. "Go to sleep and don't come out till morning."

In my own bedroom I snuggled into the covers on the four-poster bed in which I was growing up. Its once-red cherry-wood spools were scarred from wads of gum I'd saved during the war, while still a tomboy who climbed trees and preferred playing animal doctor with kittens to playing house with dolls.

Before we became the first family in the subdivision carved from strawberry fields owned by Japanese-American gardeners, who'd been interned in prisoner-of-war camps in Northern California, strange things were happening to my body and mind. Boys with whom I'd played poker, kick-the-can, and baseball now caused hot flushes if we faced each other.

By the time we moved into the new house near smelly swine and dairy farms, I'd scraped, hacked, and filed the gum from the wood, and used Daddy's brown shoe polish to shine the damaged veneer, as if to give it new life.

As I drifted toward sleep, the hall floor squeaked. The toilet flushed. Then Daddy peeked in, asked if I was awake, and closed it when I didn't answer.

A loud "Merry Christmas!" startled me awake. Jan, with Mother and Daddy behind her, was standing in my doorway. "Look at what Santa gave me in my sock!"

Jan waved three Superman comics, a tube of pale pink lipstick and bottle of matching nail polish, five pairs of lace-trimmed pink rayon panties, a pack of chewing gum, and a red patent-leather wallet holding a five-dollar bill and handwritten note. "Read it." She handed me the paper.

Mother's handwritten note said, "Buy yourself something pretty to wear. Love, Santa."

Jan handed my stocking to me. "What did you get?"

Mother grimaced. Daddy grinned. And I knew that they knew that all of us but Jan knew secrets about Santa that we'd probably never discuss.

Daddy winked when I held up a jumbo Dumbo coloring book, a box of crayons, a book of paper dolls and
clothes, a pink yo-yo, five tiny pairs of thick white cotton
panties, a pack of chewing gum, and a one-dollar bill.

Later, when I threatened to tattle about her bed-
wetting, Jan agreed to trade her stocking stuffers for
mine.

That Christmas was never discussed, but every
ensuing holiday, while Jan and I still lived at home, we
were allowed to visit the bathroom on Christmas Eve,
provided we kept our eyes shut.

Also, our stockings were hung on the correct doors
with care, and we all knew exactly who had been there.

E very year Jannice Fadely tells her granddaughters this story that until now, stayed within the
family.

"You can use it in your book with my permission,"
she said. "Many people will read your book—and they
need to know the true magic of Santa Claus."

Years ago when my son Jed was about eight years
old, we sat in our living room together on Christmas
eve as I put the finishing details on the wooden soldiers I had made him. It was eleven thirty at night. I
sat at the table, carefully painting the wooden soldiers.
My son was playing quietly on the floor next to me.

We heard a heavy object land and skid to a stop on
the roof of our home. We both looked up in complete

surprise. It sounded like a car had landed on our roof; the thud was that loud and heavy.

We followed with our eyes the sounds of footsteps of a very large person walking up the side of the roof over the top, down to the chimney on the other side.

Completely dismayed, we both flew outdoors to see what was on our roof. There was no way for anything to land or walk on our roof—it was an A frame with a steep pitch.

The walls are 8-feet-high before you can reach the roof. There were no ladders in view. Nor were there any trees nearby. To add to the mystery, it was a very cold night, and the roof was covered in ice.

My son and I raced around the outside of the house, looking up on the roof for whatever had walked up one side of the roof and down the other. Later, we walked around the house slowly to check more carefully for something or someone on our roof.

The land around the house was completely clear of any trees or obstructions, so no one could hide anywhere on the roof. The only tracks in the snow were made by my son and me. Jed and I just stared at each other in disbelief. We shook our heads. There was no way it could have been Santa Claus.

The more we talked it over, the more convinced we were that Santa had actually landed on our roof. There was no other possible explanation.

From that night on, we both knew without a doubt that Santa Claus was real. Christmas became a very special time of year for us.

My son and I rarely tell about Santa's visit to anyone—it is just too special to share with everyone. But we tell my granddaughters the story every Christmas. It is a wonderful feeling, even at fifty-nine as I am, and thirty, as my son is, to know that Santa is real.

While some people may doubt Santa's existence, we *know* he is real.

I n these days when critically acclaimed motion pictures such as *The Dark Knight* based on the comic book characters of Batman and his nemesis The Joker are hot box office tickets and offer Academy Award winning acting, comic books have taken on a respectability that they have never before enjoyed. Therefore, we were not greatly surprised that our friend Dr. Franklin Ruehl, Ph.D, a nuclear physicist, should have as one of his Santa Miracles as a child the gift of a number of cherished comic book titles.

According to Dr. Ruehl, he experienced a "heartwarming comic book mini-Santa Miracle."

Donald Duck! Bugs Bunny! Mickey Mouse! Tom and Jerry! Sylvester and Tweety!

As a youngster, these were among my very favorite cartoon characters! I always looked forward to seeing them at the theater, far more than the movies they were paired with. Then, in the first grade, I discovered comic books which featured these very same characters, and I was immediately hooked! I would buy as many as I could afford on my tiny allowance.

Of course, in those days, comic books were only a dime apiece, so I could purchase several at a time! I never tired of reading and re-reading the episodes within.

My very favorite was "Walt Disney's Comics and Stories," which typically began with a Donald Duck feature along with his nephews, Huey, Dewey, and Louie, and often included Daisy Duck, Uncle Scrooge McDuck, and Gander Goose, followed by a Mickey Mouse entry along with Pluto and Minnie Mouse.

While in the second grade, I became seriously ill right after Halloween with what appeared to be an unrelenting cold or even possibly influenza.

My mother speculated that I might have caught a bug from staying out late on a particularly nippy evening trick-or-treating, as was my wont. I would go out until my first bag was filled, return home, then go out again for a second and even a third trip. My dad advanced the idea that I might have contracted an illness from some item that I had collected.

Whatever the cause, I began missing significant time from school which I had never done before. Extreme respiratory symptoms were plaguing me day and night.

My birthday, November 8, was ruined as well as Thanksgiving. And I was missing out on buying my beloved comic books. I was suffering both physiologically and psychologically

Two different physicians had simply prescribed the standard therapy of rest, aspirin, and chicken soup, asserting that I would recover in a brief amount of time. But, if anything, my condition was worsening.

Finally, a few days before Christmas, a third doctor diagnosed me with tonsillitis, declaring that it was one of the worst cases he had ever seen. I went into a hospital shortly thereafter for a tonsillectomy and immediately improved physically.

But I was still anguished over the time that I had lost from school, which I thoroughly enjoyed, and missing out on my cherished comic books.

A minor Santa Miracle took place on Christmas morning when I raced out to check the presents under the tree. In one large box that I opened were perhaps twenty-five comic books, including not just the ones that I had missed purchasing, but a clutch of new ones I had never seen before. My parents had been buying my favorites as well as some others as a surprise for me when I recovered. I was absolutely delighted.

For me, at that age, it was the best gift that I could have received. And that box of comic books at Christmas became a tradition for several years to come. Again, while perhaps relatively insignificant on the cosmic scale, it was very significant on my scale!

The fact that my parents would fulfill my most heartfelt wish by bringing me the comic books that I most wanted proved that they were the best Santas in the world. Although I would go on in the field of physics, the tales of fantasy and imagination that were in those comic books helped to make me a more complete scientist, unafraid to use my creative as well as my cognitive abilities.

"Is it possible, just possible, that fate can move its huge hand occasionally in even seemingly insignificant ways?" Dr. Ruehl asked rhetorically, before launching into the story of his Santa Miracle.

While shopping with my mother, Florence, right after Thanksgiving at Buffum's Department Store Glendale, California, she admired an eye-catching beige Stetson cowboy hat adorned with a tuft of raccoon fur on one side and a trio of raccoon tails dangling from it on the other side.

I sensed immediately that she had fallen in love with that hat, although she did not try it on. She probably hoped that I would surprise her with it as a

Christmas gift. A collector of hats, each with a nickname, this would have been the ideal present for her.

I returned to the store a few days later, fully intending to purchase the hat. To my great disappointment, someone else had grabbed it. I was kicking myself for procrastinating, especially when the clerk told me they had no more in stock and could not re-order one this close to the holidays.

Embarking on a quest for the hat, I went from one store to another, from small shops to chain department stores, all to no avail. No one had any hat even remotely resembling it. I was berating myself for not going back that first day and buying it.

A few days before Christmas, as I was riding with my dad, Franklin, who had also kept an eye out futilely for that cherished hat, we hit some traffic. Trying to avoid the congestion, he decided to take a right turn that he normally would not have. On our route, we passed by a small boutique I had not seen previously. "Stop!" I cried at my father. While he waited in the car, I dashed inside for one last chance to find that hat.

After a quick examination of their offerings, I didn't find it, and I turned to leave. I was almost to the door when I caught sight of the very gem for which I had been prospecting on the bottom shelf of a glass case! Of course, I immediately purchased it.

As an added surprise, instead of putting it under the Christmas tree, we sneaked it in her closet.

It was not until later on Christmas morning, after opening her other gifts, that she discovered the hat awaiting her, a surprise find that genuinely delighted her. She christened the hat "My Three Raccoons" and has worn it many times with great pleasure, invariably receiving compliments about it.

Amazingly, I talked her into letting me wear the hat for a TV pilot I produced entitled, *The Amazing World of Western Fact and Fiction*. And recently, I have also worn it on a few editions of my webisode, *The Amazing World of Bizarre News*, on Videojug.com. Indeed, a female producer there was pleased with the hat the first time that she saw it and encouraged me to wear it more often!

It is probably presumptuous of me to suggest that fate intervened so that I would find the hat, but my mother and I like to think so, and we regard this a minor Santa Miracle!

Reverend Ann Palmer has affirmed that she has received at least two Santa Miracles—and probably a great many more.

Ann's childhood memories began when our nation was coming out of the Great Depression. "Our family would probably be considered very poor by today's standards," she said, "but we didn't know the difference because nearly every family we knew was facing the same kind of financial problems."

She recalled that her sister and brother were near the same age, and seemed to form a kind of "team" against her, the baby of the family. She jokes that she could have confused her real name with "Tag Along" as that was her older siblings' constant complaint to their father: "Does she have to tag along?"

Her family lived in the Panhandle of Texas, and Ann thinks that from the time she was born they had never visited her parents' relatives who lived in far East Texas. When Ann was five, though, the family planned to visit their relatives for Christmas. Her parents had bought a new car for the trip. "It could have been a used car," Ann considered. "It was a black and shiny Chevrolet, because black seemed to be the only color cars came in in those days."

At age five, Ann recalled that she probably believed in Santa Claus more than Jesus or God. "I was very upset to be driving across Texas on Christmas Eve," Ann said. "How would Santa Claus ever be able to find us while we were on the road?

"Are we there yet?" is certainly a question that children wear out with repetition on a long automobile drive, and Ann remembers asking it many times.

"We must have driven all night and stopped at a restaurant for breakfast," Ann said. "I roused from my sleep in the backseat along with my brother and sister. I was not a happy traveler, sleeping cramped up in the backseat next to my older siblings, and grumbling about how we should be home for Christmas and how Santa would never find them in the middle of Nowhere, Texas."

When the family returned to the car after breakfast, Ann had the surprise of her young life.

"Somehow, Santa had found our car while we had breakfast because as we returned, there in the back seat was a brush and mirror set on the left side of the back seat for my sister, a truck for my brother on the right side and there in the middle was a beautiful doll for me. Maybe there were other trinkets but I don't remember them. The thing I do remember is thinking, 'How could Santa possibly find us while we were traveling in a car across Texas?' To my fiveyear-old mind, that was the first miracle I had ever experienced."

Since the miraculous visit of Santa when she was five, Ann has experienced many miracles in her life. When she was thirteen she began modeling for major department stores in Dallas. After a few more years of experience, she became a runway model at fashion shows. And then one miracle after another occurred in her life. Ann went to Hollywood and was placed under contract by 20th Century Fox. Within a few months she was in Italy, appearing in the film *Cleopatra* and socializing with the likes of Elizabeth Taylor, Richard Burton, Rex Harrison, and Roddy McDowell. When she returned to the States, she had small parts in such films as *Love with the Proper Stranger* with Steve McQueen and Natalie Wood, *Bonnie and*

Clyde with Warren Beatty and Faye Dunaway, and many others.

Another Santa Miracle occurred for Anne when she was working as a commentator for Cadillac at the new car Motor Shows.

"I had flown in from California to work an auto show in Dallas just before Christmas," Ann recalled. "This job would give me the opportunity to visit my parents for Christmas Eve in their home 30 miles east of Dallas."

At the show, Ann was growing tired of working. "I had trumpeted the wonders of Cadillac automobiles for about six hours," she said. "I got off work at 11:00 P.M. and had to change out of my evening dress before I began the drive to my parents' home. About half way between Dallas and my parents' house, I got a flat tire. I was so tired from stepping in and out of cars all day, but I had to get my strength together and say 'I can do this!'"

Ann got the spare tire out of the trunk and rolled it over to the flat. "I got the car jacked up but when I tried to turn the wrench on the lug nuts, I found I couldn't get the wheel off."

Ann struggled. It could be dangerous flagging down a passerby, especially after midnight on a Saturday night, but she felt she had no choice. She happened to have a pair of red pajamas in her luggage, and she removed them from the suitcase and started waving them—but no one stopped.

"Off in the distance I could see a truck driving toward the highway," Ann said. "I just *knew* it was coming to help me. Sure enough, the truck pulled over and the driver got out of the clean, white medium-sized truck. He was very neatly dressed in a clean uniform. He turned on a large flashlight and showed me that on that particular model, there was a reversed bolt that was sort of inside a hole, which I could not see without a flashlight."

In moments, the courteous truck driver had changed the tire.

"He wouldn't accept money, and he told me not to worry as he would follow me all the way to my parents' house," Anne recalls. She was stunned, because her parents' home was at least 20 miles farther.

On the way to her final destination, Ann resolved to write to the company that employed the driver and tell them what a helpful and courteous driver they employed. She kept looking in the rearview mirror, trying to make out the license number, but she could never quite see it. She decided that she would wait until she turned to her parents' home, and then she would get the name of the company off the side of the truck as he passed her.

"I turned to go to my parents' house, and I stopped to see him pass so I could get the name of the company—but the truck was no longer there," Ann said. "I had seen the headlights and the cab with the smiling driver following me all the way to my parents' home, but now it wasn't there. It had vanished."

Ann realized at that moment that she had been the recipient of a Santa Miracle. "Why was such a neatly dressed truck driver in a pristine white truck going somewhere at midnight on a Saturday night? And why would even the most courteous and thoughtful of truck drivers volunteer to follow me all the way to my parents' home, at least twenty miles out of his way? And, of course, how could such a large truck completely disappear when it was only a couple of car lengths behind me?"

Anne concluded her story, "I know that it was an angel that manifested for my help."

Our friends and fellow authors Jeff Belanger and Megan Peckman Belanger have been collecting stories of children's encounters with Santa Claus. When they learned of *Santa Miracles* they generously sent us the following stories for use in our book.

Betty Jane Medved of Pittsburgh, Pennsylvania, recalled that her first meeting with Santa was in the basement of their church when she was in second or third grade.

"We were in a Sunday school program, singing those little Sunday school songs," Betty Jane recalled. "Nobody ever expected Santa Claus. Even when I look

back I'm surprised, because Santa Claus is almost ver-
boten in our church. They don't even talk about him.

"There was a small stage in the basement, and
our parents were there. We were all sitting in our
seats when the Sunday school director came up and
announced, "I have one more surprise for everybody."
And here Santa Claus came bounding out onto the
stage, waving and ho-ho-ho-ing and everything.

"We just all went crazy, because we never expected
him. All of us kids got in a long line, waiting to get up
on the stage and talk to him. We were laughing and
giggling, jumping up and down, and squealing. It was
so much wilder than the excitement that you would
have at a department store, because it was such a surprise—and in church, it felt kind of forbidden.

"It was Santa, and he was on the stage at our Sunday School program! We just couldn't believe it. We
kept saying to each other, 'It's him! It's him! It's him!'

"And by the time we got up on stage, it had
changed to 'It's you! It's you!' Then Santa handed out
little presents to everybody.

"I remember looking around for my mother, looking for direction on how I should behave during all
this; but she was just laughing and having a good
time."

When Elizabeth Judd, from San Francisco, California, was ten, and her brother Shawn was four, he still believed in Santa.

"I hadn't believed for years since I'd seen my dad putting gifts under the tree," Elizabeth said. "On Christmas morning, Shawn woke me up around five to go open presents. My parents, who were still half-asleep, made us lie in bed with them for a while, telling my brother that Santa may not have come yet, so he needed to wait.

"After lying there for a little bit, we all heard a thump on the roof. My brother got *so excited* that Santa was here.

"My parents and I went along with his excitement to add to Shawn's thrill about hearing Santa. Then we heard another thump—and suddenly, a bright red light filled the room as it passed by the window.

"Needless to say, we were shocked. We never figured out what it was, but to this day, my brother still believes it was Santa."

Dave Gotcher from Dallas, Texas, played Santa Claus at Universal Studios Hollywood for five years.

"My favorite memory as a Santa," Dave fondly remembers, "was when I went out with a group of volunteer performers to a place that was basically an adult day care center for senior citizens. That's where I met Frank.

"Frank had a stroke and couldn't speak anymore. An aide wheeled him up to me and said, 'Frank, tell Santa what you want.'

"I watched as this man struggled to try to speak and saw the tears build in his eyes when he couldn't.

"I heard myself say, 'It's all right, Frank. Santa never forgets a friend, and we go way back. I know what you want and I'll do my best. Bless you Frank.'

"I'd *never* said 'bless you' to anyone before. Frank then grabbed me in a hug so tight I thought my ribs would break. We were both crying openly.

"As we were leaving, the nurse said Frank had been unresponsive for a week before that visit.

"I went back the next year, and all they knew was that Frank was no longer there. I sure hope he got that wish."

Norma Joiner, one of our favorite e-mail buddies, recalled growing up in Hawaii, on the island of Kauai, she and her two sisters had great childhood experiences.

"We spent many weekends with family camping on the beach, fishing, swimming in the ocean or a stream, hiking, picking fruits in the mountains, and exploring. There was adventure all the time."

Norma's memories of Santa and Christmas are mingled with recollections of the days in the 1940s and '50s when times were tough and her father worked as a stevedore on the docks.

"My mother was a stay at home Mom, and I remember how washing the laundry meant boiling the water in a large drum, stirring it with a wooden stick, and then rinsing it in another drum filled with cold water. She would wring out the clothes by hand and then hang each item on clotheslines nailed to the side of the house and stretched across the yard to a tree at the side of the garage. Poles were used to lift the lines and raise them to a safe height from the ground. We learned, early on, that laundry days were not the time to play chase in the back yard.

"My father worked long hours and there came a time when he got involved in organizing a union on the docks for better wages and benefits for the minority workers. In representing the workers, he also got involved in special occasions where there were parties.

"One of the memories my sisters and I cherish was helping at Christmas when our living room was crowded with boxes of apples, oranges, nuts, and candies. My two sisters and I would fill brown bags with goodies and make sure everything was counted twice. It was a very exciting time for us as we got to be helpers for the big Christmas party for the families of the stevedores. Our living room smelled wonderful and the feeling of Christmas was alive!

"The night of the party, the stevedores and their families would gather at a large warehouse and there were decorations, a huge tree with lots of presents, and

Santa was there. There was laughter, music, singing, and food.

"Helping my father getting those bags ready so he could play Santa to his men was always the highlight of Christmas at our house. To this day, my sisters and I still remember the smiles on the faces of the children as they got their bags of goodies and a present from Santa.

"We are grateful for a mother and father who taught us at a young age to share with others—and that is a precious gift that no one can ever take away. That was our Santa Miracle."

Well-known as an author of inspirational works, Beverly Hale Watson of Grapevine, Texas, also devotes her time to many charitable groups and organizations, including sending regular packages of gifts and personal items to our men and women serving in Iraq and Afghanistan. Beverly is a firm believer in miracles of all kinds, including Christmas miracles, angel miracles, and Santa Miracles. For this book, she has contributed the timetable during which an extraordinary miracle occurred—and Beverly herself was a participant:

December 22

Anna Thompson was nestled under a heavy down-filled comforter listening to crackling wood and watching embers burn in the fireplace. Cool air flowed through cracks in the barren wood floor as wind whistled through the uncovered window frames. Scattered thoughts filled her mind while she lay in bed. Tomorrow her class was taking a field trip from their school in Virginia to Mallard Creek Mall in Charlotte, North Carolina. She was filled with anticipation, but had other issues on her mind.

Her mother had been hospitalized four times since March with back problems. Her father, Arlis, was a coal miner, who had been laid-off from work in June. Soon their debts exceeded their income and their savings, and put them in bankruptcy. In October, they were evicted from their home. Out of desperation her father had roamed the back roads searching for an abandoned house where they could live. This house was hidden in a holler. The living room, kitchen, and three bedrooms were empty, but each had a beautiful fireplace with logs neatly stacked on the right side. In the backyard he found a well with running water. It wasn't a palace, but certainly better than living out of their van. His family would have a home.

December 23

Anna awoke to the loud buzzing of her alarm clock. The fire had died during the night causing the air to become quite brisk. Getting her muscular arms into position, she quickly lifted her body into the wheelchair sitting next to her bed. Both legs had been amputated above her knees due to an automobile accident.

"It was a drag being confined to this contraption," Anna recalls. But, she had no choice. Although her father wanted to get her artificial legs, he could not afford them. She knew it pained him to see her in the wheelchair. He often prayed that things could be different. For Anna, it was an inconvenience; she hated that people considered her handicapped, but made the best of her situation.

Anna rushed through her normal morning routine, not wanting to miss the school bus.

The bus driver tooted his horn as he drove up the lane leading to her house. She emptied her piggy bank, grabbed her coat and headed for the door. Two hefty boys loaded her onto the bus and strapped her in place; they were happy she only weighed 90 pounds. The bus started on the three-hour journey to Charlotte.

As the students approached Mallard Creek Mall there were traffic jams, impatient people seeking parking spaces, and last minute shoppers scurrying to get inside. "My holler in Virginia is nothing like this!" Anna exclaimed.

Judy Brickle arrived at the mall an hour ahead of schedule. Her youthful appearance, warm smile, and abundance of energy belied her fifty years of age.

She was headed for the large spruce tree decorated with colorful paper angels furnished by The Salvation Army. Each one contained the name and age of a boy or girl, plus their Christmas wish list. Shoppers would stop by, select an angel, purchase the items requested, and return them to the Angel Tree for delivery. It was Judy's job to answer questions, give out angel names, and keep track of the gifts purchased. Every Christmas, she bought gifts for other kids, as she had none of her own. She felt it was always more blessed to give than receive.

Next to the Angel Tree were 500 dolls on display. Each one wore a handmade outfit sewn to perfection. These dolls would be given to some "special angels" whose names were on the tree.

Anna couldn't believe her eyes as she worked her way through the department store aisles in awe of all the Christmas decorations. Her friends couldn't wait to shop. Anna wanted to take her time, so she decided to go it alone.

Quickly she spotted the Angel Tree and the 500 dolls on display next to it. She maneuvered her wheel chair through the crowds and parked herself in front of the display.

Judy noticed Anna and her curly blond hair, small face, and sparkling blue eyes. When she smiled, her deep dimples became even more pronounced. Judy wondered what could have caused one so young to be left without legs.

"The dolls you are looking at are to be given to the girls whose names are on the Angel Tree." Judy commented as she approached Anna. "Which one do you like?" Judy asked, not knowing what else to say.

"I really love the bride doll on the end of the top shelf," Anna answered. "It is beautiful! Her white lace top with all those pearls just glisten under the lights. Her long satin skirt and fluffy petticoats are gorgeous. She even has a crown holding her veil, all trimmed with lace and tiny pearls. You know, I have always wanted a doll like that, but my parents could never afford to buy me one. She looks like something out of a dream!"

As other people approached Judy to ask questions about the Angel Tree, she found herself leaving Anna alone to look at the dolls. Anna would leave the exhibit and then return. Her focus was always on the bride doll she so admired.

As Judy observed this child, she knew in her heart that there had to be some way she could arrange for Anna to receive this doll. Without missing a beat, she reached into her sweater pocket to retrieve a pencil and pad of paper to write down Anna's name and address. She planned to add an angel to the Angel Tree with her name on it.

However, when Judy reached into her pocket it was empty. She forgot that she had left the items on a table on the other side of the tree. Quickly, she headed over to the table to reclaim her pencil and paper.

At that moment, another woman approached Judy requesting information about the Angel Tree. When Judy returned to the doll display, Anna was gone. Frustrated with the way this incident unfolded, Judy was bound and determined to locate Anna in the mall. Anxiously, she waited for the relief volunteer to arrive.

Not wanting to waste any time, Judy removed the bride doll from the display and put it in a box with a blank angel tag on it. Then she contacted me and requested a list of all the schools that had scheduled visits to the mall on that day.

While I was busy securing the requested list of schools, Judy and the relief volunteer continued their search for Anna. They asked other teenagers if they knew her, hoping to obtain her full name, but to no avail, so Judy returned to the Salvation Army's Office.

I arranged for her and two other women to start calling the various schools listed. We were sure it wouldn't be difficult to find Anna because of the fact that she was in a wheelchair.

First they called all the local schools—no matches. Next long distance phone calls were made to schools in surrounding states.

Twenty-three schools down the list and "Bingo"— they had a match! The student was from Tazewell County, Virginia. Judy couldn't believe they had found her.

It was two o'clock, and there was still much to do. Judy quickly relayed what had taken place earlier in the day to the school principal, Mr. Martin. If he would provide her with an address, the bride doll would be mailed tonight for delivery on Christmas Eve. She sincerely needed his assistance in this matter.

"Mrs. Brickle," Mr. Martin said, "I truly want to help you, but there are a few other concerns that we must address. First of all, the Thompson family lives in a holler. They have no street address. The only way the doll would get to her would be if it was sent to me or to my secretary's home. I would be delighted to drop off the doll, but I'm leaving town in the morning. That means it will be up to my secretary to handle this. Secondly, there are three other girls in the family. If you send something for Anna, you really need to include something for the other children so there are no hurt feelings."

"I will be glad to take care of them, too," Judy replied. "Just give me their names and ages. Can you check with your secretary to see if she can deliver the packages?"

The principal put Judy on hold while he telephoned his secretary, Mrs. Wiley. He asked her if it would be possible for her to run by the Thompsons' home that next day.

"I really don't have the time!" Mrs. Wiley answered. "We have company coming in from out of town. I still have presents to wrap, food to prepare, and a house to clean. Plus, the Thompson family lives an hour's drive from my house. I would be happy to do it some other day, but not tomorrow," she replied.

After hanging up the telephone, Mrs. Wiley realized that Christmas was no time to be selfish. Feeling guilty about her response, she quickly picked up the telephone and called her boss back. "I'll be glad to deliver the packages to the Thompsons," she told him. "Just send them to my home address."

By that time, it was four o'clock—time for the kids from Virginia to leave for home. Anna and her friends were headed for the school bus when she decided to go by the doll display for one more glimpse of her dream doll.

As she approached the area, a look of bewilderment came over her face. The doll was gone!

Scanning the display she realized it was the only one not there. "Where could it be?" she wondered.

Anna looked at her watch. She had ten minutes to catch the bus. "Darn, I wish I had returned to the Angel Tree sooner. It would have been wonderful if my three sisters' names could have been added," she thought to herself. Quickly turning her wheelchair around, she zoomed for the exit doors.

As Anna made her journey home, Judy got the names, ages, and "wish lists" of Anna's siblings. Filled with enthusiasm, Judy headed for the nearest department store at the mall. She had ninety minutes to gather up an assortment of clothing and toys and bring them to the gift-wrapping department. While the items were being wrapped, she went to the Angel Tree to pick up four dolls. By the time she returned, the clerk was ready to wrap them.

"These gifts need to be boxed up and shipped overnight delivery," Judy explained to the clerk.

"Sorry ma'am, the mail truck left here fifteen minutes ago," the clerk told her. "I can box the stuff up, but they won't go out until tomorrow."

Judy knew that time was of the essence. "Will you please send the boxes downstairs to Parcel Pick-Up?" she asked the clerk. "I'll take them to the post office myself. Hopefully, I won't be too late to have them put on a truck bound for Virginia."

Her adrenaline was pumping as Judy weaved through hundreds of people moving like a herd of cattle down the escalator. Judy exited the mall and found her car. Everywhere she turned, there was traffic. Cars were moving so slowly. They reminded her of swamp turtles taking a stroll on an extremely hot day.

Thanks to a polite driver who let her cut in line, she inched her way over to Parcel Pick-Up. As Judy approached, a man rushed through the doors before she had a chance to get out of her car.

"Open your trunk, ma'am, and I'll put your boxes inside for you," he remarked. Wasting no time, Judy happily complied.

As she drove the ten blocks to the post office, she prayed that there would be a parking spot near the front door and that the lines would be short inside. She had to get these packages mailed out that night! Judy spotted an open space and wheeled into the slot.

Inside there were people standing in two long lines. Not wanting to waste any time, she got the attention of a supervisor who was willing to assist her. "I need these shipped overnight delivery," Judy explained, sliding the boxes onto the counter.

The packages were heavier than she anticipated, and she was thankful when she could set them down. Other customers voiced their annoyance that she was getting preferential treatment after they had been waiting patiently in line. Judy smiled meekly and continued with her transaction.

"That will be $20.25," said the mail clerk.

Judy opened her purse, pulling out her wallet. All she had was $15.25. "Sir, I am short $5. It is imperative that these packages are shipped out tonight," she said in a desperate voice.

"I 'm sorry lady, I can't ship them until you pay for the postage," he stated firmly, knowing he had to abide by the rules.

Judy's mouth went into high gear. She explained what had happened earlier and why it was necessary that the boxes got out that night.

The mail clerk sympathized with her, but legally he couldn't mail them "overnight delivery" without her paying for them. He would hold the boxes until she came up with the additional $5.

Knowing that he was not going to budge, she headed for her car to see if there was any money in her coat pocket.

Before she left the post office, a stranger approached her. "I couldn't help overhearing what happened to you at the counter," he said. "Here's $5. Don't worry about paying me back, just have a Merry Christmas."

Dumbfounded, Judy thanked the man and ran back to the counter, waving the $5 bill in her hand, yelling to the mailman who had waited on her. He quickly took her money, grabbed her boxes, and headed for the trucks loading up at the back dock. The Virginia-bound truck hadn't left yet.

December 24

Mrs. Wiley's house was filled with friends and relatives. It was all she could do to keep her wits about her. Between preparing food, settling disputes amongst the children, and trying to tend to everyone's needs, her patience was running thin.

Just then the doorbell rang. Her husband opened the door. "Special Delivery," the mailman shouted as he climbed back into his truck. "Have a Merry Christmas."

Mr. Wiley slid the boxes inside the house.

Mrs. Wiley called everyone together and explained what had to be done. Did anyone want to ride out to the Thompsons' place with her?

The response was overwhelming. All ten guests wanted to go and to share in the surprise. After all, the real meaning of Christmas was to bring love, joy, and happiness to others.

Anna and her family were sitting around the fireplace in the living room singing Christmas carols. They didn't have any electricity, so candles and lanterns provided their light. Paper ornaments and popcorn threaded on string decorated their Christmas tree, which Arlis had brought in from the woods. He felt bad that he could not provide better for his family during this time of year. However, considering all that had happened to them, this was a very blessed Christmas. He was thankful for a roof over their heads. Besides they had the necessities and plenty of love.

Hearing a knock on the door, one of Anna's sister rushed to open it. A dozen people were standing on the porch. Some were carrying baskets filled with fruit and food. Others had beautifully wrapped packages tucked under their arms.

"Mrs. Wiley what are you doing here?" she asked totally surprised.

"We just stopped by to wish you a Merry Christmas and deliver some presents for you and your family," she replied.

Tears filled Arlis's eyes as his children jumped up and down, squealing with joy.

"We can't stay and celebrate with you, but do hope you have a wonderful evening." Mrs. Wiley said as she passed along the gifts to the family members.

Excitement filled the air as the girls opened their presents. Anna took her time savoring the moment. She opened her smaller packages first, leaving the largest box to the last.

As she removed the paper from it, tears streamed down her face. It was the beautiful bride doll she had seen at the mall! An angel tag was attached to her dress with this message: *"Please report to Dr. Brickle's office on January 2 at 10:00 A.M. to be fitted for artificial legs. The prostheses and medical services will be provided at no charge. Merry Christmas!"*

As Arlis sat in his chair observing his family, he knew that his prayers had been answered. His family was safe and warm; his children had a real Christmas; and Anna would no longer be in a wheelchair. Indeed, he was a blessed man for he had witnessed the miracle of Christmas.

Some years ago when we were presenting a sem-inar in the Los Angeles area in early Decem-ber, we began to feel in a rather festive mood toward the close of our final session. It was our last seminar of the year, and it was growing close to Christmas. While our topics of the past three days had covered a wide variety of metaphysical sub-jects, we decided to delve into an area of mysticism that nearly everyone has experienced—a belief in Santa Claus.

"When you were a child," we asked the group col-lectively, "what one thing made you believe in Santa Claus?" Our question created small explosions of laugh-ter from many of our seminar participants. It wasn't long, though, before many individuals got into the spirit of our question.

While we heard a number of great answers, a few favorites stand out in our memories. Matt told us of the following experience that convinced him of Santa's existence.

"I was only three or so. I saw my older brother and sister writing in their note pads for school, and when I asked them what they were doing, they said that they were writing their letters to Santa Claus. They explained that this was how Santa found out what kids wanted for Christmas. So, naturally, I took a crayon and began to scribble my list on a sheet of paper.

"I remember being very upset when neither my brother nor my sister would take my letter with theirs to school the next day. My sister said not to worry. One of Santa's elves would find my letter and bring it to Santa at the North Pole.

"After they left for school and Mom had me bundled up to go outside and play in the snow banks next to the house in Montana, I toddled to our grove and put my letter to Santa in a hollow in one of the trees.

"When Christmas morning came, I got everything that I had asked for," Matt concluded his story. "That convinced me that Santa could work miracles. One of his elves retrieved my letter and brought it to Santa. That was totally magical and completely convincing in my mind. Of course at that age, it didn't occur to me that my 'letter' was just scribbles and that I might have mentioned what I wanted for Christmas within earshot of Mom or Dad once or twice."

Alyssa is a California girl, and when she was around four, her older sister told her one day that Santa could find out what she wanted for Christmas if she talked into a seashell and threw it as far as she could into the ocean.

Alyssa's parents had taken her to see a department store Santa and young Alyssa had become frightened and started screaming at his first "ho-ho." She thought that she had completely blown it with the Big Man, and she moped around the house in total despair. That was when her sister took her out on the beach one chilly Saturday afternoon and told her about an alternate method of giving Santa your "want list."

"After I thought I had found just the right sea shell," Alyssa remembers, "I shouted all the things that I wanted from Santa into the sea shell just as quickly as I could. I threw it as far as I could into the oncoming tide. My sister cried, 'Good job!'"

Her sister must have been right, as Alyssa got nearly everything that she had asked for from Santa.

"I could only think that Santa was truly a most wonderful miracle worker," Alyssa said. "I mean, even the fish and other creatures of the sea would deliver a kid's Christmas list to him at the North Pole. That was some kind of wonderful."

Ella also had a somewhat unorthodox method of getting her wish list to Santa.

"I grew up on a small ranch in Wyoming," she said. "I watched my older brother Ethan writing his list to Santa just before he left the house and ran for the school bus. Since I was only three at the time, I wasn't quite certain that I understood how the process worked."

Ella's mother explained that Ethan's third grade teacher had asked each of the students to write a letter to Santa Claus. When they brought them to class that morning, the teacher would put them in a special box for direct delivery to Santa.

Ella didn't understand letter writing, but she certainly knew who Santa Claus was.

"Sometime that afternoon," Ella recalls, "I opened the drawer in Mom's dresser where I knew she kept the special stationery that she used when she wrote letters to Grandma in Kansas. Of course, at the time, I just knew that Grandma lived far away, but I knew that it took this special paper to get to her. Such special paper would surely get to Santa."

Ella knew that her mother wouldn't mind if she borrowed a sheet, so she carefully removed a piece of the stationery from the blue cardboard box with the blue ribbon that kept the papers from falling out.

"I told Santa that I wanted a Barbie doll and a toy stove and a bunch of other things that I had seen advertised on television. I ended by telling Santa how much I loved him and Mrs. Santa Claus and all the elves that made the toys."

When Ethan returned from school late that afternoon, Ella showed him her list and asked him to put in the special box to Santa that they had at school.

Ethan laughed and said that Ella's letter was just a bunch of scribbles and squiggles. "Santa can't read that, you little nut," he told her. "And that box for letters to Santa at school is just for us third graders."

When Ella started to cry and sob and wonder how she would let Santa know what she wanted for Christmas, Ethan relented.

"My big brother was always good to me," Ella said, "and when he saw how upset I was, he told me that there was another way to get my wish list to Santa."

Ethan reminded her that the little manger scene that they had on the fireplace mantel had a lot of animals, like sheep, donkeys, and camels along with the wise men, the shepherds, Joseph, Mary, and the baby Jesus.

"You just pick out an animal that you think knows how to pass the word to Santa, and the job gets done," Ethan informed his little sister. "Remember the little song that you sing in Sunday school, 'Away in a Manger'? Remember what it says about the cattle waking Baby Jesus? We got a lot of cattle on this ranch."

Ethan walked Ella down to the pen where some of the calves that were being weaned from the milking cows were kept. He told her to watch them carefully, pick the one that looked the most trustworthy, and whisper her list in its ear.

"It was pretty easy to whisper in the calves' ears," Ella explained, "because it was feeding time and one of Ethan's chores was to see that the calves got fed. Five or six of them were sticking their heads out between the boards of the pen."

It didn't take Ella long to pick the one that she felt was most capable of beginning the long line of communication to Santa Claus. "We had Hereford cattle on the range," she explained, "and some Guernsey cattle for milking. I picked the calf with brown patches over his eyes that made him look very wise."

And the animal telephone system obviously worked, Ella laughed. She got everything she wanted for Christmas that year.

Ella recalls fondly, "I whispered my Santa list into a calf's ear every year until I was in second grade,"

Hunter was quite a bit older than some of our seminar participants and he could remember a radio program back in the late 1930s or early 1940s that had a bear with a high tenor singing voice who could place direct messages to Santa by having the North Wind carry them to him in the North Pole.

"I think this singing bear was called 'the Cinnamon Bear,' but I could be misremembering," Hunter said. "Anyway, I was very much taken with the program. It came on right after school, and I couldn't get into any snowball fights or build any snowmen or construct any snow forts if I wanted to get home in time to hear the latest updates on Santa's workshop progress from the Cinnamon Bear."

Hunter was in second grade, and had no trouble writing his letter to Santa. "Maybe all the words weren't spelled correctly," he conceded, "but I figured Santa or one of his elves could make out all of my Christmas wishes."

Completely convinced by the Cinnamon Bear's testimonial for the efficiency of the North Wind to deliver children's Christmas lists to Santa, Hunter found the highest spot around him on a windy day and let his letter fly to the North Pole.

She had sat up late one Christmas Eve, hoping to see Santa.

Her parents warned her that Santa wouldn't come as long as she sat cuddled up in her blankie on the sofa.

"I am the first to concede that I was a rather willful child when I was four," Hailey said, "but I was determined to sit up all night so that I might see Santa at work. I was also going to check off the items on my list to see if he had brought everything that I wanted."

Hailey was sound asleep by ten o'clock or so, but when she awakened during the night, she saw a most astonishing sight.

"There, moving around the Christmas tree, were two balls of light, one red, one green," she recalled.

"They bobbed up and down around the tree, and I knew that I was watching Santa and one of his elves bringing the presents."

There was a part of Hailey that wanted to jump off the sofa and run to hug Santa and tell him how much she loved him. "But I knew better than to make a single peep," Hailey said, "or up the chimney they would go, taking my presents along with them. I had been warned about the great, inviolable rule that no child was allowed to see Santa or his elves in the act of putting presents around the Christmas tree or in the Christmas stockings, so I snuggled deep under the cover of my blankie. I think I might even have snored just a little bit to convince Santa and his elf that I was really sleeping."

When Hailey awakened the next morning, she was in her bed.

"I ran downstairs and told Mommy and Daddy that I had really seen Santa and his elf putting the presents under the tree," Hailey said. "Both of them kind of scolded me and said that I was very lucky that Santa didn't know that I was awake. I told them that I made certain that Santa and his elf thought I was asleep by making little snoring sounds.

Growing up, Andrea's grandfather had her convinced that Santa miracles filled every day in December.

"Grandpa Lars's hobby was magic," Andrea told us. "As a child, he had me completely convinced that the world was filled with wonder and excitement at every turn. During the Christmas season, he was at his height of glory. Every night after he returned from his job as an accountant, he would transform himself into The Wonderful Wizard of Oz or of Copenhagen or of somewhere. He had been an actor who had appeared in amateur stage productions in Denmark, so he was also very skilled in the art of theatrical makeup."

Andrea explained that when she was four, she and her mother lived with Grandma and Grandpa

Kristofferson while her father was serving in Korea in 1950. She missed her father very much, and the entire family watched the war news every night. Andrea could tell that her mother was very worried about the situation, and each night at bedtime, they would pray for her father's safe return.

"In this time of great emotional stress for my mother and me, Grandpa Lars literally created an alternate reality for me," Andrea remembers. "I will always, always, bless him for that."

Every Christmas Eve, Grandpa would manage somehow to slip away on an "errand" and change into his Santa Claus suit. Soon, seemingly from out of nowhere, Santa would suddenly appear beside the Christmas tree and begin to pass out presents.

"He was such a master of makeup that I never once even guessed that Santa Claus was really Grandpa," Andrea laughs. "Remember, I was only four years old. Then, a little while later, after Santa had taken off again in his sleigh, Grandpa would come back with a sack of groceries or something in his hands to explain his absence from the scene when Santa was there. Grandpa would stomp one of his feet and moan, 'Oh, no! Did I miss him again?'"

In 1952, God blessed the Kristofferson family with the safe return of Andrea's father from the Korean conflict. In a few more months, Dad had returned to the

Minnesota city in which they lived, and he got an apartment for them not far from Andrea's grandparents.

"When I was older, I understood that the proximity to my grandparents' home was a matter of necessity," Andrea told us. "Both Dad and Mom had to get jobs to get the family on its feet, and it was convenient for me to be able to stop at Grandma's after school to stay until Mom or Dad came home to take me to our apartment."

Andrea reminded us that she was now six, going on seven, and stated that, like most children of that age, she had begun to hear some ugly rumors about Santa Claus at school. After dinner one night at her grandparents, she confronted her grandfather with the gossip going around the playgrounds at recess that there was no Santa Claus.

"Grandpa Lars's eyes widened and he looked at me as if I had just said a naughty word in church," Andrea recalled with an infectious laugh. "He assured me that there most certainly was a Santa Claus and all those kids who were spreading such awful stories were very sadly mistaken."

Andrea said that her beloved grandfather's reassurances steeled her against the most advanced logic that any of her classmates could put forward about Santa Claus not being real.

On Christmas Eve, Andrea and her parents joined Grandma and Grandpa Kristofferson in their home to decorate the tree. As usual, Grandpa Lars excused himself, saying that he had forgotten to pick up a couple of items at the market.

Only this time, after her grandfather had been absent for a few minutes, Andrea heard a strange scuffling sound in a back room. As she listened more closely, she thought her heard Grandpa Lars groaning.

"My curiosity had reached the bubbling over point," Andrea said, "so I followed the peculiar grunts and groans to a back room that Grandma and Grandpa very seldom used. I opened the door and was shocked to see Grandpa Lars trying to pull on the bright red trousers of a Santa Claus suit."

For a moment, Andrea said that she was struck speechless. Then with a pitiful cry of shock and despair, she managed to blurt out, "Grandpa Lars! What are you doing? Are you pretending to be Santa? Does this mean . . ."

Grandpa Lars shushed her. "Honey," he said, "it's not what it looks like. I got word that Santa was running late to our house, and he asked me to fill in for him until he got here. And these darn red trousers are just too tight."

Andrea stood there, her head swirling with confusion. "Have you . . . I mean, are you Santa? I mean, have you always pretended to be Santa?"

She had barely uttered those words and asked that damning question when a loud voice boomed behind her: "Of course, not, little girl! I'm Santa Claus!"

Andrea whirled around to behold a very large, very plump man in a bright red Santa Claus suit with a bag over his shoulder coming in through the back door.

"It's a wonder that I didn't faint," Andrea said. "I was seeing the real Santa with his bright red cheeks, his full white beard, his red cap and his red suit! The rest of the night was a blur of excitement."

Andrea has a dim memory of Santa leading her by the hand back to the living room and the Christmas tree. Everyone in the family greeted Santa, and he had a present for everyone. And then he was gone.

"But I had seen the real Santa," Andrea said. "He had taken me by the hand. I had felt him, seen him, heard him. And Santa was *not* Grandpa, that was for certain."

When he was a senior in high school, Jimmy worked in a drugstore as a clerk, errand boy, stock boy, and occasional cashier.

"In other words, I worked wherever Mr. Rodriguez, the manager, needed me on that particular day," Jimmy said. "There were days when I really didn't think he needed me at all. There were three other regular employees. But he was a kind man, and he knew that our family was running on empty financially. I really needed to bring home any money that I could to help Pop and Mom with the bills that had accumulated after my little brother Brandon got hit by a car when he was walking home from school in

October. Both legs were broken and he had needed back surgery."

On December 22, Mr. Rodriquez asked Jimmy if he would be able to work on Christmas Eve until the early closing hours of 8:00 P.M. "I wasn't scheduled to work that night," Jimmy said, "but one of the employees, Hilda, had four kids and asked if she could leave at noon to begin preparing a big Christmas dinner for her family. I agreed, because I really needed the extra hours."

Jimmy knew that his own family would like to have him home early in the afternoon, but he also was quite aware of their financial bind and that his parents would be grateful for his willingness to earn a few extra dollars.

Jimmy did throw in one condition for his working late. "I asked Mr. Rodriquez if I could have the big, life-sized plastic Santa Claus that stood next to the Christmas cards on Aisle 13. It was Christmas Eve. We wouldn't need Santa to encourage shoppers to buy Christmas presents after that night, and I knew that Brandon would really get a charge out of having Santa come home with me on Christmas Eve."

Mr. Rodriquez smiled and nodded his agreement. "I only wish I had a sleigh and eight tiny reindeer for you to take home to Brandon, as well!"

About half an hour before closing, Jimmy saw three boys that he knew very casually at high school come into the store. Jimmy knew that they were trouble.

"They were thugs, plain and simple," Jimmy said. "Their black leather jackets announced to the outside world that they belonged to the Trompers. "The first time I saw a couple of those creeps, I thought they had misspelled the word 'Troopers' on the back of their jackets," Jimmy said. "Then I found out from my best friend Mason that 'tromp' was just another word for 'stomp.'"

One of the hoodlums recognized Jimmy from high school and called the others attention to the skinny kid behind the cash register.

"Hey, Jimbo," he chuckled as he swaggered up to the cash register, "you got change for a hundred?"

The other two gang members joined in their buddy's little joke by laughing as if he had just uttered the funniest joke ever heard.

Jimmy didn't answer the smart-guy's question, but he kept an eye on the trio as they moved through the store.

Mr. Rodriquez was busy filling prescriptions, and the other two clerks were helping customers with last-minute Christmas shopping.

Deftly, with practiced skill, the three Trompers shoved packages of cigarettes, candy bars, and several bottles of an expensive perfume under their jackets, then, casually, began to head for the front door.

"Hey, you guys, put the stuff you stole back or I'll call the police," Jimmy yelled as they neared the cash register.

The three Trompers looked as surprised as if a dog had suddenly spoken to them.

"Now you wouldn't want to do that, Jimbo," one of the trio warned him. "Really bad things happen to punks who mess with the Trompers."

Jimmy didn't back down. "The forefinger of my left hand is on a red button," he informed them. "If you guys don't take the stuff you stole out of your jackets, I push the button and the cops will be here before you can get away."

"Hey, Jimbo, where's your Christmas spirit?" The comedian among them tried another little joke. "This here stuff we took are your Christmas presents to us."

Jimmy didn't display the slightest sign of emotion when he fibbed and told the thugs that he had already pushed the button that would summon the police. The Trompers dropped their loot on the floor and ran out of the drug store, bombarding Jimmy with a firestorm of curses that could have singed his hair.

Mr. Rodriquez came out from behind the prescription counter and walked up to the cash register. "I didn't see everything that happened, Jimmy," he said, "but judging from all the things that I see on the floor, I think you just stopped a robbery in progress. Good man, Jimmy."

Jimmy admitted that he was more than a little nervous when he left the store later that night after closing. From what he had heard around high school, the Trompers enjoyed demonstrating how the name of their gang originated.

Jimmy shifted the large plastic Santa that Mr. Rodriquez had given him from arm to arm, hoping to remain on the ready if he should get jumped by the hoods between the store and his car in the parking lot.

Jimmy walked to his car without incident. No tires slashed. No paint scratched by keys. And no one was anywhere to be seen in the lot.

Jimmy put the large image of Santa on the passenger seat, then walked around to the driver's side, careful to scan every shadow in the lot as if it were a potential attacker. All clear.

His next worry was that the nearly twenty-year-old Chevy wouldn't start, but the motor jumped right into mechanical action as he turned the key in the ignition.

When he arrived home, he was pleased that his mother had kept a chicken dinner warm for him in the oven—and he was moved almost to tears by the reception that the life-sized Santa received from Brandon.

"Mom and Dad were pleased, too," Jimmy said. "They said that the Santa Claus that I had brought home would always be a part of the family Christmases."

Christmas Day, late in the afternoon, Jimmy got a telephone call from his friend Mason, asking him details about the run-in with the Trompers the night before. Jimmy was stunned that news had traveled so fast among the teenaged community.

Jimmy told Mason all about what had happened the night before.

"So who did you get to be your bodyguard on the drive home?" Mason asked.

When Jimmy told Mason he had no idea what he was talking about, his friend told him that the Trompers had been waiting in their car for Jimmy to leave the drugstore. They had intended to follow him until he got on the old park road, then force him over, and beat the living daylights out of him. But when the Trompers had edged their car up close behind Jimmy's, they saw that he had someone with him, some really big guy, so they pulled back and decided to jump him sometime when he was alone.

"You know those punks always like to outnumber someone at least three to one before they jump him," Mason said. "They decided your buddy looked too big for them to handle. So who the heck was he?"

Jimmy laughed as he told Mason that he was protected by Santa Claus: a big, life-sized, plastic image of good old St. Nick. From the back, in the beam of the Trompers' headlights, the store decoration must have looked like a real person.

Mason enjoyed the joke on the Trompers, but Jimmy was still worried about the threat of the hoods jumping him and beating him up.

"You got two Santa Miracles on Christmas Eve. After they decided to let you go for the time being, those thugs decided to rob a liquor store. The owner had been robbed twice before, so he was ready for trouble. He held them frozen in their tracks with a double-barreled shotgun until the police arrived. Those jerks will get put away for quite a while in some juvenile prison."

Jimmy still worried about the rest of the gang.

"Looks like you got three Santa Miracles," Mason said, "The three tough guys weren't so tough when the police leaned on them a bit. They gave up the address of the Trompers' hangout, and the other two hoods in the gang are also in the slammer."

Jimmy thanked Mason for the terrific news and enjoyed his day off with his family.

Jimmy concluded his story by stating that when he came back to work after Christmas, Mr. Rodriquez gave him a raise because of the way that he had handled a potential robbery.

Beaming from ear to ear, Jimmy said, "I actually received four Santa Miracles that year."

Kenneth's Santa Miracle is one of the strangest ones that we have ever heard.

"In 1955, my cousin Russ and I were really dyed-in-the-wool UFO buffs, though they called them 'flying saucers' in those days," Kenneth began his strange story. "We were both fourteen that summer and we saw every flying saucer movie released and read every flying saucer book we could find. Our parents—our mothers are sisters—thought we had lost our marbles over flying saucers, but Russ and I considered ourselves serious investigators."

It was their Christmas tradition to meet in the very large and beautifully furnished family lodge in northern Wisconsin that had been built by their great-grandfather, who had arrived from Sweden a wealthy man and soon tripled his income in the New World.

"I lived in Milwaukee and Russ lived in a little town near La Crosse," Ken explained, "so family gatherings were a great time for us to get together and spend hours talking about our research. Otherwise, we had to rely on letters, and a once-a-week telephone call, limited to fifteen minutes. Besides the excitement of Christmas, Russ and I were revved up to go out into the woods, because there had been a bunch of flying saucer reports from that area of Wisconsin."

Once all the families had arrived, the two cousins isolated themselves from the rest of the kids in one of the upstairs bedrooms. In retrospect, Ken realizes that he and Russ were extremely rude to their cousins— including Russ' younger brother, Ken's older sister, and three other female cousins—but they had important research to discuss.

"It gets dark early in northern Wisconsin in December," Ken said. "Since we only had about an hour of daylight, Russ and I decided to go out and get the lay of the land so when we went out after dinner, we'd already have our posts picked where we could scan the night sky."

There was a fresh fall of snow, so neither of them feared getting lost in the thick stand of woods. They could just follow their tracks back to the cabin.

Being "city boys," Ken admitted, they had forgotten that deer, raccoons, and bears also made tracks in the snow when they walked around in the woods.

And, then, just as if the environment followed a strict sense of rules, the woods suddenly became very, very dark about a quarter to five.

Just as quickly, a strong wind began to roar through the trees.

"Where did that wind come from?" Russ wondered, adding: "I think we should get back to the lodge."

Ken agreed that was an excellent idea, but it soon came down to a hard reality that neither of them knew where they were.

"We haven't gone that far into the woods," Russ said. "Our tracks should be easy to follow."

Ken agreed.

In spite of their confidence, their flashlights could pick up only a hodge-podge of both four-legged and two-legged footprints.

And then the beam of their flashlights picked up something very intimidating to two young boys lost in the woods. It was beginning to snow.

Russ and Ken were both fourteen, but Ken remembers quite clearly that he felt very much like crying.

"And then we saw it," Ken said. "The very Holy Grail for which we yearned to see for so long: a flying saucer."

Ken pointed to the dark sky and Russ saw it also. A brightly glowing ball of light, perhaps a yard or so in circumference, was bobbing up and down near the top branches of a tall tree.

"I thought they would be larger," Russ whispered.

"They come in all sizes," Ken said, attempting to sound authoritative.

As if it had been eavesdropping on their conversation, the brilliant orb dropped down to skim near the tops of their heads.

Ken and Russ both shouted in terror.

Seemingly satisfied with their response, the flying saucer moved just ahead on them on the trail, then seemed again to be bobbing up and down.

"I think it wants us to follow it," Russ said, a slight waver of fear distorting his voice.

"Maybe it will soon open up and some aliens will come out and grab us."

Ken argued that for aliens to be passengers in that orb, they would only be a few inches tall.

"Maybe it will expand into a huge craft," Russ suggested nervously.

Ken said that he liked Russ' interpretation of the object's bobbing up and down as a gesture to follow it much better than the abduction scenario that he was spinning.

"The light is so bright, we won't stumble in the brush," Ken argued. "What do we have to lose? We're already lost."

The brilliant orb stayed just far enough ahead of the boys to safely lead them out of the woods. By this time, Ken said, they really didn't think it was a flying saucer. They had no idea what it was.

"But within what I would guess to be ten or fifteen minutes, we could see the lights of Great-Grandpa's lodge ahead of us," Ken said.

Simultaneously with the boys' sighting of their family lodge, the glowing object soared high into the night sky, so high, in fact, that Ken and Russ thought that it looked like a star.

"But it wasn't finished with its display of power and majesty," Ken said. "It was like it was showing off for us. It came zooming back down, faster than we could imagine anything flying, and seemed to crash into the lodge."

Ken and Russ screamed in horror. It seemed to them that the mysterious object had led them back to the lodge, only to destroy it. Clearly, from where they stood, the great hall of the lodge was filled with flames.

As the boys got closer to the lodge, running as fast as possible in the ankle-length snow, they saw that they were mistaken. The bright lights inside were streaming from the Christmas tree that the other members of the family had decorated while the boys were out hunting flying saucers in the woods.

When Ken and Russ entered the lodge, they received the anticipated scolding from their mothers for missing the trimming of the Christmas tree. "However," Ken said, "they were relieved and thankful that we hadn't got lost in the woods. They had heard the weather forecast only minutes before and a major storm warning had been issued for that region.

"Russ and I just looked at each other in complete, almost reverent, silence," Ken said. "Whatever that glowing object was, it had saved our lives by leading us back to the lodge before the big snow storm hit. As lost as we were in the woods, we would have been frozen snowmen before any search parties found us. And that would be a terrible way to spend Christmas, frozen like a popsicle."

Ken said that his and Russ' enthusiasm for researching flying saucers was only heightened by the strange experience that they had undergone in the woods that Christmas. But they had many long discussions concerning what they had actually seen that night.

After a great deal of research, they began to consider that they may not have interacted with a spacecraft from an extraterrestrial world, but some mysterious glowing object piloted by elf-like or fairy creatures.

On the other hand, they would laugh, why couldn't it have been Santa Claus and his elves in their own high-tech transport?

Everything seemed just fine to Ronald Griffin when his family moved to an old house in a suburb of Flint, Michigan. Ron's father had been transferred because of his job, and the family moved in time for Ron and his sister Donna to start school at the beginning of the semester.

"Donna was in ninth grade that year and I was in seventh," Ron explains. "We were both really nervous that first day in school. We had lived in Indianapolis before we moved, and we had always lived in the same neighborhood and gone to the same school with class-mates that we had known since we were little kids. It is really difficult to just up and move to a different city, state, and school when you are a kid."

Donna and Ron quickly learned that their fears were unjustified. They both made new friends on the first day, and they received none of the teasing that they worried they might as "new kids." Within the first week of school, each had friends come home with them to watch television and have cookies and milk as an after-school treat.

After dinner, one night when Donna and Ron had gone to their rooms to do homework, Donna knocked on Ron's door and asked if she could come in.

After she settled herself comfortably in his bean-bag chair, she asked what kinds of things he and Logan talked about over cookies and milk.

Ron remembers shrugging and answering "just stuff."

Then Donna came right to the point. "Briana said today that the reason that Daddy got such a good buy on this house was because it is haunted."

Ron laughed. "Haunted?" he echoed. "She must have been kidding you. Just trying to get a rise out of you. Maybe that's the way kids in this town initiate the newbies."

Donna also laughed off the suggestion that there were spooks in their house as "ludicrous." She prided herself on learning a new vocabulary word every day.

The next day in school, Ron told Logan what Briana had said about their home being haunted. Logan snorted derisively and dismissed such a statement as something that a silly junior high school girl would say.

"The house sat empty for quite awhile after old man Fredericson died a couple of years ago," Logan theorized. "That old guy must have been nearly a hundred years old. He was really a nice man. He would stand in his walker on his porch and give out Christmas treats to kids. It would be just like some weirdo girls to come up with a haunted house story and say that the ghost of old man Fredricson was still clumping the house around in his walker."

Ron admitted that even though Briana might well be a "silly junior high school girl," he was a bit on guard as he moved through their house after dark.

"I didn't really believe in ghosts," he said, "but on the other hand, I had read some books about stranger than science stuff, and I had seen some really spooky movies. I watched *The X-Files* and Fox Mulder believed in ghosts, and he was a very cool guy."

But, as Ron began his account, nothing eerie or spooky visited their home until the first week in December.

"I was brushing my teeth before school one day, and Donna came up behind me and slapped me on the back," Ron said. "She was warning me for the last time not to mess with her collection of horse figurines."

Ron protested that he hadn't touched her precious little glass horses, and Donna had screamed in rebuttal that there surely hadn't been an earthquake to move them around on their selves.

Then Ron counterattacked with the accusation that maybe she was putting on some weight and jarring the floorboards of her room so the little horsies bounced all over the shelves.

It was at that point that their mother put her head in the bathroom and told them both to stop fighting and finish getting ready for school.

The next incident occurred two nights later when Donna asked Ron to turn down his radio because she was studying for a history test.

Ron yelled back that he wasn't listening to his radio. He had a test of his own the next day.

In about half an hour, Donna came storming into Ron's room, yelling that she loved Christmas music as much as the next person, but to turn down his radio or she would throw it out the window.

"She kind of turned pale when she was in my room and could see and hear that my radio stood mute at my bedside," Ron said.

"Don't you hear that music," Donna whispered. "Right now. Hear it? 'Jolly Old St. Nicholas' is playing."

Ron felt a genuine shiver go up his back. "When I really stopped to listen, I could hear the music. It was faint and sounded like it was coming from faraway, but I could hear it."

The obvious first place to look was downstairs to check if Mom and Dad were watching a television program that featured music of the holiday season. As it turned out, they were watching a basketball game.

Just at the point where Ron and Donna felt like they were going crazy, the music stopped.

"But the music returned almost every night at about the same time and continued for about an hour," Ron said. "Every night, from about nine until ten, we were serenaded with Christmas music."

After enduring two or three nights of the mystery, they called Mom and Dad upstairs to hear it. Dad never admitted that he could hear it, but Mom said it must be one of the neighbors listening to music before bedtime.

How can we hear music from a neighbor's house?

They must have the window open.

In December?

Maybe it's someone who likes fresh air and likes to sleep in a really cold bedroom.

"We went back and forth like that for several minutes," Ron said, "and then Dad came up with an explanation. He had once upon a time read somewhere that old water pipes and other fixtures could sometimes pick up radio stations. This was an old house with old plumbing. He bet that was the explanation."

Ron and Donna had an hour concert of Christmas music nearly every night. Some nights, he remembered, the music was louder than other nights.

"On the nights when there was no music, Donna and I would be waiting on edge for it to begin," Ron said. "Those nights of silence were actually worse, because we just kept waiting for it to start up again."

After about ten days of intermittent concerts of Christmas music, Donna found the first card.

"Oh, how beautiful, Ron," Donna said one morning. "Did you put this card on my dresser?"

It was a lovely Christmas card with an antique flavor, suggestive of the turn of the century or perhaps the 1920s. Charming it was, but Ron hadn't placed it in his sister's room.

Nor did he place the next six cards in her room, either.

Mom and Dad denied doing so, as well.

Donna and Ron theorized that it must be his friend Logan, who had developed quite an obvious crush on her. He was probably slipping into Donna's room when he came by after school to study with Ron.

"So we checked Donna's room carefully after Logan left one night," Ron said. "There was no card there then or when Donna went to bed—but there was a card awaiting her on her dresser when she awakened."

By this time, Ron admitted, Donna and he were getting pretty freaked out. Their house was haunted. Briana was no silly teenager, after all.

On the other hand, if they had a ghost in the house, it was a nice one. It was a ghost who liked Christmas music and Christmas cards.

One night, just before Christmas vacation, when Ron and Donna sat talking in her room, Ron jokingly said that he hoped the ghost wasn't peeking at him in the shower and that he was kind of jealous because Donna got all the cards.

When he returned to his room, he found two cards at the foot of his bed.

"I barely slept at all that night," Ron said. "I really gave my best Fox Mulder pitch to Mom and Dad that there was a ghost in the house, but they explained everything away –they just thought we and our friends were playing jokes on each other."

The first day of school vacation, Ron and Donna had their mother drop them off at the mall so they could begin their Christmas shopping.

One of the places they enjoyed most at the mall was a shop just off the food court that had been made to look as much as possible like an old-fashioned ice cream and soda parlor. After they had their favorite sundaes in hand, they sat down at a glass-topped table on wire-backed chairs, replicas of popular soda fountain furniture from decades gone by.

An elderly gentleman who sat squeezed in the crowded shop with his shoulders nearly touching Ron's asked if they were "new kids in town"?

"We moved to town that fall, in time for the beginning of the school semester." In the spirit of holiday cheer, he asked the man if he, too, were a "new kid in town"?

The man laughed, introduced himself as William, and said that he was once a new kid in town about seventy years ago. His family had moved to the Michigan city from Indianapolis when he was 10 years old.

With that common ground of origin, the three began to laugh and joke with one another. When William asked where they lived, Donna supplied their address.

"Oh, my goodness," the man laughed. "You live in Father Christmas's old place."

"As we listened, with our mouths hanging open our new friend told us that Mr. Fredricson was called Father Christmas by all his neighbors because of his love of Christmas. Way back in the 1930s, William said, Fredricson had his house covered with lights and his lawn decorated with images of Santa and his sleigh and a small army of elves."

As Ron and Donna sat there spellbound, their elderly friend regaled them with lovely story after story of Mr. Fredricson's love of Christmas and his generosity toward everyone—men, women, and especially children. Dressed in full regalia in a very elaborate Santa Claus suit, Fredericson would drop off boxes of food, toys, and clothing to needy families. In that very same Santa Claus suit, he would stand on his porch on Christmas Eve day and give out candy canes to every kid who came to his door.

Fredricson had no children of his own, but his love for his wife was legendary in the city. The story was that he gave his wife a Christmas card and a small gift on every day of the month from December 1 to the 25.

During the War years of the 1940s, Fredericson had to tone down the lights a bit because of the occasional blackout, but, dressed in his Santa Claus suit, he would drop off boxes of toys on the doorstep of every family whose father was serving in the Armed Forces. In December 1945, the lights shone brightly from the Fredricson house once again. And they continued, until 1991 when Mr. Fredricson died.

Donna asked William if he had ever heard any stories about the house being haunted.

William laughed and said that he wouldn't be at all surprised. Especially around Christmastime.

"When Donna and I got home that evening, we seemed to have some unspoken agreement that passed between us that we should go up to the attic," Ron said. "I suppose Mom and Dad had been up there to inspect the roof before they bought the house, but Donna and I had never investigated the area."

Because there were no lights in the attic, Ron and Donna walked up the steep stairs with flashlights in hand.

"Over in a corner, we found a pile of boxes that didn't belong to our family," Ron said. "In one of them, we found several cartons of old Christmas cards."

"Enough for eternity," Donna whispered over his shoulder.

On Christmas Eve, after the family returned from church services, Ron and Donna went up to their rooms to change out of their dress clothes into sweatshirts and jeans.

"On each of our desks," Ron said, "we found an old-fashioned pressboard figure of Santa, like they used to make during the thirties. The paint on each of them seemed as bright as new. Donna and I had seen them up in the attic when we had found the cards. We didn't need to ask Mom and Dad if they had brought the Santas downstairs. We knew that it was a gift from Father Christmas."

I t is often said that no good deed goes unnoticed, but in the case of Ted Horn, waiter, cook, and the owner of Dixie Diner, he had no idea that a simple act of kindness displayed toward a customer in need, would be the inspiration for none other than Santa himself.

Larry Stewart worked as a door-to-door salesman in the small town of Bruce, Mississippi. When the company went out of business, Larry soon found himself out of money. He was so broke that he went for days without having the money to even eat. Cold, desperate, and hungry, Larry wandered into Ted Horn's diner and ordered himself a big breakfast, not disclosing that he didn't have any money to pay for it.

When the time came for the bill to be presented, Larry went to reach for his wallet, then pretended to discover that it was missing. Conducting a search of all possible pockets where his wallet might have been "misplaced," Larry played out his little drama of how embarrassed he was that he should find himself in such an awkward situation.

Ted Horn, chief bottle-washer, cook, waiter, and diner owner, walked over to the stool where Larry was sitting and bent down to pick something up off the floor. Ted straightened back up, with money in hand, looked Larry straight in the eyes, and with no hint that he was on to the missing wallet scheme, he placed a $20 bill on the table in front of him, saying: "Son, you must have dropped this."

That $20 bill was a fortune to Larry as he paid for his breakfast, left a tip, said a silent prayer of thanks. As he walked out of that diner, he pushed his car to a gas station and was able to buy enough gas to get out of town.

While driving, Larry became aware of his thoughts drifting back to the diner, in an attempt to reconstruct his "lucky break." In an aha moment, he realized that nobody else in the diner had dropped that $20 bill. It must have been a deliberate act, out of the kindness and graciousness of the Dixie Diner owner.

Right there and then, Larry Stewart promised himself that if the Lord would ever put him in the position to help others in such a manner, he would do it. And indeed he did. Over the years, Larry Stewart was to settle in the Lee Summit, Missouri area, marry, have a family, and work his way into a major change of fortune. Eventually he would become a *millionaire*.

Years later, Stewart began giving cash to the needy, but remembering the way *his* dignity was spared, he gave birth to the idea of being a *Secret Santa*—disguising himself in the full regalia of Santa Claus and handing out money to people who appeared to be in need, whether he found them in a Laundromat, or on the street, or in a shelter. Feeling the joy, warmth, and glow deep in his heart and soul, Larry knew this would be how he would fulfill his promise. It would be his *mission* to be a Secret Santa.

His wishing to remain anonymous as Secret Santa would affect the lives of thousands upon thousands of people in need, launching what was to become the largest world-wide Secret Santa movement and foundation.

He did not forget the random act of kindness that started it all, as he retraced and tracked down Horn almost thirty years after their first fateful meeting. Stewart found him in Tupelo, Mississipi, and handed eighty-eight-year-old Ted Horn an envelope containing $10,000!

In March 2008, a trained archeologist made a fascinating discovery in the Nine Mile Canyon in central Utah. There, high on the side of a sheer cliff, Pam Miller, Chair of the Nine Mile Canyon Coalition, found a petroglyph, at least 1,000 years old, that clearly appeared to depict Santa, an elf, and nine reindeer.

A petroglyph is a work of art that was chiseled into rock, most often into a dark patina surface by a prehistoric artist. In the case of the ancient Santa Claus and crew in Nine Mile Canyon, the picture had to be chiseled or pecked into rock by some anonymous—and ancient—Native American craftsman.

Did some long-forgotten tribal artist see the original Santa Claus and an elf as they stopped to feed and water the reindeer on their way back to the North Pole? The artist who captured this momentous sighting on rock might have been a member of the tribe of the Shoshone, the Hopi, the Zuni, the Paiute, all of whom, among other early tribes, visited or occupied the area around Nine Mile Canyon.

Interestingly, the Santa petroglyph is located very high on a sheer cliff in a very rugged area of the canyon. Photographer Bill Bryant managed to photograph "Santa" using a super-telephoto lens.

Archaeologist Pam Miller told Cathy Zander of *Newswire* that the aboriginal artist quite likely did not have Santa, an elf, and Santa's particular team of reindeer in mind when he made the petroglyphs. The beauty of such rock art, she emphasized, is that future generations can be inspired by it.

According to Ms. Miller, Santa Claus and his helpers is but one of 10,000 petroglyphs to be found in Nine Mile Canyon. At the time of the announcement of the unique discovery, the Nine Mile Canyon Coalition was doing its best to alert the public that the petroglyphs and pictoglyphs (prehistoric paintings) were in danger of being obliterated or destroyed by heavy industrial traffic, including massive trucks, drill rigs, bulldozers, and trucks spraying dust-suppressant chemicals. The drilling for possible oil deposits in the Nine Mile Canyon area could quite possibly destroy the unique petroglyph of Santa Claus—and all the other priceless works of prehistoric Native American art. Perhaps the public, once alerted to the possible obliteration of these many ancient masterworks, may perform a Santa Miracle and work to preserve this national treasure.

On the other hand, in spite of the learned archaeologists and their many theories, could not this discovery signify more than some intellectual curiosity? May it not beg the question: How long has Santa Claus really been around?

If nothing else, the discovery of this petroglyph gives evidence of the multicultural diversity of Santa Claus and the innate spiritual truth of an unselfish, giving spirit. And interestingly, the estimated age of the Santa petroglyph is very close to time when he began to appear in Europe—and may even predate his earliest manifestation in France.

Lori Jean Flory remembers Christmas best for the Santa Miracle that her parents would provide a needy family.

Lori, who lives near Denver, didn't begin to doubt the reality of Santa until she was about six years old. Her father, an attorney, would keep her gifts in a safe in his office. Then, on Christmas Eve, when she was sleeping, he would bring the presents home and place them around the tree where Lori would find what Santa had brought on Christmas morning.

When little Lori would misbehave and need an attitude adjustment, she remembers her mother picking up the telephone and pretend to talk to Santa Claus, suggesting that he might bypass their home because there was a naughty little girl who lived there.

"I guess this was a Santa Miracle for Mom," Lori joked, "because it really worked on me. I would shift my grumpy attitude immediately and beg her to tell Santa not to skip our house. I would be a good little girl."

Each year, Lori's parents would choose a needy family, and on Christmas Eve would play Santa Claus. "We would all be standing on the doorstep of this family, and when they opened their door to our knocking, they would see us there holding boxes of food, clothing, and toys for the children," Lori said. "I remember smiles, tears, and joy on the faces of those unfortunate families."

Lori said that she will always remember the miracles that her parents brought to those needy families. "Mom and Dad were not dressed up like Santa and Mrs. Claus, but they were playing them in spirit. They were truly enacting the essence of Santa, which is love."

When Jada was six years old, she saw Santa Claus. Since then, she has always considered his appearance some kind of miracle.

"That year, what I really wanted was for Santa to bring me a Christie Barbie doll and leave it under our little Christmas tree. I had been begging my parents all year, but my parents told me that we were living in hard times."

"How can it be hard times for Santa way up in the North Pole?" I would ask my parents. "He must have plenty to eat—why else would he be so fat and jolly?"

That Christmas Eve, young Jada got up to go to the bathroom and heard sounds of laughter coming from the kitchen area.

"I peeked into the kitchen and nearly fell over at the sight my little eyes beheld," Jada said. "Santa Claus himself was just leaving our apartment, and he turned to give Daddy a high-five before he went out the door."

There was no question that it was Santa Claus. Jada saw his bright red cheeks, his long white beard, his red suit lined with white fur, his black boots. It was him.

Jada ran back to bed as fast and as quietly as she could. She knew that if Santa saw her, he just might take back whatever gifts he had left. Kids had to be in bed when he came or he would just leave with his precious bag of goodies.

"I had a really hard time going back to sleep," Jada said. "My little heart was pounding so loud that I was afraid I would wake my sisters Kayla and Ruthie. Ruthie was just a baby, so if she woke up she was likely to start crying—and that would really get me in trouble with both my parents and Santa."

Somehow, Jada recalled, she managed to keep her eyes closed and finally get back to sleep.

"It was really early in the morning when I felt Kayla tugging my arm and telling me that it was time to see what Santa had put under the tree," Jada said. "Ruthie was still asleep, and I motioned to Kayla not to wake her."

It was hard not to start screaming some serious whoops of joy when Jada opened the package with her name on it and found a Christie doll. Kayla got a cloth doll like the kind that their grandmother made for kids. Both the girls agreed that Kayla's doll had come from Santa, though, not from Grandma's sewing basket. Besides, Kayla also got a brush and some stockings.

Later, after her parents got out of bed, Jada proudly displayed her Christie doll. "See," Jada said, "I told you that Santa didn't have any hard times at the North Pole."

She remembers both her parents getting a good laugh out of her economic assessment of conditions outside of the Chicago area. That's when Jada decided to make her confession to her parents.

"I saw you talking to Santa Claus before he left our apartment," Jada said, expecting to get a scolding for sneaking out of bed and violating one of Santa's most sacred rules. "But Mommy and Daddy just smiled, like it was no big deal. I surely had little Kayla's attention though. She was bug-eyed."

Kayla was nearly four, and a firm believer in Santa. "Really?" she asked, her mouth opening wide in total awe. "You really saw Santa with Mommy and Daddy?"

"I suddenly felt endowed and trusted with one of the world's greatest secrets," Jada said. "I was probably one of the few children in the world who had actually seen Santa delivering presents. This wasn't some old fake Santa sitting in a department store. I had seen the real Santa."

"Don't be silly, Jada. You only dreamt you saw Santa," Jada's mom said.

Jada held firmly to her assertion. "I did see Santa, laughing with you and Daddy in the kitchen. Daddy even gave Santa a high-five as Santa left."

Jada thought her father was going to choke with laughter on the piece of toast he was eating. "Well, I know that Santa is one cool cat," he acknowledged. "I would surely like to give the old gent a high-five. I surely would."

In spite of her parents' insistence that she had only been dreaming, Jada persisted in her story, telling every friend, relative, and neighbor that she had really seen Santa Claus on Christmas Eve.

"Now that I am in my mid-forties, I still believe that I saw Santa Claus that night," Jada said. "Somehow, my parents' memories must have been blocked. Maybe they weren't supposed to see Santa, either. Maybe Santa put them in some kind of trance. Who knows?"

Jada has always had what she believes is a solid argument in favor of her really seeing Santa on that magical Christmas Eve. "I clearly saw Santa's red cheeks, his twinkling blue eyes, and all the rest of Santa's features that weren't covered by his white beard," she said. "This was 1968. We lived in the Projects in Chicago. I can't imagine a white man stopping by to visit my parents in the middle of the night unless it really was Santa Claus. And that's why this will always be my Santa Miracle."

Natalie Harrison experienced her Santa Miracle when she was just three-years-old and living with her family in a suburb of Cincinnati.

"My brother Tyler, who was nearly eight, had started in on my parents before Thanksgiving, begging to get a puppy for Christmas," Natalie said. "Since at that time my big brother constituted a large share of my worldview and opinions about nearly every subject, I joined him each night at the dinner table in his perpetual lobbying for a puppy."

Their parents' standard answer was that Tyler was too young to care for a puppy. When Natalie would add her desire for a puppy, she would receive a patronizing chuckle that she was far too young to have a puppy. She could have a puppy doll.

"Tyler is asking for a real, live doggy," her mother would explain. "Not a stuffed toy to have next to you when you sleep. A real live doggy would need to eat and play and go outside to go potty."

Natalie recalled that the argument about going outside to "go potty" would always crack her up. She remembered that she would ask in astonishment why the puppy couldn't use their bathroom like "big girls did." She had just accomplished that major social skill of being potty trained not long before the regular evening discussions about acquiring a dog.

On one occasion, Tyler bribed Natalie with a candy cane to cry at the dinner table that she wanted a puppy for Christmas.

"All that gained me was to be told to stop crying or I wouldn't get any ice cream for dessert," Natalie said. "Then, in a desperate moment of confusion and fear of being deprived a scoop of ice cream, I, for the first and only time in my life, betrayed my big brother. 'Tyler made me say it,' I said, and then really started crying in shame."

Natalie recalled that her father put a hand to his face and exclaimed, "I am absolutely surprised to hear that. I never would have guessed it."

Natalie was too young to understand sarcasm, but she did comprehend that she had cost Tyler his ice cream for dessert.

Natalie was well aware of Tyler saying his prayers at night, kneeling at his bed, asking God, the Baby Jesus, and Santa Claus for a puppy.

"After Mommy had read us a story, she would hear our prayers," Natalie said. "I knew that I pleased Tyler lying in his bed across the room when I also asked the same trinity of sacred figures for a puppy."

Just a week before Christmas, their parents took them to a department story that harbored a Santa Claus in his workshop.

Natalie remembers the layout of Santa Land as a very impressive display. "It was an incredibly awesome place." Tyler, firm in his puppy-quest, marched bravely to the line leading to Santa's Workshop and, when it was his turn, crawled courageously up on Santa's lap and boldly asked for a puppy.

"I wanted to help Tyler in his magnificent effort and add my personal plea to Santa, but as soon as one of Santa's elves set me on the big guy's lap, I screamed bloody murder," Natalie said. "I had seen lots of pictures of Santa. I had seen him on television. On one program he was even dancing with a lot of chorus girls. But facing him in person was just too much. For some reason, Santa just didn't look jolly to me."

Natalie will always remember how Tyler put a comforting arm around her and whispered, "That's all right, Sis. I know you tried."

Christmas Eve brought the Harrison kids a pretty darn nice collection of toys. Among the treasures were a couple of new dolls for Natalie, some G.I. Joe action figures for Tyler, and a number of assorted items to be highly prized. And then there was the underwear that Tyler always got from Aunt Olivia.

But no puppy.

Tyler told Natalie that they still had one more chance. Santa might bring one during the night and leave it under their stockings.

"We were out of bed shortly after sunrise," Natalie said. "Tyler took one of my hands in one of his, put his other hand on the railing, and we went downstairs as quickly as we could."

In their stockings they found candy canes, some new storybooks, and a tiny flashlight for each of them.

Under their stockings was a large stuffed dog.

Natalie looked up at her brother and saw tears forming in his eyes.

"Santa didn't understand me, Nats," Tyler said between sharp intakes of breath, trying desperately to keep from crying. "We wanted a real, live puppy."

At about that very moment, their parents came down the stairs to see what Santa had brought.

"I will always remember Dad walking over and picking up the stuffed dog," Natalie said. "He looked at it with exaggerated puzzlement, turned to Mom, and asked what it was. Mom played right along and said that it must be the dog that the children wanted."

Dad walked around the room, holding the dog under one of his arms. "You know, kids, I think Santa Claus misunderstood you," he said, shaking his head in bewilderment. "Didn't you want a real dog for Christmas?"

Tyler wiped his eyes with a sleeve of his pajamas. "Yes, we did want a real puppy for Christmas." Natalie added her voice to the disappointment, saying, "we wanted a real puppy real bad."

"Well, then," their father said, "it is a good thing that I have been studying magic these past few weeks."

Now it was Natalie's and Tyler's turn to be puzzled.

"Yes," Dad said. "I can turn this stuffed dog into a real puppy by saying a few magic words."

Tyler had shaken off all disbelief and was filled with wonder. "Can you really, Dad?"

At barely three years old, Natalie recalled, she didn't doubt her father's abilities at anything. "If Daddy had said that he could fly, I wouldn't have doubted him for a second."

Their father told them to lie down on the floor under the magical Christmas tree and to close their eyes.

"We heard Dad mumbling abracadabra and a few other magic words," Natalie said, "then I heard Tyler screaming that something was attacking him."

That did it for Natalie. "I opened my eyes and saw Tyler rolling around on the floor with his eyes still shut," she said. "Because his eyes were shut, he couldn't see the puppy that was jumping all over him."

And then Natalie screamed at the top of her lungs. Santa was standing there in the middle of their living room.

"Our neighbor, dressed as Santa, had brought over a puppy for us," Natalie said. "If I had been a little older, I would have recognized Mr. Ellenbecker in the Santa suit and false beard, but at three, it was Santa himself, so I lay on the floor screaming while Tyler at last opened his eyes and began to shout for joy over the puppy that was now tugging on one of his pajama legs with little teeth that we would soon learn were very, very sharp."

Natalie will always consider the jolly old elf's personal delivery of the puppy that they so wanted for Christmas as her greatest Santa Miracle.

"We named the little terrier Bosco," she said, "and he became our friend and defender for many years. Bosco was our living reminder that our father's magic, our prayers, and the miracle of Santa and Christmas can accomplish wonders."

Tuesday Miles, an author and radio host, has observed that in the eyes of a child, seeing is believing and believing is seeing. For one child, however, it was more than merely believing—there really was a Santa Claus; he did have a sleigh; he lived in the North Pole; and in his barn, he had eight very real reindeer.

As Tuesday Miles tells her story:

The date was December 14, 1992. I could smell rain on the horizon, and I had some errands to run. One of them was to drive clear across town to pay a late gas bill so it wouldn't be shut off.

I hated going into this part of town, where you tucked your purse up under your shirt, looking behind you as you walked, fearing someone was about to hit you over the head and steal what little money you had. The only parking was inside a parking garage with five levels of parking. It was dark and cold, and you could hear the sound of your shoes echo as you walked through the garage.

As I finally reached the double glass doors to the office where I had to pay my bill, my eyes were fixated on the ground. I was not a happy camper, having to pay a bill clear across town. My grouchy face announced that I was not in the mood to be nice to anybody even though Christmas was a couple of weeks away.

As I walked across the lobby floor, I raised my eyes, looking up to see where the sound of children's laughter was coming from. I turned the corner, heading toward the counter to pay my bill, and saw a man in a red suit, reading a Christmas story to sixty children in front of him.

It was like an old-fashioned black-and-white movie. My pace slowed and my jaw dropped. I recall saying to myself, *Holy Cow! It can't be. No way. Oh, my God. If there ever was a real Santa Claus, he's right in front of me.*

I was about to stop and listen to the story he was reading when my bill dropped from my hands, reminding me of my errand.

I took a number and sat down in front of the customer service woman. I had already gone over in my head a dozen times what I was going to complain about. I was going to give it to her a piece of my mind.

"Can I help you?" she said.

"I need to pay my bill," I answered. I was also thinking, to myself, *even though I don't have the money and if I paid all of it at once I can kiss my kids' Christmas goodbye.*

The women handed me back my bill and told me to go pay the bill around the corner.

When I got to the front of the line, I braced myself to hear the woman behind the counter say, "You owe $250."

Instead, something odd and unexpected happened. The cashier said to me, "Your total is $35."

A look of shock spread across my face as I asked her if she was certain.

"I am positive," she said. "There was a mistake on your bill. You only owe thirty five dollars."

I knew with no doubt in my mind that I owed an amount of over two hundred dollars. Why all of a sudden did my bill change? Should I speak up and ask again? After all, I did not want to have my gas and water shut off. I turned around and went back to the cashier.

"Are you sure without a doubt that this is correct?"

She took my account number, looked it up, and said, "Yes, this is the amount you owe."

Well, twice was enough. I shut up about it and turned to go back to my car. I started to walk toward another door, hoping to escape from all the children and Santa crowd. When I got to the other doors, they were locked, forcing me to have to walk by the large group. I could hear Santa saying bye-bye to the children and adding a robust, "Merry Christmas to all and to all a good night!"

How cute, I thought to myself.

I walked past them, trying not to make eye contact with anybody. Then I hear this deep, jolly, man's voice say to me, "Merry Christmas young lady!" Not wishing to be impolite, I replied by saying, "Merry Christmas to you also, Santa," and I continued to walk by.

The strangest feeling came over me as I was about to open the two huge doors. I found myself turning around and looking to see if Santa was still standing there.

Yes, he sure was, and he was staring right at me. I let out a sigh and turned around to go say hello to Santa.

"My goodness is your beard real?" I asked.

He nodded yes.

"And your glasses, real?

He nodded yes.

"The tummy all of you?"

"Yep," he replied as he patted his jelly belly.

Then he released a deep and strong, "HO HO HO! That was real, too."

I laughed. How could you not when hearing the sound of jolly ole Saint Nick?

Curious, I began to ask him some questions about his job being Santa each year.

"How much do you charge for special guest appearances?"

"$350 dollars an hour," Santa answered. "I'm booked solid for the rest of the season. People start reserving my services in August."

"Wow!" I exclaimed, impressed by his reputation.

Then I began to tell him about my son who has Cerebral Palsy, mild Autism, and additional intellectual disabilities. I told Santa that for the first five years of his life, my son had a difficult time understanding what the meaning of Christmas was and he barely wanted to open up his presents. Then the year before, he awakened to the Christmas season. I had taken him to go see a Santa and since then, that was all he talked about—Santa this and Santa that. He played Christmas music all year long. My son was in love with Santa.

I soon realized I had taken up enough of Santa's time and I needed to get home. The traffic would start to thicken. I wished him a Merry Christmas and thanked him for all the wonderful smiles he gives children each year. "God bless you," I said, and left.

As I was walking across the cold windy walkway—which always gave me the creeps and is a place where women are not safe to walk alone—I heard footsteps running behind me. I thought to myself, *oh, no please, don't let somebody mug me . . . don't take the little money I have.*

I started to walk faster and faster until I heard this man's voice yell at me, "Miss, Hello? Miss, could you wait for a minute, please?"

It was Santa. Did I forget something?

"I have some extra time Christmas morning," he said when he caught up to me. "I would love to come out and pay a visit to your son and daughter."

I was grateful he asked, but I had to turn him down. "I am so sorry," I apologized. "I would love for you to come. I just can't afford the amount of money you charge for your visits, though I am sure it's worth every penny."

I was just about to turn to leave when Santa grabbed my arm and said, "No, this is my treat. Please, I would love to come visit."

I stood there staring at him, not saying a word. I could not hold my tears. First, the right eye started dripping, then the left.

Santa reached under his sleeve to give me a tissue to wipe my tears, then he reached out and gave me a hug.

"Merry Christmas," he said. "I will see you Christmas morning around eight o'clock. I will bring your children some gifts."

I cried all the way home. I had been blessed twice in one day. The lowered gas bill gave me the extra money I needed for Christmas, and I was able to give my son the gift he had asked for—a visit from Santa. Shaking my head in disbelief as I drove home, I knew I was touched by an angel that day. There was no doubt in my mind that something of a divine order was holding my hand and helping me.

On Christmas morning, both of my kids came into our bedroom, saying that Santa had come and asking if they could open their presents.

After the kids were finished opening the gifts that my husband and I had bought for them, my son walked over to me. "I guess Santa must have forgotten about my wish," he said. "Santa must be busy with all the rest of the kids."

At that moment, the doorbell rang. My son went to see who was at the front door, and right before he opened the door, he heard sleigh bells. He stopped dead in his tracks. He turned to look at me, then ran for the door yelling, "He didn't forget me . . . it's him . . . it's him!"

Then the door slowly swung open, and there stood Santa and Mrs. Claus. Santa had a red velvet bag of toys slung over his shoulders.

Never in my whole life have I ever seen a kid so happy. Santa was his hero. He was the man in the big red suit who flew in his sleigh with eight tiny reindeer from home to home all around the world. And not just to children's homes, but to all who wanted to believe in him.

It never was about the presents. It was always about this person, Santa Claus, who for one night each year didn't care about the color of your skin, how much you had in the bank, whether you were rich or poor. It was about love—unconditional love.

Nineteen years later, my son's love for Santa has not changed. He honors him, loves him, demands respect for him, and waits until Christmas Eve, the night in which he reunites with his hero each year.

That Christmas morning I took a photo of Santa and my son. Above their heads, you can clearly see an amber light glowing. To me, this is the angel who brought my son his hero, Santa Claus.

When Leigh and her husband adopted their son Wes at six years old, Wes was scared of God and had trouble separating him from the devil. Churches scared him, because they had a ghost inside. He had heard people say so. There was a holy ghost that lived in the churches. He also thought Santa was a bunch of hooey.

Leigh found that there didn't seem to be a clear pathway to teach Wes about God and His trustworthiness and other spiritual lessons. Six-year-old Wes was very cynical about everything. There was no joy in fairy tales or in childhood stories that taught lessons about life. Leigh and her husband had a little curmudgeon on their hands. When she talked about Santa or Christmas, she could just hear him thinking, *Bah! Humbug.*

"So I sat there with little Wes week after week, paying attention to every wish he seemed to make as we watched cartoons or went shopping or any other moment which might present some kind of opening," Leigh said. "Then as if they were reading my mind, the school had a Santa Calling program where a child would get a phone call from Santa a few weeks before the big day."

Leigh had no clue how she would pay for all the things that Wes told Santa that he wanted, but she bought every single thing he asked for. Plus stuff he didn't ask Santa for, but Leigh knew he would love. His uncle bought him a train set, and Leigh's husband sent wonderful gifts from overseas where he was serving in the military. All these gifts would appear for Wes at the big moment.

"But," Leigh said, "the most effective part was this: I took the little guy to grandma and grandpa's house for Christmas. Then we went home."

A true cornucopia of gifts was waiting for Wes when we walked in the door.

"A good friend of ours had sneaked into the house and put all the Santa gifts under the tree," Leigh said. "In addition, there were the gifts that I had wrapped from me and my husband. The tree was hidden by everything. Half the room was packed.

"When Wes walked into the room, he saw that everything was there—everything. And it was just as Mommy had said: Santa had missed him all those years because Santa couldn't find him when he was moving so many times. This year, Santa made sure that Wes got exactly what he wanted because it was the first year that Santa could find him. And Santa always keeps his word."

Leigh explained further to Wes that Santa wasn't God. He couldn't find Wes during those "bad years," but Santa could be trusted.

"That was the beginning," Leigh said. "After that positive experience with Santa, Wes began to give God a second chance. Wes began to flip his values, back to being able to trust."

Maybe Mom was right about some things. He needed to look into the Tooth Fairy and the Easter Bunny, but they all got a second chance.

"Everybody had a second chance, because Wes had finally understood that somebody could be trusted," Leigh concluded. "Thus, little Wes had his second chance! Just what I needed. Just what little Wes needed."

R ay Garcia will always remember the way his mother would sing "Santa Claus is Coming to Town," before Christmas. She would carefully accent the words and make a production number out of the song.

"Mom could easily have been a professional singer," Ray says proudly. "And she did fantastic impressions. I was seven years old in 1968, and, honest to gosh, Mom would do 'To Santa With Love," in the style of Lulu one night, then, the next, she would be Connie Francis asking 'Where the Elves Are?' She was fantastic as Brenda Lee, 'Rockin' Around the Christmas Tree' and her Streisand version of 'People Who Believe in Santa Are the Luckiest People in the World' was fabulous.

But always, every night, her signature piece was 'Santa Claus Is Coming to Town.'"

It was easy to see why Ray had his own garage rock and roll band when he was eleven, and became a professional musician at seventeen.

"Education was big with Mom," Ray explained, "so I went to college because I promised her that I would. I played a few weekend gigs my first couple of years, but I got a taste of just how hard it would be to make a living as a full-time musician. During my junior year, I began taking education courses, and I became a high school band instructor in 1982."

Ray was so grateful that his mother lived to see him graduate and accept a job with a good-sized high school. "She got cancer when I was a senior in high school," Ray said. "She was a fighter and really did her best to lick the disease, but she died in late August of 1982."

As Ray looks back on his life over a quarter of a century later, he is glad that he was facing the new challenges of teaching music and directing a band in high school to at least partially distract him from his grief.

"I thought of Mom every day," he said, "but if I hadn't been handling the hundred and one daily crises that a high school teacher faces, I undoubtedly would have gone into a deep and total depression. I loved my mother so much."

Ray had a great relationship with his father and his two sisters, but his mother had always been his shining star of inspiration.

"I was such a Mama's boy as a kid," he admitted. "I never stayed overnight at any friend's house until I was in high school. When I was a little kid, I really couldn't bear to be away from Mom. I only liked her cooking, and I avoided restaurants, even hamburger or taco stands, until I started dating."

When Ray graduated from college, he had been seeing someone pretty steadily. "I almost asked her to marry me," he said, "but she was still in college and the high school where I was teaching was more than a hundred miles away, so we decided to see if our love could last the distance. It didn't."

After Thanksgiving, Ray found it impossible not to think about his mother nearly all the time. Again, he was grateful for the multitude of tasks on his plate as the high school bands, choirs, and small musical groups prepared for the annual Christmas program.

"But despite how busy I was with extra rehearsals before and after school, I still found myself missing her. It was, after all, the first Christmas without Mom."

Regardless of what musical piece he was directing, the melody for "Santa Claus Is Coming to Town" kept playing over and over in the echo chamber of his mind.

On occasion, he thought he saw his mother watching him out of the corner of his eye. "This was not a startling or frightening experience," Ray said. "If anything, it was comforting and left me feeling at peace within myself. Mom had been an audience at all my garage band practices. Sometimes, she had delighted the guys by singing along, often doing one of her impressions of some popular singer. All my friends loved her. They all said that I had the neatest mom in all of California. And I always heartily agreed."

At the Christmas concert, the new bandmaster received a standing ovation. Ray was so shocked and surprised at the thunderous approval that he couldn't prevent tears from streaming down his face.

Back at his apartment, Ray poured himself a glass of wine and toasted the photograph of his mother. "We were a success, Mom," he said, tears once again welling in his eyes.

It was at that moment that his elbow bumped the small radio set that he kept in the kitchen. The volume button had been somehow turned on high, and Ray heard, loud and clear, a popular singer's version of "Santa Claus Is Coming to Town."

Ray quickly switched to another station. He didn't need any greater reminder of the loss of his mother that night than to hear her favorite Christmas song blaring out of the radio.

On the next station to which he tuned, he again heard the familiar—the all-too familiar—lyrics of "Santa Claus Is Coming to Town."

As he moved across the dial to all the stations available to his small radio, every station he brought in played the same Christmas song—"Santa Claus Is Coming to Town."

Ray knew that that unique and rather show biz method of communication was his beloved mother's way of telling him that she was with him on this Christmas as she had been on so many others.

Ray knows that not everyone will accept that it was any more than coincidence that station after station was playing the same Christmas song. After all, it was only a few days before Santa really would be coming to town. However, Ray will always believe that it was his mother coming to say "Merry Christmas" and to reach out in a special way to bless him with her love.

Karen recalled the Christmas when she was a senior in high school in 2006. She was inspired by the Assistant Pastor who challenged their Church Youth Group to be creative, bold, imaginative, and come up with some new project to celebrate Christmas by helping others.

"I admit that what I came up with wasn't that new," Karen admitted, "but it had never been practiced in our little city in North Dakota."

In early December, while doing research for a paper on women's voting rights for her sociology class, Karen came across the interesting story of Arianna VanDoorn, assistant to the pastor of Park Congregational Church in Grand Rapids, Michigan, who, in

1908, founded the Santa Claus Girls. Ms. VanDoorn and other Sunday School teachers set out to provide a cheerful Christmas for those unfortunate boys and girls who would not be receiving any gifts from Santa Claus that year. As word spread of the Santa Claus Girls, Senator Arthur H. Vandenberg, editor of the *Grand Rapids Herald*, agreed to sponsor the group so that their funds grew considerably from the few dollars that Ms. VanDoorn's friends had collected. In that first year, more than 150 boys and girls from poor homes received a joyous visit from the Santa Claus Girls.

Karen shared her discovery of Arianna VanDoorn and the Santa Claus Girls with her best friends Lisa and Sandy, who were excited by the idea and agreed with her that it would be wonderful to start their own version of North Dakota Santa Claus Girls in their hometown. They all agreed that their goal would not be to be sponsored by the editor of the local paper or win any support from a state senator, but the three of them could become Santa Claus Girls and help as many poor kids as their limited funds would permit. Among the three of them, they quickly named twenty or so families in their community whose children would be finding empty stockings on Christmas morning.

Karen and Lisa had worked full-time at a fast food restaurant that summer and had been able to set aside quite a nest egg for their college tuition. In addition, they continued to work at the restaurant part-time during the school year. Both of them were willing to contribute a hundred dollars to the cause. Sandy had spent her summer babysitting for her neighbors, so her savings were not as plump as her friends, but she would contribute what she could, maybe fifteen dollars or so.

Karen and Lisa said that since Sandy was an accomplished mistress of the knitting needles, she could compensate by knitting the sides of the cloth Santa Bags that they had assembled from scraps that a fabric store had donated to them. Sandy had knitted matching sweaters for each of them, as well as for her brothers and sisters and her boyfriend, so dressing up some Santa Bags would be a breeze for her. Karen and Lisa freely admitted that they would be more likely to jab themselves with the needles than neatly knit up the sides of the bags.

When other members of the church youth group heard of the project, many of their friends contributed to the cause. Their parents, proud of the unselfish nature of their daughters' project, also donated generously. Within a short period of time, the Santa Claus Girls had collected enough money to be able to put some holiday items and a gift certificate in each Santa Bag.

Since their town was small enough where everyone knew a little bit about everyone else, the Santa Claus Girls were somewhat aware of the needs of the families on their list. In each Santa Bag they placed a bright ornament, some Christmas candy, and a gift certificate to a store where the family could acquire the things they really needed.

On December 21, the Santa Claus Girls set out on their first mission. Their plan was simple and effective. They hung a Santa Bag on the doorknob, rang the bell, or knocked on the door, then ran back into the darkness to await the surprised family member who came to answer the bell. As soon as the Santa Bag was discovered, the three girls shouted, "Merry Christmas from the Santa Claus Girls!" and ran off into the night.

That first night, the girls had distributed nine bags before the temperature turned so cold that they called it a successful initial run and retreated to Lisa's house for some hot chocolate.

December 22 was just too cold to venture out, and their parents forbade their being Santa Claus Girls that night for fear of their being frostbitten.

The next evening, severe cold or not, the girls knew that they simply had to deliver the remaining eleven bags or a lot of poor kids would be liable to receive nothing from Santa Claus that Christmas.

They began their mission just as soon as it grew dark enough to hide their identities and to be able to approach the homes unnoticed. Within a couple of hours, they had delivered eight of the special Santa Bags.

Although Karen said that her nose was as red as Rudolph's because of the cold, she said that she really wanted to deliver the final three bags to three particular families who lived across the city, several blocks away.

Lisa, always a stalwart supporter of any sensible enterprise, declared her friend's goal to be unreasonable—and admitted in no uncertain terms that she was freezing. Sandy nodded in agreement, adding that her toes were frozen. Together, almost as one voice, Lisa and Sandy argued that they could finish the delivery of the last three bags tomorrow night.

Karen reminded them that was Christmas Eve. They would be going to church, and their parents would not want them going out during their own family celebrations after the evening services. Lisa said that there was no way that her father and three brothers would delay Christmas dinner while she was out playing Santa's helper.

"Come on," Karen urged her friends, brushing aside their arguments. "I'll treat if we go into the diner and have some hot chocolate and warm up for a while. Then, if we cut across Schrader's Hill, we can save a lot of walking and time. We'll deliver the last three bags to needy families, and we'll be finished in no time."

The hot chocolate and the warmth of the diner renewed Lisa's and Sandy's enthusiasm to complete their mission, and the three Santa Claus Girls were soon on their way to deliver the last of the Santa Bags and to make some kids have a merrier Christmas.

Schrader's Hill was one of the most popular sledding areas in the city. If it hadn't been so cold that night and getting rather late, the hill would have been crowded with children zipping down the steep hill under the supervision of their parents, many of whom stayed in their cars with the motor and heater running while their kids tromped up and down the slope.

Sandy said that she had never walked across the hill after dark. "I thought they kept the bright lights on all night," she said.

Lisa had read in the local newspaper that the city—in order to conserve on energy and the city budget—would shut off all the lights on Schrader's Hill except for one security light after nine o'clock.

"Be careful," Karen warned. "Some spots are really slippery from all the sleds going up and down the hill."

Sandy had just finished commenting that she had never realized how rough and uneven the hill was when she slipped and took a nasty fall that carried her about twenty feet down the slope before she could come to a stop.

Lisa and Karen ran to help their friend, being careful not to fall on the icy areas of the hill. The moon was mostly covered by clouds, and the single light was now quite some distance away from them. It was very difficult to see the dips, bumps, and the slick spots in the shadows.

They heard Sandy whimpering in pain when they caught up to her.

"I twisted my ankle before I fell," she said. "It really hurts. I don't think I can stand up. Maybe I broke it."

Karen and Lisa tried to support Sandy as she gritted her teeth and tried to stand, but their uneven tugging and pulling on Sandy's coat only made them all fall together on another slick area of the slope.

"Oh, no," Sandy cried. "It feels like my ankle really might be broken. It really, really hurts."

"We have to get help," Karen said. "Lisa, call 911 on your cell phone."

Now Lisa was on the verge of tears. "I was going to do that when we fell," she said. "I dropped the phone. We've got to find it."

Since it had snowed earlier that day, there were several inches of fresh snow in which the cell phone could lie hidden. Karen sighed that there was little chance of finding the phone. Somehow, they would just have to carry Sandy off the hill—and try not to fall too many times doing it.

Things were looking pretty dark for the Santa Claus Girls when who should appear approaching them on a pair of skis but Santa Claus himself.

Santa pulled along beside them and began to speak.

When he could see that they hadn't understood him, he pulled down his beard. "Sorry, I forgot I still had the beard on," he apologized. "What are you three doing out here on such a cold, dark night?"

"Is that you, Jeff?" Lisa asked. "Our senior class vice-president is Santa Claus?"

Jeff agreed that it was indeed he, quickly explaining that his uncle owned the big department store in town and indulged in a bit of nepotism by hiring him to pad himself, put on a beard and a Santa suit, and earn some Christmas spending money by pulling the after-school Santa shift.

"I love to ski," Jeff said, "so I bring my skis to work and ski home across Schrader's Hill. I usually have to be careful not to run into a bunch of kids on sleds."

Sandy said she found all that very fascinating, but she was lying there in the snow in terrible pain. "I think I broke my ankle," she cried.

Jeff called the local ambulance service on his cell phone.

"They will be here in just a few minutes," he assured Sandy. "They said that they were on their way to a Christmas party at the hospital and would be driving right by the hill."

The Santa Claus Girls were stunned when the ambulance pulled up at the base of the hill, and two men dressed in elf costumes got out bearing a stretcher.

"It's a costume party," the paramedics chuckled as they gently placed Sandy on the stretcher. "And you will never guess who's driving—Harriet is dressed up like the Sugar Plum Fairy."

Karen and Lisa knew that Sandy was now in good hands. Jeff called her parents and informed them that she was being taken to the emergency room with either a broken or a sprained ankle.

Harriet, the ambulance driver, asked if she could drop Karen and Lisa anywhere along her route.

Karen explained that they were the Santa Claus Girls, and they had three more stops to make, so if she could just let them off at 400 South Street, they would be very appreciative.

Once Jeff saw that his friends were all right, he disappeared like any good Santa Claus into the night on his skis.

Karen admitted to her friend that she was pretty cold after they had rung the last of the three doorbells and ran into the night.

Lisa shivered in silent response, then moaned, "If only I hadn't lost my cell phone in the snow, I could call my parents to come pick us up."

Karen said that she thought she had an answer to their problem. If they cut across the vacant lot ahead of them and walked two blocks north, they would almost be at Jeff's front door. Since he had appeared out of nowhere and performed one Santa Miracle that night by coming to their rescue, she bet that he wouldn't mind giving the Santa Claus Girls a ride home.

Jeff didn't mind at all. And after he had dropped Lisa off at her home, he had an idea for another holiday surprise when he asked Karen to attend a New Year's Eve party with him.

Marla told us that her husband Chris was the best motorcycle mechanic in North Carolina.

"He has always had a thing about motorcycles and automobiles," she said. "He seems just to have been born with this talent. It is a genuine gift. He can fix anything with a motor. We started dating when we were sophomores in high school, and we got married two years after graduation in 1998."

In spite of his keen mechanical ability, Marla said that Chris has always had a secret ambition to be an actor. Maybe someday a talent scout would come through town, stop at the garage, and discover Chris as the next Marlon Brando, Steve McQueen, or Christian

Bale. He could be an actor and still keep riding bikes, just like Jay Leno and Arnold Schwarzenegger do.

"All of his friends know his little secret fantasy," Marla said, "but they never tease him about his yen for the stage lights, because they respect that this is his hobby. And also maybe because his next favorite hobby is martial arts."

In the summer of 2004, Chris played Captain Hook in the city's Little Theater production of *Peter Pan*. Chris' makeup was so convincing that their six-year-old son Randy didn't recognize his father on stage. When Chris came down into the audience after the play was over, Randy screamed and ran in terror when he approached him.

No way could Marla convince her son that the evil Captain Hook was his very own loving father in disguise, like at Halloween. Only when Chris began to sing "My Heroes Have Always Been Cowboys" did Randy believe that the man on his knees before him was his daddy. (Marla also said that Chris would like to be a country singer.)

At Christmas that year, Chris made a bet with Marla that his skills with makeup were so perfected that he could dress up like Santa Claus and convince Randy that Kris Kringle had paid him an in-person visit.

"I took Chris up on his bet," Marla said. "Mean old Captain Hook was one thing, but sweet, jolly Santa was another. I thought Randy would spot his daddy right away under however much stage makeup he might apply."

Under the pretense that his father had to work late at the garage on Christmas Eve, Randy and Marla began to eat the evening meal.

When a knock sounded at the door, Randy frowned his puzzlement.

"My goodness," Marla said, "who could be coming around at this time of night on Christmas Eve?"

She went to the door, opened it, and cried out in surprise, "Oh, my good gracious, Randy, it is Santa Claus himself."

Marla said that she had to admit that if she didn't know Chris' plan, he might have fooled her as to his identity.

"He had done a terrific job," she said. "The beard, the reddish complexion, the big, plump belly. Everything was perfect."

Without hesitation, Randy crawled up on Santa's lap and received each of the presents from Santa's bag with squeals and giggles of joy.

"Well, Randy, I got to be goin' now," Santa said. "I allowed you to see me in person so that you will know that Santa Claus is real. You earned this privilege because you were a good boy all year long. Now you just keep on listening to your Mommy and Daddy and saying your prayers at night, and I might stop by and see you next year. Right now, I got to get back into my sleigh and visit other good little boys and girls."

Marla said Chris left the kitchen with a dramatic flourish that tempted her to give him a round of applause.

"Well, son, what did you think about that?" Marla said. "You got to see Santa Claus."

By this time, Marla was about ready to concede to Chris that he had won his bet. It surely seemed as though he had convinced Randy that he was Santa Claus.

Randy smiled and said that it was terrific seeing Santa and getting so many terrific presents.

Then, with a twinkle in his eye, Randy added, "And I know Santa Claus is a really cool dude, too. He had a Harley-Davidson motorcycle tattoo on the back of his right hand just where Daddy has one."

Donna told us that she felt fortunate after graduating from a teacher's college in the Midwest in June 2008 when she was able to get a job as an elementary teacher in a small town in California's Central Valley. She was originally a California girl, and her securing a position in the middle of the state would bring her closer to her parents and other family members who lived not far from Fresno. Donna had last visited the almond groves near Newman with her parents when she was twelve or thirteen, and she looked forward to returning to the area as an adult.

September 2008 was an exciting time to begin teaching. The heated election campaigns were drawing to a close, and Donna took great delight in the caliber of the discussions regarding the candidates that her third-grade students exhibited. Donna was amazed at the depth that some of her nine- or ten-year-old students displayed. Some, of course, were parroting comments that they had overheard from their parents, but others seemed genuinely capable of forming surprisingly mature opinions based on their own analyses of media reports.

Donna, as was proper for an elementary-school teacher, remained impartial, nonpartisan beyond criticism. Truly, in college, after she had chosen to teach elementary rather than junior high school or high school, Donna wondered briefly if her idealism to help strengthen children's minds might have been too utopian. But now she realized with each new day that she had made the correct choice. These kids were sharp.

The election results in November brought new topics for discussion after the subjects of reading, writing, and arithmetic were put away for the day. What would happen when the new President would assume office? How thrilling it was to be a part of history with the first African American sitting behind the desk in the Oval Office.

Then, scarcely before one could believe it, it was nearly time for Thanksgiving and Christmas. Because her class contained so many members of diverse ethnic groups, Donna began a series of discussions about the various ways in which Christmas is celebrated in different countries and by different religions.

It was after two or three days of these kinds of discussions that one of the girls asked the single most power-packed question of all. "Is there really a Santa Claus?"

A few of the children giggled, but Donna noticed that suddenly all eyes were fast upon her, as if she were an oracle asked an earth-shaking question that could determine the fate of an entire civilization.

Momentarily puzzled, Donna was intrigued that her bright young nine-year-olds, who had discussed politics and elections with such seeming sophistication, should ask about the reality of Santa Claus.

"Well, I guess that's a question that you should really ask your parents," Donna answered diplomatically, after mentally weighing several possible answers.

Many of the children responded with great determination, not even bothering to raise their hands for permission. Amidst a great deal of confused and rather noisy shouting, the great majority of the class was declaring that Santa Claus was real and would bring them presents that year.

"Quiet, please," Donna said. "Let's remember our manners and courtesy."

"But tell us, please," one of the brightest students in the class asked.

Donna took a deep breath. If these kids could discuss politics and government policies with some apparent depth, they could certainly hear the truth about Santa.

"If you are asking if some chubby fellow in a sleigh drawn by eight reindeers—nine, if you count the one with the red nose—is going to come flying over and drop presents down your chimney, then, no, the answer is that there is no Santa Claus," she told them.

Dismissal bell rang, and Donna gave silent thanks for the classic "saved by the bell."

She felt very uncomfortable as the children filed out of the room in almost total silence. There were no cheery good nights or see-you-tomorrows. On some of those dear cheeks, Donna thought she saw tears.

The next morning before classes began, Donna found a note on her desk from Mrs. Campbell, the principal, requesting that Donna come to her office as soon as she arrived.

Mrs. Campbell, a tall woman who always seemed pleasant, but somewhat severe, asked Donna to sit down opposite her desk.

"I spent a good share of last evening answering telephone calls from very upset parents," she said, getting right to the point. "They were upset and angry because their children came home in tears from your class, crying and feeling in despair because you told them there was no Santa Claus."

Donna almost made the mistake of assuming that Mrs. Campbell was joking, but when she considered the tone of her voice, she concluded that she was quite serious.

"One of the reasons that you were hired," Mrs. Campbell explained, "was because of your high academic standards. Some of your professors even wrote on their recommendations that you were one of those students who always had her nose in a book."

Donna began to acknowledge such praise, but Mrs. Campbell held up her hand to silence her.

"The world of academics is often a world apart from the real world," Mrs. Campbell said. "A good teacher has to learn to straddle both."

Mrs. Campbell went on to explain that in the five years that Donna had been away obtaining her master's degree in education in the Midwest, the Central Valley had undergone three years of serious drought. In 2009, the coming year, the University of California had estimated that the drought may cause

847,000 acres to go unplanted and that there may be a loss of 70,000 jobs.

"From your visits to Central Valley in your childhood, you remember it as one of the richest farming regions in the nation," Mrs. Campbell said. "Because of the drought, many of your students' parents are broke, terribly in debt. Christmas is soon approaching. The children need Santa Claus. They need the miracle of hope. With their last pennies, these wonderful people will see that Santa Claus will come for their children. Their children will have a Christmas."

Mrs. Campbell paused to remove a book from a desk drawer. She explained that she was from New York originally, and she had always loved Betty Smith's famous novel, *A Tree Grows in Brooklyn*. In the book, Mrs. Campbell said, among her favorite passages are those in which a grandmother explains to her daughter, a young mother, why a child must be taught to believe in Santa Claus—even if the mother herself may not believe.

Mrs. Campbell asked Donna's indulgence to allow her to read a few paragraphs in which the grandmother says that a child must start out in life believing in things not of this world: "Then when the world becomes too ugly for living in, the child can reach back and live in her imagination."

Mrs. Campbell said that she would be retiring in another two years. "As a teacher, I have witnessed miracles among the children," she said. "Only by remembering these miracles in my mind can I live beyond what I have to live for."

Donna walked to her classroom in silence. One day the children would be able to decide for themselves about Santa Claus. Now it was important that they should believe with all their hearts in the true miracle of Santa.

"Good morning, class," she greeted the children seated before her. "I think I have some explaining to do. Yesterday, when you asked about Santa Claus, it was just time for dismissal, and I guess we all got excited and started talking at once. Now, about Santa Claus, what I meant to explain was that those men in department stories with pillows stuffed under their red suits were not the real Santa. Of course those men, nice as they may be, are not able to fly across the sky in a magic sleigh and bring presents to your homes.

"Now then, about the *real* Santa Claus," Donna smiled, "he lives in all of our hearts and knows everything that we want for Christmas. Don't ask me how he does it. It is just a miracle that Santa Claus is able to work."

The smiles and tears of joy and relief that shone from the children's faces provided Donna with her own Santa Miracle that she knew would last her a lifetime.

Annette Martin has become world famous as a psychic counselor and a professional singer. She is the subject of the book *Gift of the White Light: The Strange and Wonderful Story of Annette Martin* by James N. Frey.

Here is Annette's story of how she received her Santa Miracle:

When I was ten years old, my family moved to a house situated in the middle of the block in the Sunset District of San Francisco, just a few blocks from the Pacific Ocean. My back bedroom window looked out to the vast ocean, and when I opened it, I could smell the luscious salt air.

St. Gabriel's Grammar school on 38th Avenue was eight blocks toward the ocean. On sunny days I would walk to, and back from, school. On cold, foggy, and rainy days, I would hop onto the L Street car that ran up and down Taraval Street, with its metal wheels churning along the tracks.

After about two months or so, new friends were beginning to come into my life, but most of them still kept themselves an arm's length away. My singing had come into full blossom, and our principal, Sister Mary Hillary, asked me to sing in the adult choir due to my voice being so powerful at such a young age.

My singing was becoming very popular, and I was asked to do a TV show with Del Courtney at KPIX. I was studying voice, and I felt that this would be a great opportunity to sing even more. The only trouble was that my school friends began to back away even farther and not even be as superficially friendly as they were before.

As the days went by, a sadness came into my life and I felt very alone. Sure, I had my music and could see things that others could not, but something was missing.

About a month later my folks drove down to Palo Alto onto the Stanford University property. Mother had found one of her old teachers from Commerce High in San Francisco and had been invited for lunch.

We walked in and were greeted by the most beautiful thing I had ever seen—a long-haired golden retriever. I went to my knees and just started to cry. I was enveloped by this incredible creature. She was so soft and loving, and she seemed to want to be with me the entire time that we were there visiting.

When it was time to leave, I felt so sad, and I wished that I could take her home with me. Mom and Dad were quite surprised by my response to the retriever, as I had never been around dogs my entire life. I had only been exposed to one animal—Fifi, my grandmother's Persian cat.

Life went on. I continued with all of my school and professional singing engagements, but as an only child, my days were becoming more lonely. No friends to speak of and only adults that really didn't want to carry on lengthy conversations with a ten-year-old. I had such a longing to have a friend or companion. I went to church many days, asking for that special miracle . . . but nothing seemed to be happening.

December rolled around, and it was soon Christmas Eve. My grandparents were coming over for Christmas morning breakfast and the opening of gifts.

The morning arrived, and after breakfast my daddy went down to the basement and told me to close my eyes, as I was going to be the first to open packages. Keeping my eyes tightly shut and anticipating great excitement over what Santa may have brought me, Daddy said, "Okay, honey, open your eyes."

Slowly, opening first one eye and then the other, I could see a big basket in front of the tall, white-flocked Christmas tree. Moving toward the basket, I could hear something inside, and I rushed to open the lid. A little cry came from the basket, and I peered inside to discover a golden fluff looking up at me with big brown eyes.

I screamed for joy and reached in and grabbed this adorable puppy and just cried and cried, "Thank you, Daddy and Mommy. Thank you, Santa," over and over again.

My prayers had been answered. Now I had a companion with whom to play and to tell all of my inner secrets.

I named her "Rochanne," a combination of our last name, De La Roche, and Anne, being part of my first name.

Rochanne, my Santa Miracle, lived to be fifteen years old and bore ten of the most precious puppies on my bed. The memory of my dear companion still brings tears to my eyes when I think of her.

Christmas
Miracles

Christmas
Miracles

Inspirational True Stories
of Holiday Magic

Brad Steiger &
Sherry Hansen Steiger

Avon, Massachusetts

Published by
Adams Media, an F+W Publications Company
57 Littlefield Street, Avon, MA 02322 U.S.A.

ISBN-13: 978-1-60550-017-1

Printed in the United States of America.

ISBN-13: 978-1-60550-017-1

Interior photo © Falk Kienas / istockphoto.com

Previously published as *Christmas Miracles*, by Brad Steiger and Sherry Hansen
Steiger, copyright © 2001 by Brad Steiger and Sherry Hansen Steiger,
ISBN-10: 1-58062-552-5, ISBN-13: 978-1-58062-552-4.

Dedication

This book is for our parents, children, and grandchildren, with whom we have shared many Christmas miracles in the past and with whom we hope to share many more such miracles in the future.

Introduction

The story of the first Christmas, as it is told in the Gospels of Matthew and Luke, is made up of the accounts of five miracles:

1. The Angel Gabriel appears to Mary, a young girl of Nazareth, and proclaims that she has been chosen for a very special purpose. God's holy spirit will visit her, and she, without knowing a man, will become pregnant.

2. An angel manifests to Joseph, a Nazarene carpenter who is Mary's fiancé, and counsels him not to put aside the young woman, who is now very much with child, or subject her to public disgrace, but to marry her. All of this, he is told, is part of a much larger divine plan.

3. Shepherds outside of Bethlehem, keeping watch over their flocks by night, witness a chorus of angels declaring the supernatural birth of a child in a stable who, according to the joyous heavenly host, will bring peace on Earth and good will toward men.

4. A miraculous star moves in the sky to guide three wise philosopher-kings from faraway Eastern nations to worship Jesus, "the newborn king," and to bring him gifts of gold, frankincense, and myrrh.

5. An angel appears in a dream to the three wise men, advising them not to return to the duplicitous King Herod with the identity of the child that he fears will usurp his throne. The angel also manifests in another night vision to warn Joseph to flee with Mary and the child to safety in Egypt in order to avoid Herod's jealous wrath.

Since the story of Christmas is founded on the five miracles listed above, there can be little wonder that miracles of faith and love continue to occur during a holiday season that has been held sacred for 2,000 years. For those men and women who believe that Jesus was far more than an extraordinary prophet and teacher, the true meaning of Christmas far transcends the exchange of gifts, the gathering of families around the plum puddings, or the decking of halls with boughs of holly.

Although there is the general belief that Jesus was born at the hour of midnight on Christmas Eve, even the most devout cannot attest to the exact historical date of his birth. Even today, some branches of Christendom observe the holy birth in December, others in January, April, or May.

It seems very likely that December 25 was selected as the festival day because it also marked the advent of the great winter celebrations of the Britons, the Germans, and the Gauls. These days of merry-making signaled the winter solstice and a time of great feasts to honor the pagan gods. Although the early teachers of Christianity prohibited any recognition of the ancient deities or any aspect of their festivals as incompatible with the heavenly character of Jesus, numerous customs still observed today, such as the yule log, the holly, and the mistletoe, reach far back into a pagan past.

By the fifth century, the observance of the birthday of Jesus Christ on December 25 had spread to various parts of the Christian world, and by the early Middle Ages, Christmas had become the greatest and most popular of all holidays celebrated throughout Europe. By that time, churches observed the custom of colorfully decorating their usually austere interiors, and they permitted actors to present religious pageants depicting the Nativity. People sang carols in the streets, and there were numerous parades with marchers carrying aloft images of the Virgin Mary, the baby Jesus, Joseph, the shepherds, the wise men, and angels.

Since colonial times, Christmas in the United States has evolved into a period of great social activity. Because of its melting pot of cultures and customs, its unity in diversity, its blending of the contemporary and the traditional, America has fashioned a semisocial, semireligious celebration that enables everyone to wish everyone else a merry Christmas, regardless of an individual's religious expression. Christmas in the United States has become a colorful tapestry that has been woven together with the customs, beliefs, traditions, superstitions, and folklore of people who were once widely separated and culturally diverse and who are now next-door neighbors.

Washington Irving (1783–1859) wrote that during our nation's formative years Christmas ". . . awakened the strongest and most heartfelt of associations. There is a tone of solemn and sacred feeling that blends with our conviviality, and lifts the spirit to a state of hallowed and elevated enjoyment."

Christmas is a sacred time that touches many of us deep within our spirit—but it is also a time when we can put aside our solemnities and our stresses and become children again. We can stop being grown-ups and once again become the five-year-old boy or girl listening for the sound of Santa's sleigh on the rooftop.

And with so many hearts and spirits becoming open and childlike, what better time than Christmas for the manifestation of miracles?

In this book, we shall present a wide variety of miraculous occurrences that took place during the Christmas holiday. There are moving accounts of dramatic healings, inspirational stories of angelic interaction, life-altering visions, and joyous reports of the spirits of departed loved ones who briefly came home for the holidays. Christmas with all of its diverse attendant emotions truly does appear to have the power to open doorways between dimensions.

Each Christmas season, millions of men and women acknowledge the angelic promise of a peace that passes all understanding and allow themselves to perceive the world with childlike wonder and joy. Then, after the holiday has passed and they must move on with their worldly concerns, they too often permit the tensions and stresses of life to press in on them once again and squeeze the magic of the joyous holiday right out of them. And sadly, nearly all of the once hearty and cheerful expressions of peace, love, and goodwill to their fellow humans become absorbed in the day-to-day challenges of existence.

It is our earnest wish that this book might help all who read it to keep the miracles of Christmas alive in their hearts and spirits all year long.

SHERRY HANSEN STEIGER
BRAD STEIGER
Forest City, Iowa

Acknowledgements

There were many individuals who contributed their thoughts and experiences to the making of this book. Among those who must receive special thanks are Bob and Janice Kolb, Erskine and Charlotte Payton, Dr. Franklin Ruehl, Paul and Lorraine Lippold, Link and Hazel Olson, Bob Shortz, Clarisa Bernhardt, Cindy and Dave Bennett, and Dr. Bruce Goldberg.

Whenever anyone asks Pastor A.T. Vermedahl about his favorite Christmas or a special Christmas happening, he always tells the same simple, direct, and miraculous story.

He was recently out of the seminary in Chicago 1959, and he found himself the shepherd of a poor congregation in a small Wyoming parish, whose elderly pastor had died of a sudden heart attack in October.

"I had arrived about a month before Christmas, just a kid in my mid-twenties, lonely for my family back in Milwaukee, homesick for a city with a main street that stretched out longer than four or five blocks," he recalled. "I really thought that I must be being punished by God for some sin beyond my awareness to have been sent out to this wide spot in a dusty road."

Pastor Vermedahl is embarrassed today by how spoiled and self-centered he was during his first days with the congregation.

"I am afraid that I must have appeared very condescending to the farmers and ranchers who sat quietly, reverently, humbly before me," he said. "But I guess they had decided to be patient with the smart-aleck city punk preacher."

With Christmas fast approaching, Pastor Vermedahl attempted to stir up enthusiasm among the choir director and the dozen or so members of the choir to attempt a seasonal oratorio such as Handel's *Messiah*.

"Or if that was beyond their range and reach— which, of course, I presumed it was—how about creating an original cantata?" I challenged the choir director, Mrs. Olive Martindale, the sixty-eight-year-old wife of a retired high school English teacher. "Or perhaps she could at the very least arrange a medley of religious and secular carols and hymns?"

Mrs. Martindale began to tremble and tears came to her eyes. He knew that he had intimidated her, but Pastor Vermedahl barely found it within his good graces to apologize and to tell her that whatever she came up with would be fine.

Two nights before Christmas Eve, it was Pastor Vermedahl who had tears in his eyes after listening to choir practice. But his tears were precipitated by frustration. The grand Christmas mass he had imagined was not about to happen here.

"Mrs. Martindale had done her best to arrange a bright and colorful medley of Christmas music," he recalled, "but there was so little talent among her vocalists that it seemed as though they were mourning the fall of western civilization, rather than celebrating the birth of a messiah."

Later that night in his study, Pastor Vermedahl telephoned his parents back in Milwaukee to wish them a merry Christmas.

"I was much more frank with my parents than I should have been," he said, "but, alas, I had the impatience and audacity of the young. Before I had graduated from the seminary, I had envisioned myself as the pastor of a large congregation in a major city, not as the caretaker of a struggling little community of ranchers and rustics. I found myself shouting into the mouthpiece of the telephone, 'I keep asking why I was sent to this godforsaken place!'"

The words were no sooner out of his mouth when he glanced up to see the shocked face of the church secretary, Mrs. Lankford, standing in the doorway of his study with the newly mimeographed copies of the church bulletin in her trembling hands.

"Pastor Vermedahl," her voice was barely a whisper, "we don't think God has forsaken us here in our little town. We very much feel that God is with us."

With those words, she hastily set the bulletins down on the table by his desk, reached for her coat from the rack, and walked briskly from his study.

Pastor Vermedahl said a quick good-bye to his parents, clicked down the receiver, and ran after Mrs. Lankford, trying his best to apologize, to explain that he was only using a figure of speech.

"And, of course, 'godforsaken' is a figure of speech," Pastor Vermedahl sighed at his recollection of the awkward moment. "It just happens to be a very derogatory figure of speech."

When he stepped up into the pulpit on Christmas Eve, Pastor Vermedahl felt extremely uncomfortable. He had no idea how many people Mrs. Lankford may have informed that their new, young pastor considered their little community to be godforsaken.

As if to compensate for his monumental thoughtlessness, he read with great enthusiasm the Bible passages from Luke that tell the ageless story of that first Christmas Eve, emphasizing with special feeling the verses that speak of the angels on high announcing the birth of Jesus to the lowly shepherds tending their flocks outside of Bethlehem.

"At that very moment," he recalled, "the door opened in the back and a beautiful young woman in a white gown walked down the aisle directly to the front of the church where the choir stood decked out in their red and green robes, waiting to sing their next selection.

"Although I had never seen the lovely woman with the reddish-blond hair before, I assumed that Mrs. Martindale had recruited a guest choir member. If this one could sing half as good as she looked, I thought to myself, she would vastly improve the quality of the choir. Since her snow-white gown appeared in sharp contrast to the other members' red and green robes, it was obvious that she was to be a special soloist on Christmas Eve.

"Without saying a word to Mrs. Martindale, who appeared rather astonished by her sudden appearance," Pastor Vermedahl continued, "the woman turned to face the congregation and began in a rich contralto voice to sing 'He Shall Feed His Flock Like a Shepherd' from Handel's oratorio, *Messiah*. Never had I heard it sung with such majesty, such richness, such command of phrasing, such appropriate emphasis. And she had no accompanying orchestra. The lovely woman standing before us in her almost dazzling white gown, singing a cappella, provided us with an interpretation of the work that was completely magical, enchanting, unworldly."

When she had completed the selection from Handel's masterpiece, the woman stepped down from the choir loft and walked back up the aisle.

"As every one of us in the church that Christmas Eve watched the beautiful stranger's graceful exit," Pastor Vermedahl said, "she walked back out the same door through which she had entered only ten or twelve minutes before. And she was gone.

"The four men who ushered that evening were standing at the two back doors—and they swore to a man that she simply disappeared into the cold December night. There were no vehicles of any kind in the parking lot that could have been hers. All trucks, jeeps, cars, and pickups were accounted for by the members of the congregation of the church still seated within."

Before the Christmas Eve service was completed that evening, the members of Pastor Vermedahl's little church congregation were whispering that they had been visited by an angel.

"And these many years later, I have no better explanation," he conceded. "I truly believe that we were visited by an angel of the Lord that Christmas Eve. No one in that region ever saw that beautiful woman in the white gown again—and they were certainly looking for her. Perhaps an angel was sent to us that Christmas Eve to demonstrate to everyone present—and maybe especially to a spoiled big city kid preacher—that there are no places in the universe that are 'godforsaken.' I happily continued to serve that congregation for another fifteen years."

The year was 1955, and Bob Kolb, now a retired dentist from New Hampshire, remembered that it was his second consecutive Christmas away from home—and that particular Christmas Eve wasn't shaping up to be a very good one at all.

"I was sitting on a U.S. Navy ship, the USS *Piedmont AD17*. We were anchored in Subic Bay in the Philippine Islands," Bob recalled. "The temperature was in the nineties, and the ship was steel without air conditioning in the medical/dental sickbay where I worked. I was hot, despondent, and generally depressed. I just didn't want to be there."

The previous January 7, Bob had married his sweetheart, Jan, and on October 24, he had become the father of a beautiful baby girl whom he had never seen. He had no idea when he finally would lay eyes on her.

"I desperately wanted to see my wife, Jan," he said. "This was our first Christmas as a married couple, and here I was, many thousands of miles away from her, feeling worthless, defeated, and very sorry for myself."

Bob recalled that Jan was a marvelous correspondent. "She actually wrote a long and newsy letter to me every single day that I was away," he said. "And of course the letters since the baby's birth were filled with pictures and stories of this 'wonder child' that was ours. How I wanted to see my little daughter, June, and wrap my arms around her and my wife. But it was not to be this Christmas."

To make the men's pain of separation from their loved ones at Christmas even worse, a postal glitch had caused the USS *Piedmont*'s mail to be sent to its previous port. "So here I was in a distant land without one semblance of the things that I had previously associated with Christmas. There was no mail, no wife, no infant daughter—and a ship whose decks got so hot from the sun that even Santa's reindeer would burn their hooves if they attempted a landing.

The day their daughter was born, Bob Kolb's ship had been in the harbor of Keelung, Formosa, but he didn't receive word of her birth until a few days later. By the time that the wondrous telegram announcing her birth arrived from the Navy Department, the USS *Piedmont* was in the South China Sea heading towards Hong Kong to support the freedom efforts of the Nationalist Chinese government in their conflict with the Chinese Communist regime.

As they steamed along the coast of China, Bob recalled that they were often overflown by elements of the Chinese air force. Since one of the functions of their ship was ammunition supply, the crew often speculated on the crisis that would be caused if they were attacked by the planes overhead. An explosion of the munitions the ship carried would be horrible.

"But no attack occurred," he said, "and I arrived in Hong Kong harbor with one thought in mind—to get on the telephone and call Jan, who was staying with her parents in Philadelphia until I returned."

Bob explained that making an overseas telephone call in those days was so very different from today. It was not possible simply to dial a number. The call had to be arranged.

"The first step was to apply for liberty from my ship during the working hours of the telephone company," he said. "The second step was to go to the telephone company headquarters in downtown Hong Kong to plan the call. The call was segmented, and each leg had to be arranged individually. Initially, the call went to Tokyo, then connected to Wake or Midway Island, then to Honolulu, and finally to Seattle where it was tied into the continental United States system. Several hours later, the phone finally rang in Philadelphia, and I was talking to Jan."

Bob qualified that "talking" was hardly the correct term, because the quality of the transmission was so poor and the background noise level so high that normal conversation was impossible. The long-awaited telephone connection with his wife lasted for only a few minutes, and Bob was able to understand only two brief sentences: "*She has red hair . . . I love you.*"

"But it was Jan's voice that said those words," Bob remembered, "and I knew that she and my baby daughter were well. Such contact was so much more reassuring than a letter where you know they were well when the letter was sent—but you can only hope that everything is still fine by the time you read about it."

Bob said that the cost of that single phone call was $64 in Hong Kong dollars, and he still has the receipt to prove it.

After the USS *Piedmont* left Hong Kong, it headed for the Philippines where it was scheduled to do repairs and maintenance on some destroyers that awaited its support.

"It was early afternoon on Christmas Eve and my work in the medical/dental sickbay was over for the day," Bob said. "Because the Philippine temperatures in a steel ship became unbearable in the afternoon, we worked from 4:00 A.M. to 1:00 P.M., with an hour breakfast/lunch break from 8:00 to 9:00 A.M."

The men had several options as to how they might spend Christmas Eve. They could attend a movie that was being shown on board ship. They could read, write letters, or play the card game "acey-deucy"—the standard leisure-time activity aboard a U.S. Navy ship during that era.

"About a dozen of us from the medical, dental, and chaplain's department opted to have a little Christmas party," Bob said. "We all put our names on slips of paper, dumped them in a trash can, then drew names for the gift exchange at the party after evening chow."

The gift rules were simple, Bob explained: "The gift had to be something that you personally owned, and it had to have a monetary value not to exceed $3. Since we were all aboard ship with no stores or places to buy gifts—and since our personal belongings were so limited—it required a lot of ingenuity to come up with a present that might be of value to someone else, cost next to nothing, and yet be something that the giver would then have to be without for the rest of the duration. A real gift is one that actually diminishes what you have. A true gift is one whose loss will be felt by the giver."

That evening after chow, the men gathered in the dental department where there was also a small portable pump organ that Bob Kolb played at Sunday religious services when the USS *Piedmont* was at sea. Bob recalled that the chaplain opened their party with a short talk about home and what he considered to be the significance of Christmas. Later, while Bob played the organ, the men had some coffee and soft drinks and sang a few carols.

Then it was time to hand out the gifts.

"In order to prolong the event and the significance of the occasion, the gifts were given and opened one at a time," Bob said. "In addition, each recipient was 'roasted' a little bit to add to the fun. The gifts included such items as a can of shoe polish, a uniform belt buckle, a flashlight, a package of Navy stationery, a piece of fruit cake, a paperback book."

Bob received a toy roulette wheel: It was on a black marble base about four inches square that was painted red with black and white number slots on the wheel. In the center of the wheel, rising about three inches, was a T-shaped handle used for spinning the wheel.

The men said their thank-yous and went to bed. Work began the next morning at 4:00 A.M. Even though it was Christmas Day, the work aboard a ship must go on. And this was perhaps especially true for Bob Kolb and the men who worked in the medical/dental sickbay where there were always emergencies and people needing treatment.

As Christmas Day dawned, Bob remembered that he awoke with a new feeling of well-being. "It was as if all the depression, the heat, the frustration, and the loneliness were lifted," he said. "The feelings of desperation and despair were now replaced with a sense of accomplishment and camaraderie."

The loneliness for his wife and daughter were still there, but now Bob felt as though he were facing the sorrow of separation as part of a group of young men who served one another as members of a support team. The night before at the Christmas party, he had discovered that there were quite a few of the men who had children that they had never seen. They eventually loosely organized a group of the faraway fathers and called it the "Stork Club."

Bob's roulette wheel became a source of great fun. "I played with it for hours, using it to make charts on number probabilities," he said. "I also employed it as my personal 'guru' to answer questions and to create winner probabilities for our acey-deucy tournaments."

Bob recalled that the young dental technician who had given him the roulette wheel was Arthur Kitzman. "We were not close friends," Bob said, "but rather casual acquaintances. But his gift to me of that small roulette wheel was one of the finest gifts that I have ever received. In the nearly fifty years that have gone by since that Christmas time away from my family, I have been given many, many gifts. Many have been expensive and significant. Yet I do not really remember very many of those gifts. The roulette wheel, however, I remember in an intimate way—the moment of giving, the giver, the feeling of appreciation I experienced, even its physical feeling in my hands."

Bob Kolb began that Christmas Eve in 1955 thinking, "Why me, Lord?" Why had he been sent to a place far away from his wife and child? Why was this bad thing happening to him?

Yet, somehow, in a few short hours, his attitude had transformed him into an entirely different person. Now the meaning of "Why me, Lord?" was completely reversed: "Why have I been so blessed by you that I have been given all of this?"

Bob Kolb concluded his account of that Christmas Eve aboard the USS *Piedmont* in 1955 by affirming: "This, then, is the power of Christmas. A power that can in a miraculous way transform a young man from a state of abject depression and self-pity to a state of full acceptance and understanding. A power that can move a young man from the point where he says in anguish, 'Why me, Lord?' to a place where he looks at all the wonderful gifts and blessings that have been given to him and realizes that the wonder and beauty of Christmas is not in what you receive. Perhaps it is not even in what you give, but in God's love given in the form of an infant child, whose impact can perform a miracle.

"Night became day, apathy became excitement, and despair became a word that described my former emotional condition before the event that I now consider to have been my Christmas miracle."

*E*rskine Payton recalls Christmas 1992 as being extremely cold and snowy in Louisville, Kentucky—the coldest Christmas season that anyone could remember. Although he is now nationally known as the popular host of the syndicated radio program *Erskine Overnight,* during that particular holiday season Erskine and his wife, Charlotte, had jobs playing Santa and Mrs. Claus at the Louisville Zoo.

"By Christmas Eve, I was really tired of wearing the suit, the itchy beard, and hearing all the petty stuff that kids and adults wanted for Christmas," Erskine said. "I wanted nothing more than to go home, sit by a warm fire, and not even think of being Santa for at least nine months."

But Erskine and Charlotte had one more stop to make that night before they could relax. His beloved grandmother's birthday was on Christmas Day. She would turn 102.

"She had asked Charlotte and me to visit her on Christmas Eve at the retirement home—and she had requested that we arrive as Santa and Mrs. Claus to surprise her friends," Erskine said. "As weary as I was of being Santa Claus, there was no way that I could not do this simple thing to please my dear grandmother."

The roads were becoming slick but were still passable when Erskine and Charlotte left for the retirement home, loaded down with candy canes for the senior citizens.

"My grandmother's face really lit up when she saw us all dressed up as Santa and Mrs. Claus," Erskine recalled. "She wanted to show us off to everyone, and she asked that we visit with as many residents as possible. I did my usual grumbling protest, but with my two favorite women insisting that I be a jolly Santa, I had no choice but to utter my very best 'Ho, Ho, Ho's' and walk from room to room, itching beard, sweaty suit, and all."

After dispensing candy canes to dozens of the elderly residents and maintaining the persona of Jolly St. Nick for another couple of hours, Erskine was thankful that Christmas would soon be over. He was not yet at the "bah, humbug" stage, but he was getting there.

"I noticed a very elderly gentleman sitting at a table, head down, drooling, looking as though his mind was really some other place far away," Erskine said. "There was a young woman who I assumed to be his daughter sitting with him. In a kind of perfunctory manner, I put a candy cane in one of his trembling hands, not really paying much attention to see if he was even really aware of it."

But then Charlotte stepped forward and whispered conspiratorially to the old man: "You don't want an old candy cane from Santa. How about a little kiss from Mrs. Claus?"

She bent down and kissed the man's cheek, and he looked up at Charlotte and gave her a broad smile.

As the Paytons were about to move on to the next resident, they were somewhat startled to see the younger woman standing beside the elderly man suddenly break down in tears.

"She was sobbing uncontrollably," Erskine said. "I asked what was wrong and we tried to comfort her."

When the woman was able to regain her composure, she put her arms around Charlotte and Erskine and hugged them warmly.

"My father *smiled!*" she said. "He smiled when Mrs. Santa kissed his cheek. Dad has been here eight years and up to now he has never once changed his expression or given any sign that he is aware of anything going on around him. And now he's sitting there smiling, holding a candy cane! In all my life, I never received such a wonderful gift from Santa and Mrs. Claus as you gave me tonight."

Erskine saw that the woman was releasing blessed tears of joy. His beard stopped itching. The Santa suit no longer felt so hot and uncomfortable.

"I was now able to see the true magic of Christmas," he said. "I now understood that there is a Christmas spirit that transcends the rush to buy gifts, the rush to put up decorations, and the rush, rush, rush to spend extravagantly during the holiday. Christmas is a special time that transcends even the religious significance of this special day. That elderly man's smile was the best present imaginable for his daughter, my wife, and, yes, for Santa himself."

*J*anice Gray Kolb, author of such inspirational books as *Compassion for All Creatures*, said that residing in the woods of New Hampshire on the shore of a lake enables her each day to learn more about the wildlife that shares the beautiful environment with her and her husband Bob.

"Just a few days before Christmas 2000, I drew open the curtains on a sunny crisp morning to unwrap a stupendous surprise," she said. "There outside our sliding glass doors stood the gift of a huge moose!"

After exclamations of delight from her husband Bob and herself—and several moments spent in awe of the magnificent creature—Janice grabbed a camera and slipped quietly outdoors to begin a relationship with the moose that they would name Matilda.

The moose turned and ran into the woods when she saw Janice walk onto the front porch, but with

Janice calling gently—and Bob doing the same from the side living room window—the gentle creature gradually returned, stopping to munch on branches and shrubbery along the way. All the while, Janice was snapping wonderful close-ups of her as she walked up to linger along the side of their cottage.

"We watched her every move," Janice recalled, "and spoke to her in gentle tones, calling her Matilda. Rochester, our beloved marmalade-and-white cat, opted to observe the scene through the window from the sofa indoors. Bob and I gave up all we had planned to do that morning and spent two hours outdoors with Matilda. After all, how often does a moose come to call? Eventually, she roamed away from us, and we reluctantly went indoors. But the excitement of her visit lingered, and I wrote a poem to honor her."

Although Matilda did not return the next day, Janice had a vivid dream about her that night. "In the dream, she stared deeply into my eyes. I believed the dream was symbolic and required prayer and thought, but the initial interpretation that came forth was that she was a kind of spiritual visitation."

When the moose returned the second day, Janice could not help thinking of her as somehow "theirs."

"Matilda was so beautiful," Janice recalled, "and I was filled with awe at her size and gentle demeanor. I was so thankful that she was roaming our property."

The forest giant wandered into a deeper wooded area, and Janice followed. "She could barely be seen among the trees," Janice said. "If I had not known she was there, she would have been hidden. I moved in a bit closer, speaking gently to her. Still as statues, we both stood for an hour. Eventually, she became more comfortable with my presence, for she began to eat dead maple leaves and eventually whole branches. Another poem about her began to form, and I wrote it on some paper I had in my pocket."

And so it went during those days before Christmas 2000. "I passed many hours with this amazing moose," Janice said. "Sometimes I stood; sometimes I sat on the ground or on big fallen branches. But all the while I kept company with Matilda. When I talked to her, she would now turn her great head to look at me and make me feel acknowledged. Never once did she ever show aggression toward me. She could have walked or charged past me if she had so chosen, for I was no obstacle. Even when I occasionally took her picture, she seemed to ignore the flash. That she elected to stay made me feel honored, for I was in the company of a great, mysterious creature."

Though they had spent hours in one another's company, Janice will never forget that one particular moment when they seemed to blend awarenesses:

"Slowly she turned her massive head, and her big brown eyes stared deeply into mine from only ten feet away. I stood motionless, held by her gaze. Momentarily, I was in another realm. In my spirit I heard her say, '*I come peacefully so you may know me.*'

"My imagination? I really do not think so," Janice said. "As her eyes met mine, I was not thinking or creating, only allowing the contact. There was no fear, only peace. I could not move again until she shifted her head."

After the enchantment had been lifted, Janice took out her pen and paper to record the words left in her mind—while Matilda chewed on a green branch. Janice had always felt that the deer was her totem animal, and she had numerous pictures of deer in her writing room. Now a "family member," so to speak, had come, bringing with her a special spiritual vision.

Bob joined Janice near the lake, and they both took photographs of their mysterious visitor. Bob left as it was growing dark, encouraging Janice to accompany him back to the cottage.

"I stayed until dark," Janice remembered. "It was difficult to leave her, and I wanted to stay as long as I could in case this would be the last time that I would ever see her. I spoke loving messages to her and asked that she never leave our land or these woods near the lake."

On Sunday, Bob and Janice passed Matilda on the road as they drove up the hill to go to church. They stopped and backed up, and Janice rolled down her window and asked her to please wait until their return.

"On our arrival back at our cottage," Janice said, "we found her lying on our hill eating leaves and branches. We stood in silence as she rose to her enormous height, and we spent the rest of Sunday afternoon until sundown, observing all that we could about her."

Days passed and Bob and Janice continued to see Matilda, walking and talking with her in the woods or down by the beach as she stood next to their canoe. It was hunting season during these encounters, but Matilda was safe in their woods because they have declared them a sanctuary for animals with no hunting allowed.

"As Matilda continued to live in and roam our woods, we had a new spirit about us," Janice declared. "It was thrilling to share our lives with such a creature, and each day one or the other of us would stop for a moment and consider our blessing. Even unseen, her presence was with us, as we spoke of her and anticipated our next encounter."

Some years ago, Janice Gray Kolb discovered that in ancient Christian symbology, the deer is a symbol of Christ. "I have written about the deer being sacred to so many cultures in one of my recent books," she said. "Seeing those warning signs along New Hampshire's and Maine's highways about 'Moose Crossings' offers a signal both to pray and to think upon the marvelous creatures that roam these woods. Their very presence is transforming to us. Animals are messengers and they bring wisdom to us if we are open. I believe animals can become spiritual messengers of mystery and transformation, and when we do not seek to learn from them, we deprive ourselves of their indispensable roles in our lives."

Continuing with this line of thought, Janice said: "As I live in the woods and learn more about wildlife, I am grateful for the privilege of witnessing each day filled with miracles. I believe that an enormous and precious messenger came to us in the form of Matilda—and that she is a spiritual presence that reminds us of our Creator. We had only to look into her eyes to realize the holiness within. I will never forget those moments when her eyes looked deeply into mine and touched my soul. She has forever left her mark—and should we never meet again, I am most thankful that she is out there somewhere, roaming our woods. And may she remain so forevermore."

Shortly after the series of encounters that Bob and Janice had experienced with Matilda, they read an article in a local newspaper about a moose sighting in another small town in New Hampshire. According to the reporter, people left their homes and businesses to view the moose. Motorists parked their cars and joined the crowd to watch the wondrous creature grazing atop a grassy hill.

"The article spoke of the mystical quality of the moose and how there was a quiet and awe that had come over the spectators," Janice said. "Even the reporter said that she had felt 'other-worldly' inside. She went on to compare the experience to the appearance of religious apparitions, such as when people report sightings of Mother Mary or Moses. For those men and women who believe, the reporter affirmed, Mary can be seen and Moses was an actual flesh-and-blood prophet who carried God's laws in his hands. And a moose standing in a foggy field for an entire day can be seen as a visit once again from God."

When Janice read those words in the local newspaper, all her feelings regarding Matilda were confirmed.

"When I was with her," she recalled, "it was as if there was a suspension of time. There was nothing else that I should be doing. God wanted me there with her. He had sent her as a gift to me—a part of himself."

As Christmas drew nearer, Bob and Janice used one of the many pictures that she had taken of Matilda on their Christmas cards, accompanied by the first of the three poems that she had written in her honor.

"To know that Matilda was right outside our cottage on Christmas Eve and Christmas Day, roaming our property and woods, brought a peace beyond all understanding," Janice said. "She truly was of God—a holy visitation to Bob and me."

*B*rad Steiger remembers a Christmas story from his childhood that his parents told him about a man's rebirth of spirit during the holidays.

As his parents recalled the story, it took place in the early 1940s during a lovely, but very cold, white Christmas in Iowa. A thirteen-year-old farmboy we'll call Marlin Sheldahl was very excited to be playing one of the three wise men who would bring gifts to the Baby Jesus during the Sunday school Christmas pageant. Every Sunday afternoon since the week before Thanksgiving, Marlin and two of his classmates, Gary and Roger, had been practicing singing "We Three Kings of Orient Are" and walking solemnly before the crèche that sheltered Elaine, who was portraying Mary, and Lowell, enacting the role of Joseph. A rubber doll wrapped in "swaddling clothes" had the important, but mute, role of the Baby Jesus.

For several nights before the pageant, Marlin was barely able to sleep. He went over and over his solo part in his mind, visualizing just the way he would approach the manger and kneel with his gift before the Christ Child.

But on the evening of the big performance, disaster struck the Sheldahl home. Marlin's four-year-old brother, Jake, started running a high fever, so his mother said that she was terribly sorry, but she would not be able to attend the Christmas pageant. She would have to stay home and look after little Jake.

Although Marlin was disappointed that she would not be seated in one of the front pews appreciating every note of his solo—and telling him afterward how good he sounded—Dad would be there.

As Dad went out to warm up the car, Mom put the finishing touches on his costume. Days before she had dyed an old towel purple, and now she wrapped it skillfully around his head and pinned one of her rhinestone brooches in the middle of his turban. She festooned his robe with braided curtain strings and bright ribbons. Marlin was certain he looked like a genuine ancient Asian potentate. The other kings of the Orient would probably be jealous of the authenticity of his costume.

Then Dad came in, rubbing his hands to warm them, and Marlin could tell by the expression on his face that something was wrong. "Car won't start," he said, shrugging his shoulders and emitting a deep, defeated sigh. "Battery's dead. It's this darn cold. Must be ten degrees below zero out there. Car won't even turn over. Sorry, Marlin. We won't be able to go to the pageant."

"Sorry" was simply not acceptable. He was one of the three wise men for Pete's sake! He had been practicing the song with Gary and Roger and his solo part for weeks. This wasn't Broadway. There were no understudies waiting to go on if for any reason he didn't show up. He *had* to be there at the Sunday school Christmas pageant!

His dad tried to reason with Marlin. There was nothing to be done about it. They lived two miles out in the country. It was bitter and freezing outside. What was Marlin going to do? Walk?

"I've got no choice," Marlin said, fighting back the tears. "I can't let the Sunday school teachers down. I can't let the other kids down. I can't disappoint the audience. What would they think if there were only two wise men up there? I'll walk to church."

"Come on, Marlin," his father protested, "you'll freeze! Probably get pneumonia."

"I'll have two kids with high fevers to sit up all night with," his mother added.

Marlin started to reach for his heavy woolen coat, then hesitated. If he struggled into his winter coat, he would mash his marvelous costume. He would just walk as fast as he could the two miles to town and the church.

"Wait," Dad sighed. "You're as stubborn as your Uncle Charlie. I'll put the charger on the battery and we'll have the car started in maybe forty-five minutes or so."

Marlin shook his head. He was supposed to be at the church in thirty minutes. The pageant would begin in fifty minutes.

"So?" Dad asked. "We'll get there just in time."

Marlin argued that that would be cutting it too close. He had walked to town lots of times. He knew he could be there in thirty minutes.

"You've walked to town in the summer, spring, and fall," Mom said. "Not when it is below freezing."

Marlin could not be dissuaded. He would start out walking. If Dad got the car started in a few minutes, he could pick him up. If the car didn't start for an hour, he would see him at the church and ride home with him.

And with that, the king from the Orient went out into the night, following the Christmas star that would lead him to the Sunday school pageant.

Marlin had barely walked down their lane when he realized how foolish it had been to leave behind his heavy woolen coat.

The air was so cold that it burned his lungs and stung his nostrils. Although his royal robes had seemed warm enough in the kitchen of their farmhouse, it seemed now as though he was practically naked. And the pointed-toe slippers his mother had made him really looked like something out the *Arabian Nights,* but on the snow-covered gravel road they provided little protection and warmth.

And now the viewpoint of our story shifts to the perspective of Emil Gunderson, the older gentleman who had the farm next to the Sheldahls'. Gunderson, in his late sixties, had a reputation among the children of the rural community for being a grouch who seemed perpetually angry at life in general and kids in particular. He was known to have a vocabulary of cuss and curse words that topped anyone's in the entire county, and the only time that anyone could remember seeing him smile was when he threatened to take a switch to some boys who tried to steal some apples from his orchard.

Emil Gunderson was listening to news on the radio when he happened to glance out of his living room's south window and saw something on the road that caused him to set down his beer bottle and focus his complete attention on whatever was slowly moving into the circle of illumination cast by his yard light. It appeared to be someone dressed in clothing of biblical times, complete with flowing robes, turban, and those strange pointy-toed slippers.

Emil hadn't been to church in fifteen years. He hadn't set one foot inside its doors since the double funeral of his wife and daughter. He had once been considered a very religious man, but God had betrayed his years of faithful attendance in church and nightly prayers by snuffing out his loved ones in an automobile accident. And his attitude toward Christmas was far beyond a simple "bah, humbug!" On his desk were three Christmas cards from his two sisters and one brother in Washington State. Those were the only cards that he had received, except for the obligatory ones mailed out by the bank, Bill's service station, and the Farmer's Co-op Elevator. He hadn't sent any cards in fifteen years.

He couldn't take his eyes off the strange figure walking on the road past his farmhouse. And as much as he tried to fight off the peculiar sensations that were provoking long-dormant memories, the robed entity seemed to be triggering emotions that he had long considered decayed and forgotten.

And then the robed being was coming toward his house. Emil felt his heart quicken. When he was a boy, he had heard his grandmother speak of having seen a robed figure enter a neighbor's house the very night that the man died. She had always believed that she had witnessed the Angel of Death come to take the old man home to the other side.

When he heard the feeble knocking, Emil hesitated for a few moments before he answered the door. But he had never been afraid of man nor beast, so he wasn't about to start now.

He swung open the door and was astonished to recognize the older son of his neighbors.

"Mr. Gunderson, please," the boy was saying. "I'm freezing to death. May I please come in? Just for a little while?"

He stepped aside, asking the boy his name and wanting to know why he was dressed up like somebody from the Bible.

"I'm Marlin, Mr. Gunderson. And I'm one of the kings of the Orient, you know, one of the wise men who followed the star and brought gifts to the Baby Jesus in his manger," the boy exclaimed, all in a rush. "And I've got to get to the Sunday school pageant. Our car wouldn't start, so I have to walk. I'm going to be late."

Emil shook his head in silent appreciation of the kid's spunk and determination. "You're half frozen to death, boy."

Marlin nodded agreement. "Just please let me warm up for a minute, then I've got to be getting going. I'm going to be late."

"You're only halfway there, Marlin," Emil said. "You'll be a walking icicle if you try to walk there tonight in this below-zero cold. If it means that much to you, I'll take you there. Let me get the keys to my pickup."

At first the boy protested gamely, but he soon converted his objections to offering profuse thanks. Emil stopped by his bathroom to rinse with mouthwash to cover the beer breath.

Within a few minutes, he was dropping Marlin at the side door of the church where the young actors and singers of the evening's pageant were to enter.

"Won't you please come in and see our pageant, Mr. Gunderson?" the boy asked.

Emil grumbled something about having other plans, but almost as if another force was guiding him, he found himself parking in the church lot and finding a place in one of the back pews. He tried to ignore the heads that were turning to look at him, but when he glanced up from the program an usher had handed him, he saw that there were only warm smiles of welcome.

By the time that the Sunday school program had begun, several friends had stopped by his pew to wish him a Merry Christmas. And when Marlin and the two other boys stood up to sing "We Three Kings of Orient Are," it was as if he had been transported to another Christmas far back in time, when he was thirteen and he, Max Olson, and Dick Larson had impersonated the three wise men and had sung that very same song. In fact, he and Marlin had even had the same solo part and had probably even walked to the manger with the same old "incense burner" from the Sunday school prop department, the domed pot that symbolically held the frankincense brought by the travelers from afar.

With a soft chuckle prompted by his nostalgia, Emil recalled fondly how after each Sunday school pageant, the church deacons would hand out bags of hard candy and peanuts to each of the participants in the performance and to all the kids in the audience. How exciting it was to open those bags and look to see if yours contained a small toy, such as a tin whistle, a miniature Santa, or a decoration that you could put on your Christmas tree at home.

As he allowed the music and memories to carry him back to earlier, happier Christmas times, he saw himself no longer as a thirteen-year-old, but as a high school student, listening with open adoration as Rachel, the girl he would one day marry, sang a solo rendition of "Come, O Come Immanuel" for her part in the Sunday school pageant.

And then he moved ahead in time to another Christmas, when Rachel and he sat with pride as their daughter Connie stood before the altar with the other ten-year-olds and sang, "O Little Town of Bethlehem."

Soon tears were streaming down his cheeks, and since he hadn't brought a handkerchief, he had to get up and walk out of the church to get a tissue from the men's room in the basement. He had seen Marlin's father squeeze into a back pew just a few minutes before the three wise men sang, so he guessed he finally got the car started and Marlin would have a ride home.

Emil Gunderson sat in his pickup in the parking lot for several minutes before he turned the key, started the motor, and headed for home. He would call his sisters and his brothers in Washington state that next day and wish them a Merry Christmas. And he would discuss plans to visit them that spring before fieldwork started.

A thirteen-year-old boy in his Sunday school costume of kingly robes and turban, half-frozen in the December cold as he tried to walk to the church pageant, had rekindled the warm glow of Christmas in a heart that had forsaken the mystery of the season and exchanged it for the misery of a grief that had been nurtured for far too long. Just as the Christmas story tells of three wise men from afar who brought gifts to the newborn Prince of Peace, so did a little "wise man" prompt a gift of renewal to a reborn soul.

ᴇunice York from Tulsa, Oklahoma, remembered that on her husband Sam's last birthday before he passed away, he had received two elaborately decorated cakes—one from his family, the other from a fraternal organization in which the Yorks were active. Even at sixty-two, Sam had retained a childlike enthusiasm for birthdays and holidays—especially Christmas and Halloween—and he had been moved to receive two birthday cakes, both delivered on September 29 to their door.

Eunice's birthday fell on December 26, and because she had come from a large family that had never had any extra cash for the observation of two special days in a row, she had been accustomed since childhood to having her birthday passed over without notice. Maybe a birthday card. Perhaps a present of stockings or a handkerchief. But never a decorated cake with candles and a personalized greeting written on the frosting.

Of course, the situation had changed after her marriage to the gregarious and fun-loving Sam, but on his last birthday she teased him about his having received two extravagantly large birthday cakes when she had gone so many years without having been given any cakes at all.

"Well, then, by golly, Miss Eunice," Sam laughed. "This year I'll see to it that you receive two big special cakes on your birthday, too."

Eunice appreciated his good-natured thought, but she only shook her head and replied: "Your head will be so full of Christmas, like it is every year, that you will forget all about my receiving even one cake."

Sam placed one hand on his chest and raised the other as if he were in court, taking an oath. "Cross my heart," he said with great solemnity. "You shall have two birthdays this year or my name isn't Samuel B. York."

Eunice would be eternally grateful that Sam had not sealed his vow by saying, "Cross my heart and hope to die," because her beloved husband died of a sudden heart attack one week later.

"It would have been unbearable to consider for even one fleeting moment that such a wish, regardless of how silly its intent, may have had anything to do with Sam's sudden death," Eunice said.

Sam York's unplanned and rapid departure from his well-ordered life would seem to have freed him from all earthly promises and commitments. However, according to Eunice, this was not at all the case.

On her birthday, over two months later, Eunice York sat alone, feeling sad and depressed. Their only son had been killed in Vietnam. None of her family lived near, and the people they knew in Tulsa were mostly Sam's friends and acquaintances and none of them knew it was her birthday. Of course there were a few close lady friends with whom she occasionally went shopping or played cards, but since her birthday fell the day after Christmas, she had chosen not to bother any of them about an additional celebration—and expense—during the holidays.

With Sam in his grave for nearly three months, there seemed nothing for her to do other than spend a night in solitary misery.

But amazingly, on that cold and icy night, a friend, Lorna, traveled across the city by bus to deliver a cake and a carton of ice cream to Eunice so they might celebrate her birthday.

"How . . . how did you know?" Eunice asked, unable to take her eyes from the sumptuous cake with candles, a floral design, and a personal greeting spelled out in frosting on its sides.

"I don't know if you'll believe this or not," Lorna began, a nervous smile on her lips. "I had just gotten home from work when it seemed as though I could hear Sam talking to me as if he were standing right there in the room with me. He told me that it was your birthday and that I should hurry out and buy you a cake with all the trimmings!"

Eunice was stunned by her friend's straightforward explanation of her birthday treat, but she didn't feel like interrogating her any further. After all, it was Christmas, a time of miracles. And if anyone could come back from the other side to see that she received a cake on her birthday, it would be her beloved husband.

Eunice and Lorna had no sooner finished a good-sized portion of cake and ice cream when Anita, the young woman who had been boarding with Eunice since Sam's death, entered the front door and walked back to the kitchen carrying a box that contained a beautifully decorated birthday cake.

Eunice shook her head in astonishment. "Anita, how did you know it was my birthday?"

Anita smiled and shrugged her shoulders. "I was just walking by the bakery, and I saw this magnificent birthday cake in the window . . . and I just felt like buying it for you. I didn't even know it was your birthday. I guess . . . I just thought I should buy it for you."

Eunice was certain that she had not mentioned the fact that it was her birthday to Anita, and the young boarder had never known Sam. "My husband kept his promise," Eunice York said. "Somehow, through the miracle of Christmas, he saw to it that I received two special cakes for my birthday."

*D*uring every Christmas season since he was a young adult, Bob Shortz of Dallas, Pennsylvania, has volunteered to work in some aspect of human services to provide for the needy and the homeless. For Shortz, the true meaning and magic of the holiday began on Christmas Eve 1958, when he was eight years old.

"My twin brother, Ned, and I were in the living room with our father, who was relaxing in his favorite easy chair after setting up the Christmas tree," Bob said. "It was our family custom to decorate the tree on Christmas Eve, and my brother and I were in a hurry to get started—but Dad said he wanted a chance to sit down and rest a bit."

The twin boys could not imagine how anyone would want to sit down and relax on such an exciting night. Grown-ups were so unfathomable!

As the boys paced the room, waiting for their mother and older sister, Wendy, to join them, Bob remembered that he began to quiz his father regarding a very important matter about which he had been quite concerned but had been afraid to confront. "Daddy," he asked, "how can Santa come down the chimney? Wouldn't he just end up in the coal bin?"

Bob knew that the chimney was connected to the furnace, because one of his chores around the house was to keep the "worm," a metal corkscrewlike device, covered with lumps of coal so it could draw fresh coal from the bin into the furnace.

His father acknowledged that that could be a problem for an ordinary person, but Santa was magic.

"You mean, the furnace can't burn him?" Bob persisted. "How does he get back out of the chimney?"

His father's voice rose just a bit impatiently. "I told you, Bob. Santa is magic. He can come down in the chimney just as far as he wants and then come out. Because of his magic powers, the chimney becomes an elevator. He can get out in the kitchen and eat the snack we'll leave for him. He can stop out in Wendy's room—or wherever he wants."

Bob seemed pleased that there was an explanation for what had seemed to him to be a troublesome aspect of the whole Santa-Claus-down-the-chimney scenario.

"By the way," his father said, "how about you two going up to Wendy's room to see if she needs any help wrapping presents. Your mother and I will call you when it's time to decorate the tree."

Bob recalled how he and Ned had raced upstairs to his sister's room. "Wendy had been wrapping presents from our parents to our aunt and uncle," he said. "She had already finished when we burst into her room to offer our services, so we sat on her bed and talked about what we hoped we would be getting for Christmas."

Wendy was a year older than the twins, so Bob knew that she was keener in the ways of grown-ups. He told her about their father saying that Santa Claus had magical powers that could transform the chimney into a kind of elevator—and he asked her if such a thing could be true.

"Hmmm," Wendy said, thoughtfully. "I've never seen Santa do it, but that must be how it works. Since he's magic, he can do anything, really."

Once again, Bob recalled, he felt reassured.

"We sat on the bed, looking out the window at the Christmas lights strung across the avenue," he said. "Suddenly Wendy said, 'Look! Look up at the moon!' "

There, in front of the moon, was a strangely formed cloud that projected a silhouette of Santa's sled so perfect and so clear that Wendy didn't have to explain.

"There it was," Bob said. "You could see the runners and the curvature of the front of the sleigh—and on the back was Santa's bag full of toys!"

Bob remembered how the three of them stared at the silhouette in thrilled astonishment. "You couldn't see the reindeer pulling the sleigh, but there was no mistake *who* it was that we were seeing!"

After the initial shock, the three of them raced down the stairs to tell their parents that they had seen Santa Claus's sleigh silhouetted against the moon, and they begged them to go to the windows to look up at the amazing sight.

"Mother hurriedly ran to a window to have a look, and Dad eventually left his chair to check out the hubbub," Bob said. "But you know how it is. By the time the grown-ups had arrived at a window, well, you know."

Their mother offered a sympathetic, "I think I see it."

"My, my," said Dad.

"It didn't matter," Bob Shortz said. "I knew what we had seen—and nothing could change the magic of Christmas and Santa Claus for me that year or ever since."

*F*ive months after the start of World War I, just after midnight on Christmas morning, the vast majority of German soldiers declared a Christmas truce in the hostilities between themselves and those of the Allied troops—the Russian, French, and British. Regimental bands began to play Christmas carols and the men raised their voices in joyous celebration of the Holy Night when the Prince of Peace was born.

The Allied soldiers were understandably suspicious about the shouts of "Merry Christmas" that they heard directed at them from the German trenches. Perhaps they had snipers lined up just waiting for a curious Tommy, Ivan, or Frenchy to peek his head above the trenches.

But at the end of each hymn or cheerful carol they heard the German boys from Kaiser Bill's army calling out something about a Christmas truce. The men in the Allied trenches checked with their officers, but none of them knew anything about a truce having been declared for the holidays.

At dawn's first light on Christmas morning, the German troops rose up out of their trenches, set down their weapons, and began to walk across "no-man's land," singing carols and shouting out, "Merry Christmas," in French, Russian, and English, as well as their native German. From all appearances, from everything the Allied officers could see through their field glasses and from what the soldiers were able to witness from their frontline observation posts, all the Germans appeared to be without rifles or any kind of weaponry whatsoever.

Soon the Allied soldiers crawled up out of their trenches and walked toward the Germans who were so openly and trustfully celebrating Christmas. The men shook hands, wished each other a blessed Christmas, and exchanged gifts of cigarettes and food. Later, they sang hymns and carols, and those of the same faith worshipped together. Some accounts of the Christmas truce even state that opposing sides played a good-natured, but rousing, game of soccer. The remarkable unofficial "time-out" that was declared by the combat soldiers without any thought of obtaining permission from their superiors lasted for two or three days.

Sadly, the Christmas truce of 1914 was probably one of the very last examples of old-fashioned chivalry in modern warfare. Within another few weeks, the first great technological war would begin slaughtering human beings on a scale previously undreamt of in any military officer's most fevered nightmare of destruction. The employment of poison gas against the men in the trenches, the aerial bombing of cities and civilians beyond the frontlines, the onslaught of armored tanks crushing men and smashing walls, machine guns mowing down ranks of soldiers, aircraft swooping down from the skies and strafing troops on the ground—all of these horrors and more would make the notion of another Christmas truce during the war an impossible dream. But the 1914 Christmas miracle created by the common foot soldiers' declaration of peace and goodwill toward their fellow comrades-in-arms will live forever in memory as a triumph of the indomitable human spirit over the fatal disease of war.

$\mathcal{D}$uring the push to Berlin during the latter stages of World War II, Bryan Potter and a group of other bone-weary GIs were quartered in a brick farmhouse and told to get a good night's rest. The order was as unnecessary as telling a starving man to eat everything on his plate. The men were cold and exhausted in the bleak December of 1944, and although there was little to burn in the fireplace and the antiquated kitchen stove, any warmth at all was greatly appreciated.

They had just finished a sparse, but somehow comforting and filling meal, when one of the men started tapping his fork on his metal mess kit.

"Fellas," he said, when he had everyone's attention. "Do you know what today is?"

"Don't tell us it's your birthday, Skeeter," Potter said with a sigh of mock disappointment. "I am so sorry, I wasn't able to go shopping for a present. Every time I did try to go into town to buy something, those nasty Nazis started shooting at me."

"Can it, Potter," his buddy replied. "It's the eve of the birthday of someone a whole lot more important than this dogface GI."

And then the realization seemed to strike everyone in the crowded kitchen at the same time. It was Christmas Eve.

"For several moments, the room was silenced as we all became lost in our own thoughts of Christmas back home," Potter said.

"We were all somewhere else in time and space. Some of us were probably remembering a special Christmas Eve at home with Mom and Dad, sitting around the dining room table after a big meal, listening to Bing Crosby sing 'White Christmas' on the radio, all of the kids just waiting to tear into the presents under the tree. Or the last Christmas that we held our wives or sweethearts in our arms before we enlisted. We all wanted to be back home with our loved ones, not crowded into some German farmer's deserted home with the enemy all around us."

One of the men shifted uncomfortably on the hard wooden bench, then spoke up before he lost his nerve. "I think we should do something to observe Christmas Eve—you know, like singing a Christmas hymn.

Something like 'Silent Night' or 'Little Town of Bethlehem.' "

"If he had been expecting ridicule from the hardened, tough men around him, he received none that cold and lonely Christmas Eve far away from our homes," Potter recalled. "Softly at first, as some of us struggled to remember the words, we began singing 'Silent Night.' Then as we got more into the spirit of the hymn, our voices became stronger and stronger until the rafters of that old farmhouse were reverberating. By the time we got to the third verse, most of us were just humming along, but even that had a good Christmas sound to it."

Then, suddenly, someone carrying a bright light slammed open the kitchen door and shouted: "Everyone out! A mortar shell is about to hit!"

Potter and his buddies scrambled for the door, ran several yards, then threw themselves headlong on the frozen, snow-packed German terrain.

Seconds later, the demolished farmhouse erupted in a fiery explosion and began to rain pieces of brick down on them. Nazi mortar fire had scored a direct hit on their temporary sanctuary.

"It was a good thing for us that even though we were bone-tired, we simply reacted on our training and our war-honed instincts," Potter said. "None of us thought to stop to ask the stranger with the bright light just how he knew that a mortar shell was about to hit the specific target of our particular farmhouse.

"Whoever the guy was, he didn't burst in among us and shout, 'Heads up! The Jerries are going to start shelling!' He told us to get out because a round was about to hit us. That statement required special and specific knowledge, and if any of us had stopped to interrogate the fellow concerning the source of such intelligence, none of us would have survived the direct hit."

Potter and his buddies spent the rest of the night in the ruins of a barn, huddled around a sheltered fire. One of the men commented that Christmas Eve was the perfect night to sleep on a pile of straw near mangers and cattle pens.

"Later, when some of us had a chance to talk about the incident, a couple of the guys were already calling it a miracle," Potter said. "After discussing it at great length, we all agreed that the man who burst into the farmhouse was not carrying a bright light, he was the light.

"When we compared our collective memories, we concluded that the stranger was surrounded by a brilliant kind of illumination. We were convinced that an angel saved our lives on Christmas Eve in 1944 by warning us to get out of the farmhouse immediately before the mortar shell hit us."

When Don Checketts was a nineteen-year-old Marine stationed at Campo de Marte in Managua, Nicaragua, he became so homesick at Christmas for his family back in Ogden, Utah, that his wish to be able to be two places at once came true. A Christmas miracle enabled Checketts to visit his family in Utah and remain physically on duty at the Marine base at the same time.

According to Don H. Checketts's story in the May 1968 issue of *Fate* magazine, mail call on December 2, 1929, brought him a long, anguished letter from his mother that described in detail her great heartache at their being separated by so many miles during the Christmas season. She wrote that she would do anything if she might see him, if only for a few moments.

Checketts became very depressed by the sorrowful tone of his mother's letter, and he went to his bunk that night wishing that there existed some means by which he might establish instant communication with his mother and somehow relieve at least a portion of her grief.

At last he fell asleep. Then, after only a few minutes of deep slumber, he came wide awake with the driving compulsion that he had to go somewhere in a hurry.

Checketts got out of his cot, looked over at his buddy in the next bunk, then was startled to see his own physical body still lying on the cot beneath the draped mosquito netting.

Only momentarily shocked by the sight of his physical self lying asleep on his bunk, Checketts was more impressed by the deep awareness that he had to get moving, that he had somewhere important to go. As if he were receiving instructions from some invisible higher intelligence, he stepped outside the tent, raised his arms above his head, and looked up at the moon.

What occurred next, Checketts claimed, was breathtaking.

First, he said, he had a sensation of tremendous speed, as if he were toppling end over end in midair. Kaleidoscopic scenes of snow-covered mountaintops, river valleys, lakes, and vast areas of emptiness passed by so fast that they became blurred by the high speed at which his consciousness was moving.

When everything came to a stop, Checketts was still stretching his arms toward the moon, but now the moon shone over towering cliffs and snow-covered hills instead of tropical jungle.

Although he had never seen his parents' new home in Ogden, he somehow knew that the white house at the top of the hill before him was that very domicile.

He made his way through undisturbed snow to the porch of the house. His knock at the door produced sounds of movement within. When the door opened, his mother stood before him in her nightclothes.

Mother and son were overcome by the unexpected reunion, and tears flowed unchecked. She expressed concern that he was standing outside in the cold in his short-sleeved uniform, but Checketts told her he would be able to stay for only a few minutes, just long enough to let her know that he was all right.

With a farewell hug and kiss, he turned away from his mother, left the porch, and walked back down the hill. He looked back only once and saw his mother still standing in the open doorway, waving at him.

Soon the strange sensation of incredible speed once again captured him, and when Checketts was again aware of his surroundings, he was standing in front of his tent at the Marine base in Nicaragua. He went inside, got back into his bed, and awoke the next morning to find his pillow wet from tears.

More than ever, he was convinced that the remarkable journey to his mother's arms in Ogden, Utah, had been a real experience. Every detail was clearly defined in his mind, and he had been left with an exhilarating sense of personal freedom.

On December 28, mail call brought Checketts a letter from his mother that was dated December 3, the morning after the extraordinary adventure in his spiritual body. Both Checketts and his tentmate, to whom he had confided the experience, were able to read that his mother had confirmed the Christmas miracle in every detail.

In the early 1970s, Clarisa Bernhardt accompanied her late husband, Russ, to Los Gatos, California, where he was performing his popular one-man show, Scrooge, In Person, as part of the gala Christmas season at the Olde Towne Theatre and Shopping Center. Clarisa, who lives today in Winnipeg, Manitoba, and is currently regarded as one of North America's best-known psychic-sensitives, remembers Los Gatos as appearing like a giant Christmas card of holiday decorations and good cheer, the very picture of holiday merriment.

One morning, she dropped by the theater where Russ was rehearsing to let him know that she would be doing a special taped interview for her radio show that day, so she might be a bit later than usual. She recalls that it was fairly early, around 8:30 A.M., and a gentle, brief morning rain shower had freshened the pines with a wonderful "Christmas" fragrance.

Puzzled to discover the front door to the theater locked, Clarisa remembered a stairway that would take her to the bell tower, where she could crawl through a window and enter the theater.

"When I reached the bell tower, I paused for a moment to enjoy the gorgeous rainbow that arched over the mountains," Clarisa said, "then I found my way in. I went through the balcony and down the stairs to the main theater area."

As she entered on the right side and crossed behind the last row of seats, she was aware that she was alone in the theater. It was quite obvious that Russ was not rehearsing at this time.

As she reached the aisle on the left, she started down toward the stage—and then she stopped, as if frozen.

"There, standing in the area just below the stage, was a beautiful lady in an off-white, eggshell-colored robe with a cowl that covered her hair and accented her lovely face," Clarisa said. "She was looking directly at me. I could see a beautiful and brilliant light around her. Her countenance was glowing, yet it did not diminish my ability to see her."

Clarisa closed her eyes, quickly blinking them, then opened them again, as if to clear her vision.

"But she was still there," she said, "still looking directly at me—but now she was also smiling at me."

Clarisa could feel the power from her eyes as she looked at her. "I knew exactly who she was," she said, "and I looked at her intently, trying calmly to observe as many details as possible. I wanted to etch her image in my memory. I was in the presence of the Holy Mother!"

And then she was gone. Clarisa estimated that the experience had occurred within one minute, though she felt suspended in time.

"To this day," she said, "I can close my eyes and instantly recall that magnificent experience and see her as if it's happening all over again."

Understandably, Clarisa said that she wishes she could have asked Mother Mary many things. "But I had not attempted to speak. I was completely overwhelmed. I had just seen Mary and been in the presence of the Holy Mother."

She also knew that the visitation was something important and significant in her life. In the weeks that followed before Christmas, Clarisa recalled that she was privileged to receive numerous mystical experiences and visions.

"One very special blessing manifested to heal a terrible ache in my heart," Clarisa said. "I was reunited with my dear son, who had been separated from me following tumultuous family events some years before. No matter how desperately I had worked to mend the situation, nothing had worked. The family rift keeping us apart had seemed impossible to change—and then almost instantly and miraculously, we were together again. It was truly a Christmas miracle. I will forever be thankful to Mother Mary for accomplishing such an 'impossible' task."

*T*ammie Bissonnette knew that she would have a difficult delivery because the child was breeched within her womb. But she felt that the fact that her daughter would be a Christmas baby would be ample compensation for her discomfort.

"That was before the contractions began," she recalled. "Halfway through the delivery, I would have been happy to have settled for a Valentine's Day child." Putting the birth off until February seemed, in the moment, like a good idea.

Her family doctor, Dr. Rubenstein, had debated whether or not they should take the baby through cesarean section, but after discussing the dilemma with some of his colleagues, he decided that it would be better to wrestle with the breech problem in the delivery room. Tammie would not be anesthetized, because she, the mother, would have to help. She would be given only a mild painkiller.

"I knew all these things, and I believed that I was prepared mentally and physically for the ordeal," Tammie said. "According to my calculations, my daughter, Liza, was due around the twentieth to the twenty-fifth—but then the worst happened. My water broke on the fifteenth. My husband, Phil, was out of town on business until the seventeenth, and Dr. Rubenstein had taken an early holiday and wouldn't be back until the nineteenth."

As her mother, Carla Ackerson, drove her to the hospital, Tammie kept hearing Dr. Rubenstein's caveat: "Little Liza is due to enter the world right around Christmas Eve, just when you were praying for her arrival. Of course, only Liza knows for certain when she will arrive. Doctors can only guess."

She knew that Dr. Rubenstein had intended to be back in time for the delivery, but as he had reflected, only the baby knew for certain when her birthday would be. And, of course, Phil would be crazy with worry that he wasn't there, Liza being their first child and all.

Dr. Marisse Walker, the pediatrician with whom Dr. Rubenstein had discussed the complications of the delivery in the event that something should prevent his being there, was in the midst of a difficult surgery when they arrived. Mrs. Ackerson and Tammie were informed that she absolutely could not be disturbed.

"I am afraid that the doctor summoned to pinch-hit was not the best example of the devoted practitioner," Tammie recalled. "He seemed hardly interested in hearing the nurse's summary of the difficulty of the delivery, and he was certainly indifferent toward alleviating any of my pain."

As the dilation was nearing completion, the agony was nearly driving Tammie out of her mind, and she squeezed her mother's hand so hard she feared she would snap a couple of finger joints.

"Maybe it was the terrible pain," Tammie said. "Maybe that was what made me feel like I was whirling around the room like a propeller on an airplane. I seemed to go faster and faster . . . and then—pop! I, that is, the real me, was suddenly floating above the bed in the labor room looking down on my body, my mother, and the nurse who was trying to ease my pain."

Tammie was shocked to see how contorted her facial features were. "I thought I must have died, but then my body on the bed below threshed wildly and let out an awful cry of pain," she said. "I was baffled. That was me, Tammie Bissonnette, down on the bed, but it was also me—or some aware aspect of myself—up near the ceiling watching the scene below and feeling absolutely no pain at all."

That was when she became aware that lovely Christmas music was swirling all around her.

"I heard what I thought at first was an orchestra playing 'Hark the Herald, Angels Sing,' but then I realized it was a melody only similar to that old hymn. When I heard a magnificent choir singing words of praise to God, I thought for certain that this time I really had died and gone to Heaven."

Then Tammie's attention was focused once again on her body below on the bed.

"I saw the nurse measure my dilation, and she said. 'You're ready, honey! Now where is that idiot doctor?' "

The nurse left the room, and Tammie's out-of-body consciousness followed her as she walked down the hall and located the doctor. "I saw him scowl at the interruption, for he was talking with an attractive nurse and I could see that he hated to be bothered to deliver my baby."

Almost at once after viewing the doctor's distasteful scowl, Tammie was back in the bed in the labor room, moaning again with terrible pain. She wished that she could leave her body again and go back up near the ceiling where there was no hurt.

"I did flip out of my body again during the delivery," she said. "I saw my face pale and glistening with sweat . . . and then the most extraordinary thing occurred. I saw this beautiful angel approaching me, and she was leading this lovely young woman by the hand. Before my spiritual eyes, I saw that vivacious young woman appear to be transformed—to shrink, if you will—to the size of an infant. I remember that I took the baby from the angel's arms, and then I was conscious of the two of us being dragged into some kind of tunnel with a light at the end. And the next thing I knew, I was back in my body, lying back on the hospital bed, holding my baby, Liza, and everything was all right."

Tammie's mother, Mrs. Ackerson, bent over the bed and kissed the cheeks of her daughter and her new granddaughter. "Mom said that she had managed to get a hold of Phil in his hotel room, and he was wild with happiness. He would be home sometime the next afternoon."

Tammie told her mother that she had hoped that the baby would be born closer to Christmas Eve or on Christmas Day. "But I had a vision or dream or something, Mom, and I saw a beautiful angel hand over the care and nurturing of this lovely young woman to me," Tammie said. "That young woman became baby Liza. So just as we should keep the spirit of Christmas each day in our hearts, I will surely love this little Christmas season miracle of mine every day of my life."

On Christmas Day 1989, Melissa Bauer's father asked her if she wanted to go along with him when he took Grandmother Bauer home after her holiday visit with the family.

"I was thirteen that Christmas," Melissa said, "and I felt so special that Dad had asked me to ride with them and keep him company on the drive back. In years past, he would have asked my older sister Marilyn, who was home from college for the holidays. I was really surprised that he asked me, because I expected him to say that the drive back would give him a chance to catch up with Marilyn since she had been away for three months. After all, I had been around and underfoot during that period of time. But then, Dad and I hadn't communicated much either, because he was always so busy."

Melissa also looked forward to talking with Grandmother Bauer during the trip to her house.

"Grandma was a hoot, always laughing and telling jokes about what she did when she was a teenager back in the Roaring Twenties," Melissa said. "I think she kind of embarrassed Dad sometimes when she told anyone who would listen to her stories she had been a flapper who had frequented speakeasy hideaways. I swore that I would never tell anyone the family secrets—which was a fib, because those stories were too good to keep out of the widest possible circulation."

Grandmother Bauer lived in a nearby village in New Hampshire, and it took about twenty minutes to drive between the two homes.

"After we saw Grandma safely to her door and inside to her favorite chair in her living room, Dad and I headed back home—in a sudden sleet storm," Melissa recalled. "Grandma said that we should stay until the sleet let up, but Dad said that it could last all night and only get progressively worse. It was his responsibility to open up the supermarket the next morning, so he had to get home that night."

As the storm worsened and the roads became slick and treacherous, Melissa's father took his right hand very briefly off the steering wheel to pat her on the shoulder.

"I'm glad you're with me tonight," he said. "I wouldn't like to be alone in this mess."

Melissa remembered that the loving gesture from her father made her feel wonderful and wanted.

"I just felt all warm and fuzzy inside," she said. "I wanted so much to have Dad's approval and to know that I was as special to him as Marilyn had always seemed to have been. I guess it is only natural that the older child gets a bit more attention just because she arrived first on the planet, but I do admit to having had a little sliver of sibling rivalry stuck in my psyche."

And then it became obvious to her that her father was having difficulty negotiating the familiar New Hampshire hills and curves with their new coating of freezing sleet.

But these roads weren't familiar. Melissa and her father were somewhere on a very dark and winding road and sliding backward.

"Where are we, Dad?" Melissa asked, not recognizing the area.

"I . . . I took a shortcut," he explained. "Thought it would be safer on this old road. No one travels it much any more."

Melissa remembered how she began thinking that they could slide into the ditch and not be found on the lonely stretch of road for days.

Her father was attempting to appear very calm and confident, but she knew his mannerisms too well not to recognize that he was extremely nervous and uncertain.

"Melissa, please, roll down your window and watch very carefully that I don't get too close to the edge," he asked. "I . . . think it could be quite a drop-off around here. Can't tell in the dark, of course. But I have driven this old road in daylight; I think I remember some pretty good drop-offs along this stretch. Just keep a really sharp eye."

Melissa rolled down the window and saw by the illumination from the car's back-up lights that their rear wheels appeared to be on the very edge of the gravel. She had no idea how much control her father had on the slick road, but he appeared to have managed to stop the car from sliding.

"Don't back up another inch, Dad," she shouted. Her face was stinging from the sleet and the cold, but she felt strangely exhilarated by the precarious situation.

"I was needed," she said. "Dad and Mom had always taken such good care of me, but that night, Dad really needed my help. He couldn't see clearly out the rear window that was coated with freezing sleet. And he wouldn't dare get out of the car to check for fear it would slide away from him. He really needed me to watch for the edge of the road."

In the dim light from the dashboard, Melissa could see that her father was sweating heavily, even with the open window letting in the cold.

"I'm going to release the brake and carefully accelerate," he said, explaining his plan of action. "I hope we're on a patch of gravel where we can find enough traction to allow me to stop sliding backward and to move forward up this hill. If I can do that, we will be home free—I know it! There's an old covered bridge just over the top and then it's downhill all the way."

Melissa offered her encouragement. "Go for it, Dad."

"Easy now," he said, "I'm going very easy. Keep watching the edge, honey."

Melissa's face was numb from the cold and the sleet, but she kept looking out the window.

"That's when I saw directly behind us and just above us a brilliant white light with a bluish center," she recalled. "I don't know where it had come from. It hadn't been there moments before—and then there it was. It was strangely beautiful, and it appeared to move higher, then lower, as if it were somehow intelligently surveying our dilemma.

"I didn't hear a voice," Melissa said, "but I knew that I was receiving a message from the light that told me not to worry, that Dad and I would be all right. Somehow that light and I were connected in some mysterious and glorious way."

Melissa's father released the brake and gently pressed on the accelerator—but to his alarm, the car began sliding backward.

"Melissa, I can't control the car," he said, unable to keep the panic from his voice. "I'm sorry. We're sliding backward. Hold on, honey, we could go in the ditch and tip over. Be sure your seatbelt is buckled!"

She tried to calm her father, to tell him not to be frightened. She knew that somehow the mysterious light was in control and that they would not be harmed.

The car went backward all the way to the base of the hill, and Melissa saw the light spin off into a clump of trees, then either disappear or blink out in the darkness.

"We hadn't sat there very long when a highway patrol car pulled alongside of us," Melissa said. "The officers told us that we shouldn't try to travel up the hill. The old covered bridge had collapsed and passage would be impossible. There was nothing left up there but some broken and rotted planks and a long drop into the river. Up ahead, though, they said, was a road that would lead us back to the main highway where crews had already applied salt and sand to the slickest places."

The remainder of the drive back home was uneventful. Melissa's father praised her for being so helpful, for keeping an eye on the edge of the road, and for paying no mind to the cold and sleet that he knew had to be stinging her face.

"I had truly bonded with my father that Christmas Day," Melissa said, "but I had also bonded with something incredibly mysterious that represented a source of strength outside of myself that has returned time and again in my memory to give me courage during some very dark moments.

"I don't know if that light was an angel or an unknown intelligence of some kind. And I don't know why I felt so much a part of it. All I know for certain is that whatever it was, it became the Christmas miracle that probably saved my dad and me from injury or worse during that sleet storm."

*D*ave Bennett was recently diagnosed with Stage 4 lung and bone cancer. The cancer in his spinal column has already gnawed away at the top three discs. This kind of deterioration causes excruciating pain—add to that difficulty breathing, nausea, weakness, and debilitating tiredness from intensive chemotherapy treatments and radiation, and it becomes difficult to feel much other than agony and despair. The doctors are unable to tell Dave just how long he might expect to live. He and his wife, Cindy, are looking at an optimistic ten-year plan, yet are getting his affairs in order. That tells you something about them.

Cindy said they have had a deluge of well-meaning people offering suggestions for various techniques to try to recover. "Suggestions range from jumping up and down on a trampoline to drinking a healing Essiac Tea and all kinds of things in between," she shared. Confirming Dave would definitely not be trying the trampoline cure, she added that he does have a strong personal connection with Spirit and is able to sift through suggested cures and take what works best for him.

Dave is not afraid to die. He has done that already. In fact his near-death experience completely transformed and redirected his life many years before. While out at sea, working on a research vessel, Dave suffered an agonizing death of slowly drowning after being tossed about like a rag doll in a raging storm. He described the pain of being submersed and tossed about in dark, murky salt water with lungs near bursting and burning in need of a crucial breath of air. Just as the pain intensified to an overwhelming degree, it suddenly reverted and began to fade a little at a time until it was completely gone. Then everything went cold and dark—a cold darkness. That was how Dave described the event.

The rest of the experience is nearly the classic near-death account—of a gradual light becoming so bright and warm and full of love that one has no desire to ever leave it. Being one with the light and its love, without a physical body and no pain, suddenly other "light beings" came toward him. Dave felt he knew them and they knew him as they were supporting and helping him to adjust.

Then, before he was able to communicate with any of them, he experienced a "life review" where every minor and major thing he had said, done, and thought, and how it had affected the lives of those around him when he was alive, flashed before him. Supernaturally, he was able to review the feelings of others as the result of his actions—all the joy, happiness, heartache, disappointment, love, hurt, sorrow, grief —but all without the accompanying guilt or judgment. All the subtle interactions of his entire life were ineffably experienced. He knew the review was shown him not to be judged, but to learn and grow from.

"It felt like coming home," Dave said. "I experienced a love and acceptance like I had never felt before." Then others seemed to join the first group that had surrounded him, and Dave began to see things that were not familiar to him at all. The "others" remained supportive, but Dave felt disoriented. He thought he was looking into his future!

The clearly audible words, "This is not your time, you must return," interrupted with a bang. Like a cannon, shooting him back to his earthly body, then again, "This is not your time, you have a purpose!" Dave described the fact of "having to return" as a more painful contrast to the love and peace than the actual pain of drowning. All of this seemed to be a prelude to a miracle that was to occur on Christmas 2000.

This would be the first Christmas that Cindy would not be with the rest of her family in thirty-nine years, and she was feeling the pangs of self-inflicted guilt for not making a six-hour drive to spend even a few hours with them. Exposing Dave to any cold or flu germs could be fatal, as both radiation and chemotherapy deplete the white blood cells, thereby severely compromising the immune system of the patient.

Although she probably could have made the drive by herself, it didn't feel right leaving Dave home alone on Christmas. Even though many of the out-of-town family would have already left, Cindy planned to make the drive alone, the day after Christmas, depending on how Dave felt. She did not yet know there was likely a "higher power" at work in the decision to stay home.

Around 5 P.M. the phone rang. On days she wasn't working, Cindy says she screens calls, as they would normally be clients calling to schedule appointments, but this time she picked up the phone right away. "Hi Cindy" said the unidentified voice. It took a few seconds before Cindy recognized the voice as that of a sweet massage therapist she knew that specialized in Tai massage. "Have you ever heard of Padre Pio?" she asked. Cindy acknowledged that she had visited Padre Pio's church when she was traveling in Italy.

Padre Pio, born into a hard-working farming family in southern Italy in 1887, entered the novitiate of the

Capuchin Friars at the age of fifteen and was ordained a priest in 1910. In 1918, the five wounds of Christ's crucifixion appeared on his body, and continued to do so until his death in 1968, making him the first stigmatized priest in the history of the Church. His entire life was marked by long, arduous prayer, continual austerity, and ineffable suffering, both physical and mental as observed by those who knew him. Hundreds of thousands of devotees flock to his place of entombment in the crypt of Our Lady of Grace Church and claim spiritual and physical healings by the grace of his saintly suffering. Last year the claim of 7 million pilgrims visiting Padre Pio's mountaintop sanctuary was second only to the number of visitors to the Marian sanctuary of Lourdes, France. Padre Pio was only recently beatified as a saint by Pope John Paul II.

Even though Cindy had visited the holy site it was interesting to hear of the other woman's experience. The therapist, whose name was Nancy, continued to talk about Padre Pio. Known for his compassion and healing, it was also reported that he bilocated or was in two places at one time, the woman said. It is documented that during the Second World War, the U.S. Army air force was going to accidentally bomb an area that was occupied by allies, unbeknown to them. The fighter pilots reported seeing a monk appearing in midair, right in front of their plane, motioning for them to turn back. The fighter pilots were so frightened by the sight that they did turn back, and the impending bombing massacre was averted!

Cindy said, "She then asked me if I had heard about the healing miracles that happened around a glove that had belonged to Padre Pio."

Cindy had not, so the woman on the phone offered to put another woman who was there with her on the phone to explain. "The woman had a very sweet and calming voice and turned out to be a local television personality, but wishes to remain anonymous, so we refer to her as our 'Christmas angel,' " Cindy continued.

She told of a priest who used to be a custodian of Padre Pio's in Italy, but returned to his former parish in Brooklyn, New York, following Padre Pio's death. The priest had been given two of the gloves that Padre Pio wore on his hands to keep the blood from the Stigmata wounds from dripping on the floor. The gloves are considered sacred objects and are known for their healing properties. There were many stories of how parishioners of this Brooklyn church had miraculous healings by the gloves, which are said to give off an uncannily beautiful rose scent. The scent is always present, although emanating stronger at times, and weaker at others.

The priest kept one glove for himself and gave the other one to his sister, who felt it should be made available to all to benefit from. His sister felt that the parking-lot attendant of the church, who knew every-one in the parish, would be the best guardian for dis-seminating the healing power of the glove. The glove is kept in a box with a piece of a sheet that came from Padre Pio's bed, a book in which people write to Padre Pio, and one of those double-image pictures of Padre Pio that changes as you tilt it from side to side. Con-tinuing, she interrupted herself with a little laugh and an aside, saying the parking-lot booth used to be a shrine to Frank Sinatra, until Padre Pio's box arrived. Now it is shared—Frank Sinatra and Padre Pio!

Telling of a long waiting list for the glove, the woman on the other end of the phone said that her name came up for Christmas Eve, so she felt there was no better way she could spend her own Christmas other than to share it with whoever was in need. She had the glove for two entire days, so it was still in her possession and the English massage therapist friend had mentioned Dave's cancer, wondering if he might want to touch the glove.

Dave was not feeling up to making the trip to Brooklyn, so this wonderful woman offered to come to see them.

"Now to tell you where we live, it is known as Windy Hill," Cindy said. "Our place used to be a cross country ski resort on top of a high hill that is often buffeted with lake-effect snow, and we were having a very bad blizzard that day. Since it was Christmas Day, the landlord was out of town, so the driveway had not been plowed. We were literally snowed in, yet she offered to come to us!"

At the woman's insistence, Cindy gave her directions and over an hour and a half later, via cell phone guidance, she arrived covered with snow and bearing a canvas tote.

"We sat in our living room and she pulled out a wooden box with a little picture of Padre Pio on the top," Cindy said. "She gently opened it and took out the picture that was in the box, then a little book, then very gently brought out the glove. At first I was surprised. It was a little tiny brown glove with no fingers in it. It looked like a glove you would see on a homeless person. The funny thing to me was that it was so simple. You would think it would be ornate or at least a little bigger! Padre Pio was a large man. I remembered seeing his slippers when I saw his monk cell in Italy. They were so big!"

The little brown glove had a simple metal cross gently sown onto the top side. Later, when Cindy turned it over, she saw that someone had sown a tiny piece of cloth with a little x in the place that must have been where the hand wound from the stigmata was.

"The amazing thing to us was the aroma that came from it. Anyone who smelled this rose scent could tell you that it is like no other rose smell you had ever smelled," Cindy continued. "You couldn't create it even with the best of oils or perfume!"

Dave and Cindy described the sheet from Padre Pio's bed as having the same scent, as well. It was kept in a little plastic bag, but the glove itself was not in any container, other than the box. Dave put the glove in his hand and Cindy said you could actually see the calm come over him.

Dave explained what he felt as he held the glove in his hand: "At first, I just sensed a type of love similar to what I feel when I touch my near-death experience. When I touched the glove I was feeling with my heart and not my mind. I could feel my heart opening up and feeling that light and love. I could feel both Spirit and human emotion because it was a vast amount of unconditional love. It was like going back into the light a little bit, not all the way. In order to come back from a near death you have to accept that light back. And I have been having trouble keeping my heart open and working with my light and love because of the physical fatigue and drug induced emotions. But as I stroked the glove it felt like some of the barriers were just melting away and the light in my heart was just able to open and shine as bright as ever. Well, I could just say that my spirit was singing. Spirit gets in this joyous frame of not mind—but Spirit. When

Spirit is joyous, it feels like a song in your heart and it interacts with your human emotions. It just brings tears to my eyes. It gets you a little choked up. You can feel it emanate throughout your entire body. It isn't just your heart that expands, it expands through the entire body—physically, I could feel it!"

The fact that Dave could "feel" the glove was the first hint of the miracle. Dave sat there stroking the glove as their new friend and Christmas angel told the story of the glove in more detail and described how she happened to end up with it. Dave had permanent nerve damage in the hand that could now "feel" the glove. He had not had any sensation in it for over six months!

The woman described how Padre Pio was said to bring so much compassion and insight into his parish confessional that it seemed to aid people in knowing just exactly what it was they needed to confess and release.

"The funny thing was, that it felt to me, like a little confession of my own—as I held the glove," Dave said. He found himself talking about his near-death experience, the cancer, and what it was like having it.

"As she was telling about Padre Pio's confessionals from the heart, I felt compelled to confess feelings that had welled up within me, but that I hadn't realized were there," Dave explained.

Cindy said when Dave handed the glove to her, she could immediately feel energy coming from the center of it. She felt an indescribable peace. As she handed the glove back to Dave, she took out the piece of sheet from the little bag and was amazed by the rose scent that came from it.

As Dave continued to share his feelings, the scent of roses grew stronger and stronger until the entire room was filled with the powerful rose scent and with a pervading sense of peace and love.

After tea and cookies, the Christmas angel was on the phone calling the next person with whom she was about to share the glove, telling them that she was on her way.

Later that night in bed, Dave told Cindy he could still smell the potent smell of roses. Cindy no longer smelled them until she reached over and touched Dave's hand. Then suddenly through the physical connection with him, the scent became vivid to her, as well. Cindy said she promptly fell asleep and "missed out" on the rest of Dave's miracle.

Dave said the rose scent, still strong, seemed to envelop and maintain him in this peaceful, blissful state. He drifted off to sleep, in a more relaxed state than he could remember in a very long time.

Then, he said, at 2 A.M. he was awakened to the smell of roses. That scent had become even stronger. It

was everywhere and so overwhelming that he started
to cry.

"I could feel my heart fully open, and I could feel
my light and my spirit shining as bright as in my near-
death experience. So, I got up and meditated and just
enjoyed taking that energy in," Dave said.

It was as though Dave had a spiraling of energy
that brought together the elements of his life into a
clearer focus and design—of a ministry helping others to know of and to experience this state of grace.
Somehow, his near-death experience seemed like the
groundwork, the background, to a tapestry woven in
anticipation of a Christmas miracle that continues to
add golden threads of wonder to the mystery cloth of
life itself. Holding the glove of Padre Pio reconnected
Dave with the inner peace and love he had touched in
his near-death experience, that had been blotted out
by pain and medication, troubles and worries.

"Spirit indicated this was to be my future path—
working with others who are suffering with a terminal
illness. I know it is time to communicate what I have
experienced and learned, and now I am using it to
cope with my own terminal illness. I am to begin to
share it in a more public way," Dave said.

Cindy and Dave are hopeful and prayerful that
Dave will be completely healed. Dave said he believes
that we all have obstacles and experiences that we

must overcome and learn from so that we can evolve and grow.

"God hasn't abandoned us when things seem tough. It is necessary to see the positive and negative in all I've experienced in order to grow. God's light and love is a part of each of us and we don't have to go searching for it. We just need to open up to it," Dave said.

Even if Dave is not completely healed, Cindy and Dave feel his cancer has brought about a situation that is allowing both of them to come back to their spiritual center. That, in itself, is a wonderful gift.

When Dave went to his oncologist for the first checkup since just before Christmas, his X rays showed a miracle truly had taken place on the physical level as well. Dave's tumor had become stabilized. It was no longer growing.

"We recognize our Christmas miracle as a sign that miracles do happen and that people like our Christmas angel are around to bring miracles to us and everyone else on a daily basis," Cindy said. "We are reminded that Angels don't always have wings—sometimes they appear in a snow-covered coat and scarf!"

Padre Pio said, "Love is the first ingredient in the relief of suffering." It is clear that Padre Pio's love is continuing to touch many lives.

As an epilogue, Cindy said that in talking with their Christmas angel on the phone recently, the woman shared how deeply she herself had been touched by simply being the "courier of the glove." In addition, she learned of two more Christmas miracles with the glove after it left the Bennetts' home:

When the Christmas angel arrived at the home of the next recipient, the friend who had the tumor was unable to be present. So they called her on the phone, and while holding the glove, they all prayed for healing. In utter amazement, when the woman with the tumor went to the doctor, he declared the tumor was gone! The doctor had no way of explaining this miraculous disappearance, but the woman herself knew . . . Padre Pio's glove had healed again!

The other healing that day was that of a woman who suffered greatly with double vision. After holding the glove, she was immediately blessed with no more double vision! She was so overjoyed she was afraid to tell anybody, Cindy said, for fear the problem would return. As of now, it has not, so she has been telling everybody!

*S*herry's mom, Lorraine Lippold, was no stranger to hospitals. Many years of intense pain from scoliosis of the spine and nerve and disc problems resulted in a series of operations that would have been difficult for a young healthy person to endure, much less a woman in her seventies. Surgeons implanted metal rods in her back, from the base of her spine to her neck, that required grafting bone from the hip and leg to use in attaching the rod to the spine. This extremely complicated and dangerous surgery was performed not just once—but multiple times! For various reasons, the rods were taken out, then others reinstalled.

Enduring a body cast for six months after several surgeries, and allowing for the healing of the bone grafts, muscles, and nerves, Lorraine found the ordeals were taking a toll on her physical stamina, as it would on anyone's! They still weren't right, so yet another surgery, taking out the old rods and installing rods of a more recent technology, seemed successful. Then, over a year's time of healing and more body casts, she was able to wear a plastic cast that enabled her more freedom of movement.

While unpacking boxes in a new home, Lorraine was standing on a ladder, putting some dishes in a high cupboard, when she lost her balance and fell onto a metal serving platter in the box beneath her, which sliced her leg in a manner that looked more like a shark attack than a fall. More than half of her calf was sliced to the bone, and as if that wasn't enough, the severe fall threw out the rods in her spine. She would eventually have to go in and have all the rods removed, once more, still another major back operation.

But that would be after the long, arduous process of mending and healing from the injured leg. Infections and swelling caused major problems and pain, nearly unbearable, but Lorraine pulled through, only to be dealt other onslaughts, of lupus disease and some rare form of lung disease to boot. So over many years, she was on massive doses of antibiotics and various medications for the swelling and pain. People around her marveled at her courage and stamina.

She had just begun to gain her strength back when pneumonia moved in, not once but four times! A period of two months saw her hospitalized three times with pneumonia so serious, they weren't sure she would pull through. Each time, Sherry's dad, Paul Lippold, rarely left Lorraine's side. He would sit by her hospital bed day and night, holding her hand and deep in prayer. Their faith pulled them both through one close call after another. Lorraine, a short and petite Swede, was now confined to a wheelchair full time. The surgeons did not want to risk reinstalling the rods in her spine after having to remove them after her horrendous fall. Paul would wheel Lorraine into the kitchen/family room area to the table where they would sit and read, eat, and watch television. On this one particular day, Paul noticed that Lorraine was somewhat listless and kept slumping way down in her chair.

"I'd pull her back up and arrange the pillows, setting her straighter, only to notice a short time later she would be all slumped down again," he explained. Finally, Lorraine said her back was really hurting her and she thought she would just go and stretch out in bed, so Paul wheeled her back to the bedroom and tucked her in, then went back out and watched something on television for about an hour, before going back to check on her.

When he walked into the bedroom, he heard what sounded like the noise Lorraine made while reaching the last few drops in a glass with a straw. One of the side effects of lupus is a dry mouth, so she almost always had a glass of water, ginger ale, or some liquid in a glass with a straw. He started to head right back to the kitchen to retrieve her another glass of juice, when he realized that his ears heard one thing, but the quick glance as he headed toward the bed told him another.

Realizing Lorraine was asleep, so the "gurgle sound" must not be a hint that her glass was empty, he did a fast U-turn and returned to the bedroom. As he got closer, he could tell that noise was coming from her chest! Paul tried to awaken Lorraine, even resorting to shaking her, as he got no response. After several unsuccessful attempts, he frantically called 911.

"Everything arrived at once," Paul said. "The fire department, the police, and the ambulance. The entire townhouse was filled with emergency medical personnel and they were all doing their best to revive her, but had no response. When I heard one of them yell 'bag her,' I was terrified, thinking that meant they were to bring in the coroner's bag! Of course, it didn't, and they put a tube down her throat and rushed her to the hospital."

"There in the emergency room, they worked on her, and then needed to put her in an intensive care unit, but there wasn't a single one available. So Valley Lutheran Hospital, where she was, called the same ambulance that brought her from home to the hospital to transport her to Mesa Lutheran Hospital's intensive care unit. Lorraine was on total life support for more than three days, when neurology scheduled an encephalogram to determine the extent of brain damage. There was no knowledge of exactly how long Lorraine had been 'out' before they put her on life support, but it was a consensus that, more than likely, if she ever came around, she would be a vegetable," Paul added.

Sherry and Brad were scheduled to lecture and give a seminar in Florida, when shortly before they were to leave, came the first phone call that Lorraine was in the hospital. In prayer and turmoil, they were uncertain if they should cancel and get right to Arizona. Although Mom had pulled through so many terrible ordeals, this one sounded most serious. Then came the dreaded phone call from Sherry's dad that if she wanted to see her mother, she had better get out to Arizona immediately, as it looked like the Lord had finally called her home. It was Mom Lippold's request not to be kept alive by machinery and life support, and her wishes regarding such a situation had been made clear.

After many discussions on the phone with nurses and doctors and Sherry's dad, Brad and Sherry cancelled their Florida lecture and made plans to immediately go to Mom Lippold's bedside in Arizona. Sherry was finding this to be an extremely difficult situation to bear. Thinking miracles do occur even under extraordinary circumstances, she didn't think they should "pull the plug" and was shocked to learn that was about to happen, even though it was at her own mother's request.

Both Sherry and Brad had lost close family members at Christmas. Sherry's son, Erik; Brad's dad, Erling; and now—Sherry's mom. They would, of course, respect her wishes, and they made arrangements to make the trek from Iowa to Arizona. So, once again, not long before Christmas, Sherry and Brad began bracing themselves for what was beginning to look like another sad Christmas of losing a beloved family member.

The Lippolds' faith carried them through one crisis after another, yet Sherry knew this was going to be more difficult than she could imagine for them. They had been extremely active in their church, and now the prayers of their pastor, church members, friends, family, and other churches around the country were a strong support.

"This time, she must have been covered in so much prayer that it was a shield that blanketed her, keeping her safe for the three days she was—for all practical purposes and by definition—dead," Paul said, then recalling that a miracle of miracles had occurred.

Paul went home at the insistence of the nurses to take a shower and get at least a couple of hours of sleep, before returning to the hospital. When he came back, he thought he was seeing things as he walked into Lorraine's room and there she was sitting up in the hospital bed, reading the paper!

In just a few hours' time, she had come out of the coma, shocking the entire hospital staff! To everyone's utter amazement, just minutes before they were about to remove the life-support, a nurse who was checking on Lorraine had affectionately stroked her hand, and then holding on to it for a second, had noticed what she thought was a response from Lorraine.

The nurse screamed out that she could feel a slight squeeze back from the patient . . . so suddenly, hospital staff went right to work on her and, miraculously, she came around—and out of the coma!

After reviewing the situation again and again, all reiterated that Lorraine's coming out of the coma was stunning enough, but the fact that she demonstrated no signs of any neurological damage was something of a miracle.

Instead of another Christmas funeral, Sherry and Brad celebrated Christmas with Lorraine, who was still weak from the ordeal but gaining in strength daily, and the rest of the family. They were shown, once again, that even when the odds are "stacked against you"—as they surely seemed to be with all that Lorraine had been through—miracles can and do happen. A better Christmas gift, Sherry and her dad could not have had!

*W*hen Bernadette Lopez was a schoolgirl in Las Cruces, New Mexico, she contracted polio, which she remembers as a disease that made her burn with fever and left her right leg paralyzed and her left leg painfully twisted.

"My father or my mother had to carry me back and forth to my bed from the toilet or other rooms," Bernadette said. "My mother was so worried about me that she would sometimes sleep with me in case I needed something during the night."

The disease had quite understandably left Bernadette very depressed. "I was not yet ten years old, and the doctors told my parents that I would probably never walk again. Later, I might try leg braces and crutches, but a wheelchair would be a more likely prognosis. And along with that grim malediction came my inner sadness that I would never be a wife or a mother or have any kind of normal life—ever."

On Christmas Eve 1942, Bernadette's father had bundled her up so that she could attend mass with them. They were very poor in those days, and since most of the little money that her parents did manage to save went for Bernadette's medicines, there were few presents for her baby sister, Rosa; her parents; or herself.

"Mother said that the most important thing was that we had each other and could be together on Christmas Eve," Bernadette recalled.

Then, after they had returned from mass and had a little bit to eat, Bernadette suddenly began to run a high fever.

"Perhaps the chilly night air had affected me adversely or the night had been filled with too much excitement for me," Bernadette said, "but I was soon shivering and moaning incoherently."

In order to save on their electricity bill, Bernadette's mother would often crawl into bed with her and read to her by the light of a candle that she would set on a bedside chair. Although her husband warned her of the potential danger of such a practice, she felt that the reading of a special Christmas story would bring some cheer to their crippled daughter.

Bernadette said that she doesn't remember at all what her mother was reading to her that night. Her fever was very high, and to her nine-year-old mind, she was dying.

"When I came back to periods of semiconsciousness, I was glad that Mama was there with me," Bernadette said. "But most of the time I had no idea where I was or who was with me."

Sometime that night, Bernadette's fevered dreams became a kind of waking night vision, and she was startled to find that she was somehow out of her body and that her conscious self was floating up near the ceiling. Below her, she could see her shivering body and her mother's familiar form on the bed—and then she was astonished to see two columns of angels standing at the sides of her bed. She remembers clearly that there were six of the glorious beings on her right side and six on her left. "They began to sing the sweetest, most beautiful song that I had ever heard," Bernadette said. "And all around them was the most magnificent music being played by an unseen orchestra. I thought to myself, truly, this is the song that the shepherds had heard on high on the Christmas Eve when Christ was born."

But the angels began to sing louder and louder, until their mighty chorus of voices hurt her ears. And the angelic beings themselves appeared to grow larger and larger as they sang louder and louder.

Just as the song of the angels seemed to reach a crescendo, Bernadette awakened to the horror of discovering that she and her mother were enveloped in flames.

The girl jumped out of bed and dragged her mother from the flames that had engulfed them.

"I pulled my unconscious mother away from the burning bed," she remembered, "and then I began beating out the flames, first with my bare hands, then a bath towel. The bedclothes were badly burned, as well as half the mattress and one of the pillows."

Her father appeared at the door of her bedroom and shouted a combination of alarm and joy: "Bernadette! You are walking! The bed is on fire!"

The miracle of it all had not struck her until her father had shouted it aloud. How could she, a small girl weakened by fever and paralysis, have managed to jump out of bed and pull her mother to safety?

Although Bernadette has asked herself that question now for nearly sixty years, she always arrives at the same answer: It could only have been due to the twelve beautiful angels who appeared at her bedside on that Christmas Eve in 1942 and accomplished four miracles.

"First, they performed a miracle of healing on my legs," she said. "Then they kept singing louder and louder until I awakened to save my mother and myself from the fire that had begun when Mama had fallen asleep and knocked over the candle. The third miracle was that although Mama's dressing gown and night-dress were burned off her body on her left side and my nightgown was scorched black, neither of us had the slightest burn on our flesh.

"Fourth, and the greatest Christmas miracle of all, I continued walking without assistance. I was a bit unsteady at first, but my parents never had to carry me anywhere again. Within a couple of months, I was once again running and skipping rope with my friends, a happy schoolgirl who would never forget the angels from on high and their beautiful song of healing.

"I know that those same angels have watched over me all of my life," Bernadette said, concluding her story, "and from time to time, I have been very aware of their presence around me. And, oh, yes, I married when I was twenty-three years old, and I had three wonderful, healthy children, two of which have made me a grand-mother four times. My Christmas miracle demolished the doctors' malediction that I would spend my life in a wheelchair."

*W*hen the doctors pronounced their solemn recommendation in March 1993 that Russell Miller should be allowed to die in peace, his family rallied and vowed that he would be up and singing Christmas carols with them in December.

There was no question that the prognosis appeared very disheartening. From the medical perspective, recovery was impossible.

The fifty-three-year-old Miller had entered a coma after an aneurysm burst in his brain, and the specialists at the Colorado hospital held out no hope of his ever regaining consciousness. Although they understood what a difficult family decision they had placed before the Millers, they solemnly offered their best advice that Russell's feeding tube should be unplugged and he be permitted to die peacefully.

Kathy Ebert, Miller's twenty-six-year-old daughter, remembered vividly the shock that their family received that snowy afternoon in early March when their longtime family physician, Dr. Roberts, grimly concurred with the specialists.

"Dad and Doc Roberts had been friends for years," Kathy said, "and he had tears in his eyes when he said that there was little or no hope that Dad would ever come out of the coma. And if he ever did, Doc told us, he would be on the level of a vegetable—and he would probably never be able to recognize any of us ever again. As much as it gave him sorrow, Doc Roberts suggested that we strongly consider the specialists' advice to allow Dad to pass on."

At that point, Kathy recalled, her mother, Maureen, put her arms around Kathy and her brother, twenty-two-year-old Randy, and with a trembling voice and tears streaming down her cheeks, told them that it had to be a family decision. She alone would not—could not—be the one to pass judgment on whether their father would live or die.

Randy wiped his eyes on a handkerchief and took a deep breath, as if to fix his resolve, before he spoke: "The specialists said there is little or no chance that Dad will ever regain consciousness. Well, if there is even the slightest chance that he can wake up and live, how can we deny him that possibility? Even if it is a million or two million to one, it's still a chance, isn't it?"

Kathy and Maureen became very still, as if mentally pondering the odds. Would it be fair to Dad—or to any of them—if he simply lay there in a coma for months and months before they finally gave in to the specialists' recommendation and allowed him to die?

But Randy wasn't finished with his argument. "We've always been a praying and a Bible-reading family," he reminded his mother and sister. "We've always put our trust in God. I say we keep on praying until He cures Dad. I say we just keep on focusing on seeing Dad home with us celebrating Christmas! Dad has always loved Christmas so much. With the help of God, let's create a Christmas miracle!"

Kathy nodded her agreement. They made a pact at that very moment to make a prayerful and joyful noise around their father's bed, night and day.

They made a vow to have their father home and singing Christmas carols with them in eight months.

They would practice the faith that had begun with the miraculous birth of the Christ child, and they would never stop believing that they couldn't make another miracle happen.

From that moment on, there was always at least one member of the Miller family beside Russell's hospital bed. Each day, Maureen read the Bible with great feeling, just as if her beloved husband were awake and participating in their daily family devotions.

Randy prayed aloud and placed his hands on his father's head, citing the example of Jesus laying on hands during the course of his healing ministry. A sports enthusiast since his childhood, Randy also assumed the role of a compassionate but persistent coach. He would sit beside his father's bed and repeat words of encouragement over and over, until they became a kind of chant: "Okay, Dad, come on now. I know you can hear me. Come back to us now, Dad. You can do it, Dad."

Kathy brought her guitar and accompanied herself as she sang all of her father's favorite hymns. As often as possible, she brought her ten-year-old twin daughters to sing along with her in a family trio. When her husband was able to join them, they formed a harmonious quartet that inspired the entire corridor with their joyous gospel songs.

Once a day, all the members of the Miller family—including any friends or relatives who had come to visit—would form a circle around Russell's hospital bed and clasp hands in a silent prayer for healing.

Within about ten days after the Miller family had begun their healing regimen, an amazed nurse witnessed the impossible when Russell opened one eye.

Four weeks later, he opened both eyes, and it was apparent to all those present that he was looking around the hospital room with intelligent curiosity.

The third week in April, just six weeks after an assessment of Russell Miller's burst aneurysm had led experienced medical specialists to declare that he would remain in a coma until death overtook him, he moved most of his fingers and some of his toes.

In mid-June, less than three months after he had lost consciousness, Russell Miller was responding to sounds and recognizing members of his family. He was opening his mouth and attempting to speak to his wife, children, grandchildren, relatives, and friends.

In another month, he was able to go home.

Once he was in his familiar home environment, Russell rapidly continued to improve. In a very short time, he was able to walk and speak normally. He ate meals with the family, watched television, and began to read books, magazines, and newspapers. Soon he was joining in the family's prayers for his health to be completely restored.

By that Christmas, Russell Miller was able to participate fully in his family's celebration of the holiday. His devoted wife, daughter, and son had not accepted the doctors' grim pronouncement that he was doomed to live out his remaining days in a coma. Their unyielding love, their boundless faith, and their constant prayers had petitioned the Creator to grant them a true Christmas miracle.

*I*s it possible that a mere Christmas card can engender a miraculous healing?

Dr. Franklin Ruehl, a theoretical physicist who lives in a suburb of Los Angeles, recalled an incident from 1989 involving his mother, which seems to indicate that such a miracle is indeed within the realm of feasibility.

"Mother had long suffered from chronic back pain," Dr. Ruehl said. "In fact, as long ago as 1953, an orthopedic surgeon had diagnosed her with premature arthritis of the back and predicted that it would continue to progress with an ever-increasing rate with the passage of time. As a consequence, she was always trying new exercises in an effort to combat this problem."

In early September 1989, Mrs. Florence Ruehl saw a fitness guru on television demonstrate a supposedly ideal stretching exercise for the back. Carefully, she followed along step by step with the instructor's example—but she immediately felt a bolt of pain shoot through her lower back.

"By the time I got home, I found her lying in bed, writhing in excruciating agony," Dr. Ruehl said. "Analgesics provided some measure of relief, but only temporarily. Because of her distrust of doctors, Mother adamantly refused to see a physician, but as the days dragged on, it was evident that she had more than a transient problem. Sitting upright was especially painful, so she would end up eating her meals standing at the kitchen counter."

Dr. Ruehl said that he finally got his mother to agree to visit a female chiropractor, but the erstwhile healer spent most of the time espousing the doctrine of the natural health movement, giving Florence Ruehl only a brief session of ultrasound therapy, which proved completely ineffective.

In mid-November, she relented and allowed her son to take her to a traditional medical center where, after a battery of tests, an attending physician informed them that Mrs. Ruehl hadn't fractured any vertebrae or torn any ligaments, as they had feared, but had simply pulled some muscles. The doctor went on to express surprise at how she had virtually no signs of arthritis for a woman of her age. He prescribed a two-week regimen of the powerful drug prednisone.

"It worked wonders," Dr. Ruehl recalled. "Mother got back on her feet and immediately spent as much time as possible Christmas shopping, fearing the beneficial response to the drug would wear off. It did. And the doctor refused to renew the prescription, stating his case that the potent medication could have devastating side effects if taken over a prolonged period of time. Mother once again found herself back in bed and unable to sit up as the month of December rolled around."

Dr. Ruehl began his Christmas shopping, hunting for gifts and cards. While he purchased several items and was able to accumulate a beautiful array of cards featuring cats for his mother, an ailurophile of the first order, he continued to search for an ideal card that would somehow properly address the miserable experience she was enduring with her back problem. He had canvassed all the stores in several malls but found only the standard kind of Christmas greetings.

"Then, on Christmas Eve, I happened to chance upon a small out-of-the-way card shop," he said. "I read one verse after another, finding them all bearing the traditional blissful greetings.

"Just as I was about to leave, I spotted a large, beautiful card, obscured by frolicking Santas. Reading it, I knew instantly that it was the card for which I had been searching—the very card meant specially for my stricken mother. It was as though Fate had guided me to that very shop and that very card."

When he returned home, his mother apologized for not having had a chance to get any cards for him. Dr. Ruehl then invited her to take half of the cards that he had purchased.

"I spread them out, facedown, and told her to pick cards at random that she could then give to me," he said. "Of course, I withheld that special card."

On Christmas morning, Mrs. Ruehl came out to the living room, determined to at least sit up to read her cards and to open her gifts. When she began to read the special card that her son had found for her, they both cried.

"The card had obviously been penned by someone who appreciated that not everyone at Yuletide is happy, that serious problems may be plaguing some people in this season of joy," Dr. Ruehl said.

"The verse in that precious card that began 'With all my love, Mother,' stated that although it was Christmas when everyone else may be feeling happy, it can be very difficult to smile and pretend things are all right when they really haven't been. And while there may have been times when she wondered how she could carry on, the verse proclaimed that if anyone could do it, she could—because she had always had an inner strength that would never allow her to give up.

Because of her determination, she was a very special woman who was very easy to love and she was wished a Merry Christmas so filled with love that she would never feel alone."

Incredibly, Dr. Ruehl said, after his mother read the card, she stated that she was feeling less pain when she sat up. She was able to be seated at the dining room table and enjoy their Christmas turkey dinner.

"Within the next few days, she improved at an astounding rate," he stated, "soon resuming all her normal activities. And now, twelve years later, she still has suffered no recurrence of that terrible back pain. She has, though, limited her exercise regimen to brisk walking—and she snaps off the TV anytime an exercise expert pops up."

As a scientist, Dr. Ruehl understands that skeptics might assert that his mother would have recovered eventually, that the timing of her resurgence with the reading of the card was purely coincidental. "But Mother and I are convinced that that Christmas card possessed a miraculous healing power," he said.

*J*ust before Thanksgiving, November 1990, truck driver Ray De La Cruz was sitting in his rig at an intersection in Mesa, Arizona, eager to get home after a hard five days on the road. As a line of pedestrians moved along the crosswalk in front of him, Ray glanced at his wristwatch, once again admiring the turquoise band that his wife, Renee, had given him for his fiftieth birthday in July.

Suddenly, his eyes began to cloud with a gray mist. He felt disoriented. His surroundings began to dim, and he prayed for the light to change so he could pull his rig over to the side of the road.

Within a few moments, Ray was unable to see the traffic lights, and only the sound of the horns of irritated motorists behind him told him that the light had turned green and he could drive across the intersection. Somehow he managed to pull his truck and trailer off the street just as he went completely blind.

Later, as he told his story, Ray De La Cruz admitted that he was very frightened when this terrible thing occurred. "I felt panic," he said. "I had no idea what had happened to me."

Sadly enough, neither did the specialists at the clinic.

Renee accompanied Ray when he went for a battery of tests, because he wanted her there to hear everything the doctors said and try to understand anything that he might miss in his nervousness and anxiety.

The examining doctors were able to dismiss Ray's fear of a brain tumor or any number of dire physical conditions, but they remained puzzled as to the cause of his sudden blindness.

Renee told the specialists that Ray was never sick, that he never even complained of an occasional headache. How could such a thing as this mysterious blindness occur all of a sudden?

"And I had no pain or no headache all the time when the doctors were examining me," Ray said. "I felt fine. I just couldn't see."

Finally, one of the doctors said—perhaps more in frustration than in a medical conclusion—that what was required to restore Ray's sight was a miracle.

"Mr. De La Cruz," he said, "we cannot find anything physically wrong with your eyes or anything that could have caused your sudden blindness. What we really need to restore your sight is some kind of a miracle."

Ray endured his sightlessness for three weeks before Renee declared that he had suffered enough. It was only a few days before Christmas. She would pray to Mother Mary to lift the shutters from Ray's eyes and restore his sight by the holy day of her son's birth.

"I asked Renee if she shouldn't have given the Holy Mother a little more time," Ray said, "but she argued that since the medical specialist had said that it would take a miracle to cure my blindness, then we would ask for a miracle. And every believer in miracles knows that they can happen in a split second."

Encouraged by his wife's faith, Ray began to pray also.

"And we asked our little daughters, Michele and Teresa, to pray with us until their bedtime," Ray said. "Then, after mass on Christmas Eve, from nine o'clock until eight the next morning, Renee and I said the rosary and prayed for my healing."

About eight o'clock on Christmas Day, Ray came down with a fever. "I felt like I was burning up," he said. "It seemed as though there were flames all around me. I got hotter and hotter. I felt like I had gone to Hell. I started screaming for Mother Mary to save me from the fire and the fever."

As Ray lay back on the bed, Renee placed a cool, wet cloth on his forehead.

"And then, somehow in my inner eye, I saw Mother Mary," Ray recalled. "She wore a blue gown, a white veil, and she held a rose in her right hand. She smiled at me—and then she disappeared."

When Ray told Renee that he had been blessed with a vision of the Holy Mother, she became very excited and asked Michele what time it was. She wanted to write down the exact time of the visitation so that they had a record of the marvelous event.

In spite of his blindness, Ray had continued to wear his watch due to habit. When he heard Renee ask the time, he automatically glanced down at his wrist.

"And my eyes began to focus on my watch," he said. "Within just a few moments I could clearly see the numerals on the dial and the pattern of the turquoise band. I could see!"

Overwhelmed with joy, Ray leaped from his bed and kissed and embraced his wife and daughters. He could see! Mother Mary had restored his sight. And he could feel that the fever had also left him. The Holy Mother had brought them their Christmas miracle.

Later that joyous Christmas night, Ray and his wife sat down on the sofa in the living room to think about what had just occurred. They both knew that there was a lesson in the miracle that Mother Mary had bestowed upon Ray.

"We thought for a long time," Ray said, "and then a thought came to me. My sight left me when I looked at my watch at an intersection—and it returned when Renee wanted to know what time it was that I had the vision of Mother Mary. I knew that all of this had something to do with time."

Renee and Ray thought and prayed through most of that night about the mystery of Ray's blindness and the miracle that had restored his sight—and by morning they felt they had the answer.

When Ray had been discharged from military service, he had told his parents that he didn't have "time" to go back to school. He needed a job.

As he grew older, he could not find the "time" to get married until he was in his late thirties. Although Renee was ten years younger than he, Ray kept putting off having children, insisting that it was "not yet the right time." Now Ray was over fifty, Renee was forty, and their daughters were only nine and seven. Michele and Teresa needed a father who would spend "time" with them.

Ray always complained that he didn't have "time" to help with the housework, to maintain the yard, to play with the girls, to go to church, to visit his parents—because he had to keep long hours behind the wheel of his truck. And yet he was the one who kept volunteering for the long hauls.

"To get more money to pay the bills," he said in his defense. "My time earns money."

Renee stroked her husband's hair and pulled his head to her shoulder. "And how much time do you have left with your daughters before they are grown and married?" she challenged him in a soft voice. "How much time do we have left before we are too old to enjoy one another? How much time do we have left before God calls you—or me—home? And when you are home, how much time do you waste by playing cards with your friends when you could be having quality time with the girls and me?"

Ray had no argument against such charges. He then clearly understood that Mother Mary had given him another chance to have more time with his family and the things that really mattered in life. She had taken his sight—then restored it with a Christmas miracle—so that he might truly see.

Ray De La Cruz has enjoyed full vision ever since his dramatic Christmas miracle. He quit his job driving big rigs across the country and went to work as a dispatcher for a taxi service. He is home every night for dinner, and he spends as much time as possible with his family.

And there was even a bonus to his miracle: Before he mysteriously lost his sight, he required bifocal lenses in his glasses. Since the Christmas miracle bestowed by Mother Mary, he has not needed eyeglasses at all.

*E*ach year during the Christmas holidays, we receive numerous reports from sincere men and women who tell us that they received a visit from the spirit of a departed loved one sometime during the traditional twelve days of Christmas.

Some may theorize that such visitations may be due to the power of suggestion brought on by the nostalgia for the past that is so prevalent during the Christmas season. The sights, sounds, and smells of the holiday have an incredible power to cause us to revisit cherished memories of those dear ones who have passed to the other side.

Or is it possible that the spirits of our beloved departed truly do draw nearer to us during this wonderful, yet sometimes melancholy and introspective, time of the year?

For many men and women, the holiday season can be a time of loneliness and a great longing for what they remember as much better times in their past. And for those who have lost loved ones during the Christmas holiday, a season that was once associated with joy and family togetherness can become a time of sorrow and depression. It may be that the grief of loved ones on the earthplane can draw the departed back to offer reassurance that they are all right and that life and love truly do extend beyond death.

When Joyce Epstein's twenty-four-year-old sister, Nan, and her husband, Jason Moore, were killed in an airplane crash on September 12, 1988, she felt as if she could no longer go on living.

The children of a Roman Catholic mother and a Jewish father, Joyce had been Nan's surrogate mother since she was nine and Nan was four.

"Our mother died very young of cancer," Joyce said, "and Dad didn't remarry until I was in my second year of college, so I had a lot of years of looking out for my baby sister."

In spite of the surrogate mother relationship assumed by Joyce—or perhaps, because of it—she said that the two of them had always been closer than most sisters she knew.

"It had been pretty hard after Mom died," Joyce said. "She had been a lively Irish-American girl with sparkling green eyes and coal black hair. No one could resist her charm and her good spirits, and the sound of her laughter would encourage the most solemn of stone statues to join in the fun. Before she got sick, we would sometimes as a family go to Saturday synagogue with Dad, then get up on Sunday morning to go to mass with Mom. And in December, we celebrated both Christmas and Hanukkah, placing a crèche with the baby Jesus beneath the Christmas tree and lighting the eight candles on the menorah to commemorate the miracle of the oil that fueled the candelabrum in the Temple for eight days.

"After Mom died, I more or less floated between the two faiths," she said. "Dad wasn't a strict orthodox Jew, so he let us girls pick and choose as the spirit moved us, so to speak."

Although she kept close tabs on her sister even when she was attending city college, Joyce was delighted when Nan began dating Jason Moore during their junior year in high school.

"Jason came from a good family, and he was a decent, hard-working guy himself," she said. "I had a feeling that this would be one of those high-school romances that would last forever."

Sometimes, Joyce learned to her sorrow, "forever" on Earth may not last for a very long period of time.

"Nan and Jason were such a wonderful couple," she said. "They both got jobs right out of high school and began to save for their marriage. Jason went to night school at a junior college in the city, and he was determined to better himself."

After nearly six years of hard work and planning for their future, Jason Moore and her sister decided that they could enter comfortably into marriage. They had acquired a sizable savings account, and Jason had satisfied the graduation requirements at the junior college, been promoted several times at work, and was now taking night courses at city college. Nan's position as a cashier at the bank was secure, and it now seemed as though all systems were go to continue their lifepath together as a married couple.

But the always frugal, always practical couple did not go on their honeymoon immediately after their wedding that May. They put it off until September when they knew they could better afford it after the expense of the wedding reception.

"They got married in a civil ceremony to avoid any complications with any religious issues," Joyce said. "Jason's folks were Methodists, Nan had decided to be confirmed a Roman Catholic in Mom's honor, Dad and our stepmom were Jewish, and I was sort of a New Age blend. The newlyweds hosted a really great reception at one of the local hotels—and they paid every dime of it themselves."

It was during takeoff of their honeymoon flight that the small commuter plane crashed.

"It was supposed to take them to a larger airport where they would take off for Tahiti," Joyce said. "Instead, it rose just high enough to slam back down to the ground and take Nan and Jason, seven other passengers, and the three crew members to their deaths."

Joyce Epstein entered a period of deep depression after the fatal accident.

"For a time, I sincerely did not feel that I could go on living," she stated frankly. "My sister and Jason had become my world. Shortly after Nan had graduated from high school, Dad and our stepmother had moved to a different city, leaving me, Nan's surrogate mother, to look after her. My own plans for marriage had been dashed when my fiancé was involved in a serious automobile accident and left mentally impaired. I had compensated for the loss of my future by spending even more emotional energy on Nan and Jason. I was thirty-one, and I felt as though my life was over."

Although she had sought counsel from a rabbi, a priest, her father, and certain of her friends, Joyce could find no respite from her grief. "I barely slept. And when I did, my dreams were haunted by scenes of the crash and my deep sense of loss."

Joyce is now somewhat ashamed to admit that for a time she had even considered suicide. "I felt that since Nan and Jason had been taken from me, I would join them on the other side. Thank God, I had confessed such a plan to a priest, and he convinced me that such a drastic deed would not produce the results that I desired."

Three months after the tragic deaths of her sister and brother-in-law and between the Hanukkah and Christmas celebrations, Joyce left her home to seek rest and seclusion in a small ski resort in Colorado.

"There was absolutely no way that I could deal with the holidays in the old familiar places where Nan and I had spent so many wonderful holidays," she said, "so I found this little out-of-the-way lodge where I could seek solace of spirit."

One night as she sat reading near the fireplace in her room, Joyce unmistakably felt a physical presence behind her.

"I turned to see the images of Nan and Jason standing behind me in the center of the room," she recalled. "I saw them as solidly as they had ever appeared in life. They were smiling and holding hands—and for the first time in months, I smiled, too."

Joyce is certain she actually heard Nan speaking in her familiar, soft, lilting voice, so much like their mother's gentle Irish brogue.

"Please do not continue to grieve so for us," Nan's spirit told her. "Jason and I are all right. And our love is even stronger here than it was on Earth."

Joyce tried to fight back the tears and the sudden rush of emotion that caused her to shout: "Why did you leave me? Why did you leave me alone? I can't go on without you!"

Nan's lovely features seemed momentarily to be feeling Joyce's pain, but then she smiled and spoke with authority: "Of course you can, Sis. You know, when I was just a little girl, there were times when you had to leave me alone for a while. I would cry, fearing that if something happened to you, I wouldn't be able to live without you. But you always came back home, and we were together again. One day, my dear sister, you will join us here, and the three of us will be together again with Mom and other dear ones of our family who have already come home. Until that day, my darling, be happy and live a life of joy and fulfillment."

Before Joyce could speak again, Nan and Jason faded from sight—but the impact of her sister's words have never left her.

"The proof of my sister's immortality freed me from my deep depression," Joyce said. "And the fact that she appeared so happy permitted me to become positive about life once again."

Joyce concluded the story of her Christmas miracle by stating that all of her friends were pleased to notice her new positive attitude when she came home after the holidays.

"To all who would listen," she said, "I told the story of a sister's love that was able to push aside the dark curtain of death long enough to restore the faith of one who had felt left behind to survive only in gloom and despair. To all who would listen, I declared that love is the greatest power in the universe—and maybe that is the true message of Christmas."

There can't be any worse time to be fired than at Christmas. At twenty-six, Earl Burdick felt that he was a complete failure.

Four years before, in 1980, he had taken a job teaching high school English and journalism in a suburb of Chicago—a position that he hoped would serve as a stepping-stone to help him achieve his dream of becoming a full-time freelance writer. After the first semester, he learned that he was not cut out to be a disciplinarian—and facing the classrooms of unruly, disrespectful students until the end of the school year in June became a living hell.

A fellow faculty member who knew Earl was leaving teaching suggested that he sell insurance. "You can write during the day and make evening appointments to call on prospective clients after work," his friend said, making the schedule seem ideal.

But it took Earl less than a month to discover that he had absolutely no talent for intruding on tired and often irritable people and convincing them that the acquisition of an insurance policy and its subsequent payment obligations would be the answer to all their earthly concerns.

Finally, in the winter of 1981, he secured a job as the manager of a convenience store, and things seemed to be going well—so well that a year later, in the winter of 1982, he married Marjorie, the patient young woman to whom he had been engaged since their senior year in college.

Although he put in long hours at the store, he still managed to find time to write after work and on weekends, and he had received several encouraging rejection slips and had made one small sale to a trade journal. Yes, things were going so well that they decided they could afford to begin a family. Marjorie was expecting in May.

And now, two weeks before Christmas in 1984, the convenience store had been bought out by a national chain of similar marketplaces, and Earl had been summarily fired as its manager. Desperate, he had suggested his moving a couple of rungs down the ladder and working as a salesclerk, a stock boy, a custodian. But the new owners informed him that they would be bringing in their own specially trained crew to staff the store. They no longer required his services in any capacity.

It was two in the afternoon. Somehow Earl had to focus on the hard reality of becoming suddenly unemployed. After three years, he had come to rely mightily on a weekly paycheck. And now with a baby on the way. . . .

Oh, dear God, how was he going to tell Marjorie what had happened? How long could they stretch their meager savings until he found another job?

Although it was not his custom to do so, Earl walked into a bar, ordered a stiff drink, and sat down at a small table near the door. As he took a moment to survey his unfamiliar surroundings, the thought struck him that this was only the second or third time he had ever been in a bar in his life.

Earl knew that he had been walking the streets in a rather disoriented mental state, and he glanced at the address on the napkin under his drink to see where it was that he had randomly stopped his wandering and attempted to regain some perspective. Judging from the address on the soggy napkin, he had walked a lot farther than he had thought.

After Earl had sat in brooding silence for a few minutes, he was startled out of his interior monologue of despair by a well-dressed, pleasantly smiling stranger who asked if he might join him.

Glancing up and noticing that the man already had his hand resting on the back of one of the chairs at the table, Earl shrugged and indicated that he could sit down if it pleased him to do so.

"Thank you, Earl." The man smiled, sitting down opposite him.

"How do you know my name?" Earl asked.

"Oh, I know a lot about you, Earl," the stranger said. His eyes seemed sad and his voice concerned when he added, "It's difficult to adjust to cruel circumstances when you are suddenly fired, especially at Christmas, but you must not be discouraged."

Earl squinted over the edge of his glass and studied the man carefully. Rather tall, well built, salt-and-pepper hair at the temples. A soft voice that communicated quiet strength and confidence. Bright blue eyes that seemed to have the power to peer within one's soul.

"I'm sorry that I don't remember you," Earl said apologetically, extending his hand. "Where did we meet, Mr. . . . .?"

The man shook Earl's hand warmly. "Oh, we've never met in person," he said, "but I know of your problem, and I want to help you. It's Christmas, your wife Marjorie is expecting your first child, and you're out of work."

Earl was feeling very uncomfortable. "You know my name, my wife's name," he began. "You know that Marjorie's pregnant. You know that I just got fired. Man, you are beginning to creep me out. Are you one of the suits from the company that just fired me? If you want to give me another job, that's fine. Maybe you suddenly got a guilty conscience over firing me at Christmas time."

The stranger smiled and denied working for the company that had acquired the convenience store and terminated Earl's position as manager. And then the man proceeded to tell him just how much he really knew about the most intimate details of Earl Burdick's life.

"I have never been so mesmerized, so enraptured in my life," Earl told us recently as he recounted the story of his Christmas miracle. "The stranger spoke in this incredibly soothing voice, and he really seemed to know everything about me and my hopes and my dreams. He knew my birth date, Marjorie's birth date, how the two of us had met in college, on and on. I just sat there and listened to him with my mouth hanging open."

And then, Earl said, came the most amazing thing of all: "He told me that he knew that what I wanted most in life was to be a writer. He told me of a small community newspaper in one of the suburbs that needed a managing editor. He wrote down the address and he told me whom to see. Then he gave me a little pep talk about how newspaper work could help me polish my skills as a writer and teach me the discipline of meeting deadlines under pressure. He told me to keep my chin up and never become discouraged. 'We never walk alone,' he said. There's always someone to reach out and give us a helping hand.'"

Earl was so heartened by the man's inspirational message and the tip on the newspaper job that it took him a moment to realize that the stranger was no longer sitting at the table speaking to him. He looked up to see him walking out the front door.

"I ran after him to thank him," Earl said, "but he must have blended right in with the people walking on the street, because he was nowhere in sight. I was right behind him, but somehow I lost him."

Before Earl called Marjorie with the bad news that he had been fired, he dialed the telephone number on the slip of paper that the stranger had given him.

"The man who answered the phone was the publisher of the community newspaper," Earl said. "He was astonished that I had called that afternoon, because his managing editor had just walked out on the job that noon and left him in a desperate situation. They had to have a special Christmas edition with the last-minute shopping advertisements out in three days. We struck an instant rapport, and I told him of my background as editor of the college newspaper, as an English and journalism teacher, and as a freelance writer. I made an appointment to see him that next morning, and I got the job as managing editor that I held for over ten years."

Earl said that at first he figured that the stranger in the bar had to be some incredible psychic or a remarkable mentalist like the Amazing Kreskin.

"I went back to the bar a few times over the next several months, thinking maybe the man might frequent the place, but I never saw him again," he said. "I tried to describe him to the bartenders who work there, but none of them claimed to recognize him at all."

Later, as Earl replayed the whole strange and wonderful episode in his mind, he came to a very different conclusion.

"No ordinary human—even if he were the world's greatest psychic—could have known all the things about me that he did," he said. "And what about giving me the name of the publisher who had just lost his editor that very day? That compassionate and remarkable stranger was no psychic—he was my own special Christmas angel!"

One of our favorite Christmas miracle stories was told to us some years ago by a woman who had grown up on a farm outside a small town in North Dakota in the 1930s.

"That December we were living in an old farmhouse that had more cracks than Daddy could patch with tar paper," Julie Wilkins remembered. "We had lost our farm the year before and we had lost Mama to typhoid fever that summer. There were four of us kids—Steve, twelve; Larry, eight; Merrie, fourteen; and I was ten—who had to nestle as close as possible to the old oil burner in the front room and try to keep warm enough to do our homework at night."

It was just before Christmas that Julie came down with a really bad fever.

"We had but one blanket a piece," she remembered, but Merrie and the boys all piled the covers on me when they were doing their chores and home-work. Normally, everyone walked around that cold and drafty old house with blankets around us like Sioux Indians, but they wanted me to get warm enough to break my fever."

After losing the family farm, their father worked during the spring, summer, and fall as a hired man for Mr. Hanson, an elderly farmer. "The problem was, old man Hanson had no need of hired help during the winter months," Julie said, "but we still had need for food. Daddy was lucky to get a part-time job at the elevator until fieldwork began in the spring."

Julie remembered that her father was extremely depressed that December.

"It would be our second Christmas in the cold and drafty old farmhouse," she said. "And, of course, worst of all, it would be our first Christmas without Mama."

Julie was quick to point out that the family used to have really wonderful Christmases. "We were never rich, but we were well enough off until the Depression wiped Daddy out. But more than our nice home on the family farm, the presents around the Christmas tree, and the delicious holiday dinners, we missed Mama."

Because of the terrible melancholy that had envel-oped their father, Julie did not wish to concern him with her illness, so as much as possible, she suffered in silence.

"One entire day while the other kids were at school, I lay and prayed that we could have more blankets and just a little extra money so that we could have a nicer Christmas and so Daddy would not have to work so hard," she said.

On the afternoon of the Christmas miracle, Julie remembered that she had been huddled next to the oil burner, waiting for the kids to come home from school.

"I knew my fever was getting higher," she said. "I wanted Merrie there with me. She was the oldest, and she always seemed to know that to do. She was like another mom to us younger kids."

Julie heard the front door open. "The sound of the door opening really startled me," she said, "because I knew that Steve, the last one out the door that morning, had locked it behind him."

She turned to see a very handsome man walk into the house. "He was fairly tall, well built, and he had long blond hair that reached nearly to his shoulders," she said. "I couldn't think of any man around those parts who wore his hair so long."

Julie started to say something about trespassing, but he just smiled at her. "I will never forget his bright blue eyes," she said. "And the way he lifted one hand as if to indicate that he had come in peace, that he wouldn't hurt me."

The stranger had four thick blankets under one arm, and he set them down on the kitchen table.

For the first time, Julie noticed that he wore hardly anything at all against the cold North Dakota winter weather.

"He had on just a thin white shirt and a pair of blue jeans," Julie said. "I could see that he meant to give us those blankets, so I spoke up and told him, 'You'd better keep a couple of those for yourself, Mister. You'll like to freeze to death in this awful cold.' "

The handsome stranger smiled, and he spoke for the first time. "He spoke in this very unusual, beautiful, rich voice," Julie said. "It was kind of like he was somehow singing and talking at the same time. 'I won't need them, thank you,' he said. 'They are for you.' "

Just before he left, the man took four $20 bills from his shirt pocket and set them on top of the blankets. "A little extra money," he said with a broad smile.

He was almost to the door when he turned to her and said in that same talking/singing voice, "You'll soon be better, Julie. Merry Christmas."

And then he was gone.

"Immediately after he left," Julie said, "I knew that I had just seen an angel. He had come in answer to my prayers. I had asked for some more blankets and 'a little extra money,' and that was just what he had left us."

When Merrie, Steve, and Larry came home from school, Julie told them excitedly that an angel had brought them four new blankets and some money.

"Merrie felt my forehead and said something about how my fever felt so high," Julie said. "She covered me with the new blankets and poured hot tea down my throat until the fever broke."

That night when he came home worn out from work at the elevator, their father listened carefully to Julie's story about the angel who had brought blankets and money. Angel or benevolent neighbor, he knew that the four $20 bills that the man had left would provide just the kind of buffer he needed to catch up on some bills and to be able to provide better for his children.

"Daddy always felt that some nice young man in town or on one of the neighboring farms had learned of our hard times and had taken it upon himself to give us the blankets and the money," Julie said. "Eighty dollars might not seem like much today, but back in those days of depression in the 1930s, it really helped Daddy to start to climb back on his feet."

Julie said that her brothers and older sister always believed that her identification of the stranger as an angel who had heard her prayers for blankets and some money was the correct one. They agreed that there wasn't anyone in town or country or anywhere in the county who resembled their handsome, longhaired benefactor.

"Even then, I was a really good artist," she said, "and I was able to draw a very accurate sketch of the benevolent stranger. We lived in that community for another eight years, and none of us kids ever saw anyone who looked the way he did.

"I will always believe that it was an angel who paid us a visit just before Christmas and helped us to survive that terrible winter. I will believe that until the day I die. And then I know that I will see him again."

*W*e Steigers don't know why we were so surprised when John Fisher told us that he believed in Santa Claus. Perhaps it was because John was fifty-six years old, a graduate of an Ivy League university, and a successful New Hampshire businessman.

John motioned for the waitress to bring a fresh pot of coffee to our booth. "I believe that Santa exists," he said, "because I saw him bring gifts to my sister Ruby and me when I was eight years old."

We were sitting in an all-night restaurant with a man we had known for about five years. We had first met him when he attended one of our lectures in New York City in 1987, and we had become friends through a continued correspondence. He was an intelligent man with a quick wit and a compassionate heart, and he had managed to become extremely successful in his retail business without compromising his strict spiritual ethics.

For years, he had wanted to sponsor us in his hometown, and in 1992, we scheduled a seminar with him for the first weekend in December. It would be our final appearance for the year.

Now, we settled back in the restaurant booth and asked him to tell us about the night that he had seen Santa Claus.

When he was young, John began, his family had been very poor. "Of course, when you're a kid, you really have little concept of whether or not your family is rich or poor," he said. "My father, Stephen Fisher, always managed to have food on the table and made enough as a truck driver to allow us to keep the lights on and the furnace running—although I remember it was always set very low, even during the coldest weather. My mom and Ruby always wore heavy sweaters to keep warm. But when you're three or four, you care very little about social status as long as there is food in your tummy and a roof over your head. It's when you start school that you find out just where you belong on the social pecking order."

Although the onset of the Christmas season always posed a major challenge to Stephen and Alma Fisher, somehow they managed to come up with a few gifts for Santa to place around the tree on Christmas morning.

"I am certain that, compared to the presents that some of the children in better-off families received, our toys would have been considered cheap," John said, "but to Ruby and me, they were wonderful."

When John started school in 1943, World War II had already taken many young fathers from the small town in New Hampshire. Because Stephen Fisher had been born with his right leg considerably shorter than his left, he was not eligible for the draft. "But the fact that so many men had been drafted or had volunteered for the armed forces didn't help Dad find work," John said. "A lot of the storekeepers, wanting to help with the war effort, hired the wives of men who had left home to fight the enemies overseas, thereby contributing to the support of a fighting man's family. There was nothing wrong with this reasoning in principle, but it left Dad with only handy-man type work that paid very little."

In spite of these very difficult times, the Fishers always celebrated Christmas to the fullest extent that their meager budget would allow. And John and his sister would lie in their beds on Christmas Eve, barely able to keep from trembling, as they dreamed about Santa Claus and what he might bring them.

"When I was in first grade, all the kids believed in Santa," John recalled. "We were all true believers who knew that it was Santa Claus who brought all those gifts on Christmas morning. In second grade, the ranks of the believers began to thin, and heretics among us whispered that there was no Santa Claus.

Some insisted on voicing the absurd notion that it was only one's parents who placed those gifts under the tree while the children slept. By third grade, I was one of only a few devout believers who were keeping the faith."

In the summer of 1945, when John was in the third grade, the terrible war ended, and by the holiday season, the stores were filled once again with toys made of metal, rubber, and wood, rather than cardboard, paper, and sawdust. "It was absolutely mind-boggling to walk past the department stores and the dime stores and behold the marvelous array of toys," John said. "I spotted a red fire engine that I wanted so badly that I became dizzy with longing every time I thought of it. Ruby's dolls had always been made of stockings with button eyes, and she had fallen under the spell of a doll that had a realistic ceramic face with bright blue eyes and golden curls that cascaded down over its forehead.

"We wrote out our list to send to Santa at the North Pole; and as convincing as an eight-year-old boy and a five-year-old girl could be, we vowed our belief in the reality of his being and swore that we had been so good that the very angels adored us."

That same afternoon, the angels must have been looking the other way when John got into a fight with his friend Randy Sommers, who had called him a baby for still believing in Santa Claus. Dennis Murray, John's best friend, had to break up the fight and make the two boys shake hands.

"Dennis was an agnostic about Santa," John said. "He still wanted to believe, but I could see in his eyes as we walked home that afternoon that he had doubts."

What John didn't know at that time was that his father had run a red light with his old pickup in his haste to make as many deliveries as possible that day, and the fine levied against him in traffic court had depleted the meager savings that he had set aside to buy Christmas presents. Stephen Fisher had come home that evening, leaned his head on his wife's shoulder, and gave her the sad news. The children would receive no gifts at all that year. How could he face them on Christmas morning?

Alma Fisher wiped the tears from her eyes and told her hard-working, caring husband that they would just have to pray for a miracle that Christmas.

On Christmas Eve, John and Ruby sat quietly on the sofa in front of the Christmas tree.

"We had both noticed that Mom and Dad had acted very strangely during dinner," John said, "and a seed of doubt had entered my mind. I didn't want to spoil things for my little sister, but I had begun to wonder if maybe the kids who teased me about believing in Santa had been right. I began to figure that perhaps the reason that Mom and Dad had been so quiet and kept giving each other weird looks throughout the meal was because they had hidden away all these wonderful toys. They were probably wondering how they were going to get them out of the hiding places and under the tree without our seeing them.

"I decided that I would somehow stay awake that night and see for myself once and for all if Dad and Mom were really the ones who gave us our gifts and if Santa was just a story for little kids."

John recalled how he lay there in the dark after bedtime, listening quietly for any sound that might betray his father or mother getting out of bed and going down the stairs. "It must have been very late when I heard a peculiar kind of humming sound in the living room," he said. "I got out of bed and peered down into the darkness. I gasped out loud when I saw a bright light and a shadowy figure moving around the Christmas tree. I crept down a few more steps, and I saw a really eerie light and shadows literally bouncing around the room. I figured that it had to be Dad with a flashlight."

In the next few moments, John was puzzled when the eerily glowing light seemed to move directly through the wall and exit the house. "I got a glimpse of it outside the living room window before it disappeared," John said. "I thought that somehow Dad must have got outside, but I knew he couldn't stay out there long in his pajamas, for it was really cold. I decided to sit there on the steps until Dad came back inside. I would quietly confront him with my newly gained knowledge of the Santa subterfuge, but I would promise not to spoil things for Ruby."

John sat there for what seemed hours, drawing his bathrobe tight around him to keep warm. "Then I heard Mom and Dad speaking in their bedroom," John said. "Since I was sitting there in the middle of the stairs like a little troll on a bridge, there was no way that either of them could have come up the stairs without passing me. I got up, crossed the hall, and knocked softly on the door to their bedroom."

When he entered, John was astonished to see his father sitting up on the side of the bed, being comforted by his mother. "I had never seen Dad cry before, and I had no idea how to respond," John said. "Then Mom said that Dad was heartbroken because they had no money to buy Ruby and me even the smallest of presents for Christmas. I kind of started to giggle because I thought they were teasing me, keeping up the Santa charade. I had seen someone moving around the Christmas tree in the living room."

Fearing an intruder, his father went to investigate, baseball bat securely in hand. When he clicked on the lights, he gasped in amazement and shouted for everyone to come downstairs. There around the tree was the red fire engine that John had wanted so badly. And next to it was Ruby's doll with the golden curls. And there were other gifts, including some for Mom and Dad.

"In spite of my parents' protests to the contrary, I assumed that they had pulled off an major illusion on behalf of the Santa myth," John said. "But as the days went by with Dad and Mom insisting that they had nothing to do with the gifts, I began to believe that some kind of Christmas miracle had occurred in our humble home."

John's parents believed that Uncle Don and Aunt Jan, who were aware of their financial problems, had crept in with a flashlight and left the gifts so the children wouldn't be disappointed at Christmas. They also suggested their next door neighbors, the Murrays, as possible candidates who might have done such a good deed.

"But for years to come, Uncle Don, Aunt Jan, and the Murrays next door always denied that they had anything to do with it," John said, concluding his story. "So if Mom and Dad, my aunt and uncle, and the Murrays next door had nothing to do with our Christmas miracle, that's why I believe in Santa Claus. The skeptics can stay with the benevolent neighbors or relatives theory, but I long ago understood that what I saw that night was a holy light moving around next to the

Christmas tree. I saw the very spirit of Santa Claus and the very energy of unconditional love manifesting to fulfill two little kids' dreams of a merry Christmas."

*E*ver since he was a little boy, Rick Horton's favorite holiday had always been Christmas, and he gloried in every aspect of the season. Nothing could keep Rick from a joyful celebration of Christmas.

Then, on December 4, 1987, a sudden heart attack at the age of thirty-eight took him from his wife, Melba, his three young children, and his loving parents, Louise and Charles.

In spite of the heavy cloud of grief that hung over the family, his parents decided that they would do everything that they could to make the Christmas holiday season as happy as possible. They knew that Rick would have wanted it that way.

Louise and Charles set about decorating their house, inside and out, just as they had since Rick was a small boy. They made certain that Melba and the grandkids knew that they were to come for a big turkey dinner on Christmas Eve and that they would all go to church as a family on Christmas Day. Everything would be just as it would have been if Rick had not died—for they knew that he was very much with them in spirit.

As Louise and Charles were assembling the miniature manger scene that they had placed on the fireplace mantel ever since Rick was seven, it came to them that they should fashion a small home altar to commemorate the memory of their son. They bought a terrarium to honor Rick's love of plants and nature, and Charles filled a tall purple urn with scented water. Around Rick's picture, they placed a tall red candle in a bright green holder and a number of Christmas-tree ornaments to add the touch of holiday color that he had always loved so much. Just off to the left, they placed a small incense burner in which they burned cones of sandalwood three or four times a day.

Solemnly, just a few days before Christmas, Charles lighted the tall red candle, and Louise placed a Bible on the altar and opened it to the story of the first Christmas as recorded in the Gospel of Matthew. Both of them gave silent prayers toward the same unspoken request: that they be given some sign that Rick's spirit was a happy one.

Louise began to cry softly, then lowered her head against her husband's shoulder.

"Don't cry, Mom," he comforted her, taking one of her hands in his own. "If there is any way between Heaven and earth for Rick to make contact with us, you know that he will find it."

Louise smiled. Charles had tried to tame their son's assertive personality when he was a boy, but he had come to admire Rick's aggressiveness. Their Rick had the knack of knowing how to turn on the charm and push for what he truly believed in, and he had used this talent well through high school, college, and the business world. If only he hadn't been taken from his family when he was so young, when he was just beginning to achieve a high level of personal and professional success.

Brushing back a tear, Charles chuckled softly. "You know, there didn't seem to be anything that Rick couldn't figure out," he said. "Rick had that stubborn streak that made him just keep at things until he was satisfied he knew what they were all about. If there is a way to bring us a message, you know he will."

On Christmas Eve day, Louise was up early to begin preparing a hearty meal for the family. In her mind, she had carefully planned the events of Christmas for the Horton family: Melba and the children would arrive about five o'clock for an early dinner. When they had finished eating, everyone would help clean up and then it would be time to open the presents under the Christmas tree. After the excitement of watching the kids unwrap their gifts, they would all enjoy some tasty glasses of eggnog—with a little something special added for the grown-ups. Then Melba and the grand-kids would stay overnight so they could all attend an early church service the next morning.

Louise was somewhat annoyed when Melba and the grandkids burst into the house an hour earlier than she had mentally scheduled their arrival. Louise knew that she could be an awful perfectionist fussbudget about such matters—especially when she had every-thing worked out in her own mind—but she found herself getting a bit nervous and irritated when she felt as though the evening would not proceed as smoothly as she had visualized. She knew that the grandkids would start snooping around the presents and getting into things they shouldn't. Charles was sitting in the living room reading the evening paper, so she knew he wouldn't be doing much policing of his grandchildren. Melba asked if she could help, but Louise was fussy about finishing things that she had started.

Although she loved Christmas carols as much as anyone, Louise found the music coming from the radio getting on her nerves. Under any other circumstances, she would have enjoyed the familiar holiday melodies, but because of the stress of checking the turkey in the oven, preparing the trimmings for a perfect dinner, keeping an eye on the gifts under the tree, and feeling the pressure of guests—even if they were family—who had arrived an hour early, Louise found herself shouting at her husband: "Charlie, I know it's Christmas Eve, but can we please do without the carols for a little while?"

Charles was puzzled. "I beg your pardon, Mom. What did you say?"

With her nerves frazzled, Louise took his question to signal resistance to her subtle request to shut off the radio. She raised her voice, trying her very best not to sound really nasty: "Please, at least until I finish preparing dinner, please shut off the radio."

Charles stood in the kitchen doorway. "Mom, there's no radio, no television, no phonograph playing Christmas music anywhere in this house," he said quietly.

And then, for the first time, they all began to pay attention to the music that was filtering through the house. It was a lovely, haunting melody, strangely familiar, yet none of them could identify it. Sometimes there would be a chorus of voices with the music; other times, there would be only the lovely orchestral sounds filling the air around them.

"It definitely has a Christmas flavor to it," Melba said. "But it is no hymn or popular holiday song that I know."

Louise, Charles, Melba, and the three children looked everywhere for the source of the beautiful melody. Charles even went outside to see if someone had left a radio or tape player going in a car parked somewhere in the street. But search as they might—downstairs, upstairs, in the basement and attic—they could not locate the source of the wonderful music.

And then they all began to move to the one place that they had, on one level of awareness, been avoiding.

"We began to move toward the altar that Charles and I had prepared to commemorate Rick's passing," Louise said.

Melba began to weep as the entire family, including the children, heard the ethereal, angelic music coming from the Christmas ornaments arranged around Rick's photographs.

"It was a true Christmas miracle," Louise said. "It was as if each of the ornaments was some kind of receiving set for the beautiful, unearthly music that was being broadcast from Heaven."

"Rick always loved Christmas music," Charles said, his eyes misting with tears. "And now he's somehow arranged to send some very special Christmas music to us from the angels on high."

And then, just as suddenly as the music had begun, it stopped.

Louise suddenly had a clear mental image of what was occurring on that most remarkable Christmas Eve.

"The radio," she said. "Rick wants us to turn on the radio. While I was fussing that I wanted a radio off, Rick was trying to get us to turn the radio on."

Charles clicked on the old console model they still kept in the living room. The very first sounds that flowed from the radio were the words from the poignant holiday song that promises that the singer will be home for Christmas.

"We all stood there, tears flowing freely," Louise said. "We all hugged each other, and those of us who knew the words sang along with the radio. We all felt Rick right there in the midst of us, hugging us, and singing along."

Charles smiled, his voice quavering as he spoke: "I told you Rick would find a way to let us know that he was all right. He did it. Rick came home for Christmas."

Louise concluded by saying that she believes that her son gave his family the greatest Christmas gift possible. "His spirit demonstrated the truth of the Christmas promise. He gave his children a proof of life everlasting that will strengthen them all the days of their lives."

*W*henever seventy-three-year-old Lanette Willert tells the story of her Christmas miracle, her voice grows soft and you can see tears begin to well up in the corners of her eyes; for even though it took place many years ago, the memory of that long-ago Christmas remains as fresh in her mind as if it had occurred only yesterday.

When she was a young girl, Lanette's family lived in a small town in Minnesota, far enough north where they seldom had to worry whether or not they would have a white Christmas. She was Lanette Petersen then, and she remembers December 1943 as seeming particularly cold and beset with one blizzard after another.

"I was sixteen that winter and considered myself quite a grown lady," Lanette said. "Because so many of our hometown boys had enlisted to fight the Nazis and the Japanese in the war, I read the paper and listened to the news on the radio so I could take part in conversations with the adults who gathered to discuss current events at the soda fountain and the restaurant. And I never missed going to church every Sunday to pray for all the GIs—and especially our hometown boys—and ask God that they come home safely. Since Christmas was just around the corner, the church was going to have a couple of special programs to remind everyone of the true spirit of Christmas, which was to bring peace to Earth."

Lanette's little brother, Karl, was going to play a piano solo at the Sunday school program. "We were so proud of Karl," she said. "He was only ten years old, but he could really play the piano. He had started lessons when he was seven, and by the time he was eight, folks in town were calling him a little genius. He had played solos at several school band concerts and even a couple of times with the adults at the summer concerts in the park. At the Christmas Sunday school program that December, Karl would first play 'Away in a Manger' as a solo, then the third and fourth graders would assemble around the piano and Karl would accompany their singing of the carol. Of course, being Lutherans, we knew that Martin Luther had written 'Away in a Manger,' so this really had special meaning to us."

Every night Karl would practice, perfecting his talent, improving his skill. In those days, families provided most of their own entertainment in the evenings, and the Petersen family had little Karl on the keys to supplement the radio or phonograph.

"Dad and Mom—Virgil and Dorothy Petersen—would usually read books or magazines in the evenings, and sometimes, after homework, I would listen to some news or comedy shows on the radio," Lanette said, "but Karl provided excellent background music for whatever the family was doing."

For many years afterward, Lanette blamed herself for what occurred late one afternoon as she was walking home from her part-time job at the soda fountain.

"Karl had hung around the store waiting to walk home with me," she said. "Although Mr. Monson had a sign tacked to the magazine rack that warned, 'This isn't the public library. No free reading,' I would let Karl read some comic books if he stayed out of sight in a back booth."

Lanette remembered that it was several degrees below zero and it was already dark when her boyfriend, Robert, suddenly appeared beside them and asked her to go sledding on Martinson's Hill. Lanette replied with great resolve and told him that she was due at home for supper—and besides, she couldn't let Karl walk home alone after he had waited so long for her at the soda fountain.

"Robert was really convincing," Lanette said, "arguing that just a couple of runs down the hill wouldn't take that long. And he played up to Karl, saying that he just knew that my little brother would love to go sledding with the big kids."

Karl was excited by the prospect of joining a group of teenagers on their bobsleds on Martinson's Hill. "We just called them bobsleds," Lanette said. "They were just big sleds that two or three of us kids could sit on at the same time. Martinson's Hill had the advantage of a long slope that seemed to go on forever, and it was fun sledding with the gang. And the fact that it was after dark made it seem all the more exciting."

Lanette insisted that they would join Robert for only a couple of runs down the hill, and the three of them set out for Martinson's Hill on the edge of town.

"I will never forget how the wind seemed to slice right through my parka," Lanette said. "It was crazy to go sledding when it was so cold, but we were Scandinavian-Americans from Minnesota who were supposed to have fun in freezing temperatures, just as our Viking ancestors had romped about on the ice floes above the Arctic Circle."

Lanette kept a scarf over her mouth and nose so that she could breathe without the wind blowing frigid air down her throat, but Karl had neither a scarf nor a parka.

"He had a heavy wool coat and a stocking cap that he pulled down over his ears," she said. "He seemed to be having so much fun, and he wasn't complaining about being cold—so we probably took five or six runs down the hill. But when we finally decided that we had better get home for supper, Karl was shivering. We still had quite a ways to walk from the sledding hill to our home, so his lips seemed almost blue with cold before we walked in the front door."

Two or three nights later, when Karl was practicing his solo for the Christmas pageant, Lanette heard him stop playing to put a hand to his chest and release a series of hoarse, barking coughs.

"Mom was instantly alert to the sounds of any colds or sickness in the Petersen household," Lanette recalled, "so she advised Karl that she would be rubbing his chest with Vicks when he went to bed. Dad set aside his newspaper and asked Karl if he was feeling okay."

Karl nodded and continued playing "Away in a Manger." He admitted that he had a sore throat and a tickle that made him cough. That night, the family was kept awake by the ten-year-old's rasping cough. The next morning, Dorothy insisted that he be taken to Dr. Wayne to have him see to that ugly cough.

"I'm feeling better, Mom," Karl protested. "I'll pick up some cough drops on the way to school."

Seemingly pacified by Karl's apparent improvement, Dorothy let him go to school, but a bleary-eyed Virgil announced in a grumpy tone that he would also pick up some cough medicine at the drugstore so they could all get some sleep that night.

After supper that evening, as Karl was practicing the piano, he began coughing and pressed a hand to his chest. "Mom, I have such a terrible pain here."

Lanette watched her mother rush to Karl and feel his forehead. "Virgil, this boy is burning with fever," she said, her face drawn and anxious. "Call Dr. Wayne."

Those were the days when doctors made house calls—but those were also the days before modern miracle drugs and antibiotics.

Lanette recalled listening outside Karl's bedroom door as Dr. Wayne examined her brother. She will always remember her mother's cry of fear when the doctor cautiously diagnosed pneumonia.

Dr. Wayne did his best to sustain a mother's hope: "Now, Dorothy, the fever, the chills, the sharp pain in the chest indicate pneumonia, but let's be strong and not give in to anxiety. We'll just work hard with Karl and break that congestion right out of him. After all, we can't disappoint his audience at the Sunday school program, can we?"

"For ten days and nights, we all did whatever we could to help Karl get better," Lanette said. "Karl kept saying over and over how he would get well, how he would play 'Away in a Manger' for the pageant. But he insisted that I help him walk downstairs to practice.

The Sunday school program was only a few days away. It just broke my heart to have to tell him that he had to stay in bed."

Once, Lanette recalled, she entered Karl's room to find him moving his fingers on the bed covers as if he were playing the piano. He explained that he could "play" the stripes on the blankets as if they were piano keys.

And then Karl took a sad and pronounced turn for the worst, and he could only lie still in bed, trembling with fever, fighting for every breath of air that he could force into his lungs.

On a cold and awful winter's night just six days before Christmas, Dr. Wayne slowly moved the blankets over Karl's silent face and body. Through Lanette's grief and guilt, she heard the doctor say something about "edema in the lungs" having quieted forever her brother's talent and spirit.

A few nights after the funeral, the Petersen family was seated in the front room at the table, trying their best to appreciate the chicken dinner that Grandmother Sorenson had brought over for their family meal.

"I saw Mom look over at the Christmas tree," Lanette said, "and she began to cry when she saw the gaily wrapped presents that Karl would never open. I guess that's when I remembered that it was Christmas Eve and I felt sad that that holiest of nights would never again be the same for any of us."

Grandma Sorenson managed to get the family around the table, urging them to eat some dinner and try to bring something of the Christmas spirit into their hearts. She had just asked the blessing for the meal when they all heard the first notes come from the piano.

"We were all startled, and we all turned in our chairs to look at the keyboard," Lanette said. "I remember that I felt a shiver run up my spine. Then once again the keys sounded—and we all recognized the opening notes of 'Away in a Manger.' We all heard it as clearly as if Karl were sitting there in front of us, playing the piano."

Virgil Petersen reached out to take his wife's hand firmly in his own. "It's Karl," he said softly, tears moving over his cheeks. "It sounds just as he would play it."

Dorothy lowered her head, not daring to believe. "Is . . . is it possible?"

Once again, the notes sounded from the piano, and Lanette whispered the words of the familiar Christmas hymn: "Away in a manger, no crib for his bed, the little Lord Jesus lay down his sweet head. . . ."

Grandmother Sorenson nodded solemnly. "Our Lord promises that we will all be joined together once again in heaven. The angels are giving us a sign right now, letting our little Karl come to play the piano for us one last time."

"Can it really be Karl?" Dorothy cried out from the depth of her mother's heart.

The notes sounded louder than before, then, once again, very faintly. "Thank the blessed Lord," Lanette heard her mother say, "our little Karl is now playing for the angels in Heaven."

Lanette concluded her Christmas miracle story by saying that after that special Christmas Eve, they never again heard any heavenly notes sounding from the old upright piano. "Even though God had taken our beloved brother at Christmastime, he also granted us all the greatest Christmas gift of all—proof of the survival of the spirit after death. We were all able to lead more spiritual lives after that Christmas Eve because of our certainty that the soul lives on."

Susan Klemp was half asleep when she thought she heard her infant daughter crying. She opened her eyes, looked about the room, and was startled to see that the bed lamp had been turned on and a man was leaning over the cradle.

"My God!" she gasped. Her brain struggled with a hundred different fears.

Her husband, Gus, was on a three-day ice fishing trip with friends. She was alone.

Did the intruder mean to injure little Gretchen?

Why had she let Gus go on that silly trip so close to Christmas? All right, so he was a high school sociology teacher and those few days during Christmas vacation gave him his only chance to indulge in his favorite hobby—but it was only three days until Christmas Eve!

And now there was a burglar in the house.

Then she heard the man singing softly to the infant, "Silent Night," in German, just as Gus liked to do, the way his grandmother had taught him when he was a boy.

Susan got out of bed, forgetting for the moment that she should either be calling the police or getting Gus's revolver out of its hiding place in a dresser drawer.

"Who are you?" she asked the man. He had drawn the hood of his heavy coat over his face so she couldn't distinguish any of his features in the dim light.

"Who are you?" she repeated, trying her best to dismiss all inflections of fear from her voice.

The man raised his head, and Susan was shocked to recognize her husband.

"Oh, Gus, you big lug, why did you come home without telling me?" she asked, tears of relief clouding her eyes.

Susan collapsed on the edge of the bed, nervous laughter releasing her pent-up tensions. "Do you know that you nearly scared the life out of me?" she scolded.

Then she noticed that his coat was soaked and that it was dripping water that smelled strongly of fish and Canadian lake.

"Don't get Gretchen wet with your stinky fish water!" she said sharply. "How did you get so wet?"

Susan walked into the bathroom and got Gus a thick towel.

"You get those wet things off," she told him, "while I go make you some hot coffee. I'm so glad you're home in plenty of time for us to get some last-minute Christmas presents for your brother's family."

As Susan was putting on her robe, she heard Gus once again humming "Silent Night" over Gretchen's cradle. She was just leaving the room when the bed lamp went out.

Susan called for Gus to turn the light back on, but he didn't answer. She fumbled for the light switch for the ceiling light, found it at last, and turned it on.

Gus was gone.

Susan never saw him again.

On the same night that his image had stood over their infant daughter's cradle, singing a Christmas hymn, he had broken through the ice in a faraway Canadian lake. Gus Klemp's body was never recovered, but his spirit had come home to say farewell and to share a Christmas miracle with his wife and baby daughter.

*D*aniel Gomez felt his heart sink to his knees. How could this have happened again, and so close to Christmas? For the third time in six years, he was laid off his job, only this time it looked like the company was going to be permanently out of business.

Each time before, he and several other employees were promised an increase in pay and benefits as soon as the company could reorganize and restructure things. Although it often took longer than expected, each time they called Daniel back to work, his boss reassured him that the problems were being worked out. Since the commitments of a slight increase in salary and a few extra "perks" had been honored, Daniel had no reason to doubt the current solidity of his employer. Things had been going very well for the last several years, with no hint of the impending calamity, when this, the final notification—the dreaded pink slip—came. The timing couldn't have been worse. His wife, Sarah, was pregnant with their third child, and not in good health. For several weeks, she had been experiencing tightness in her chest and was having a difficult time breathing, but she insisted she was probably just suffering from allergies or a winter cold that would soon pass. She refused to go to the doctor, not wanting to add any more bills to their already overstretched budget. With two other children, one seven years old and one four, there never seemed to be an extra dollar left after their monthly expenses were met. But now, when Daniel arrived home, he knew there was no choice but to take Sarah to the doctor—no matter how much she protested.

The second he kissed Sarah hello, Daniel knew that she had a fever and had taken a turn for the worse. There was now an audible wheezing in her chest, so without saying another word, he went to the phone, called the doctor, rounded up seven-year-old Katie and little Jonathan, then returned to the bedroom with a pile of winter snowsuits, coats, hats, boots, and mittens, which he dumped on the floor. As he started to sort out whose coat belonged to whom—he announced to his wife that Dr. Zachariah was waiting for her and he wouldn't take no for an answer. He decided it best not to mention anything about their current employment status, fearing the stress of the news would further aggravate her condition.

It took every ounce of energy Daniel could muster up from deep within him to entertain the children with a positive spirit and remain hopeful while their mama was in the examination room with the doctor. Unfortunately, little Jonathan brought up Santa Claus and what he wanted for Christmas, which was now only three and a half weeks away. Daniel suddenly felt a growing tightness in his own chest as the mere mention of Santa reminded him that he was without a job, so there might not be a Santa this year. Then, as he glanced up, he noticed the doctor approaching with a not-so-pleasant look on his face. Noticing the presence of the children, Dr. Zachariah turned to the reception desk and requested several lollipops and some assistance to watch over the kids while he talked with Mr. Gomez.

"How is she, Doctor . . . do you know anything yet?" Daniel blurted out.

Sensing Daniel's anxiety, Dr. Zachariah tried to tone down the seriousness of Sarah's condition, yet emphasize the importance of medical attention. "Your wife told me you have been trying to get her to come in for the last several weeks, and that she refused, thinking she would be fine. But," he continued, "I can tell you this, if you had not insisted in bringing her now—even another twelve hours might have been too late. She is down getting X rays that I think will confirm my suspicions of pneumonia. It won't be much longer before we know."

The doctor barely finished speaking when he spotted an attendant pushing a wheel chair with Sarah holding an envelope with the X rays on her lap. At that very second, a page calling for Dr. Zachariah was the X ray technician who was relaying his findings to the doctor. It seemed that everything was happening at once. Dr. Zachariah made a motion with his hand that signaled Sarah's being wheeled directly back into the examination room, while he maintained the other arm around Daniel, guiding him to follow along.

Putting the X rays up on the light box, he proclaimed, "Yes, sorry young lady, it will be the hospital for you," he semiscolded, but tempered his words with a wink, adding, "it's a good thing your husband loves you and saw to it to get you in here—in the knick of time. And now we have no time to waste in getting you checked in and started on treatment—immediately! You don't mess around with pneumonia, and it is most definitely what you have." Daniel squeezed Sarah's hand affectionately, kissed it, then attempted to lighten up the moment by teasing her, saying, "See, what did I tell you? You should listen to your hubby!"

With tears in his eyes, he did all he could to hide his desperation. In a moment of near panic, he felt his throat clamp as he swallowed the huge lump that seemed to be welling up from the pit of boiling worries in his stomach, as he realized he didn't even know if they had hospital coverage now—and Sarah didn't even know the other bad news of the day. Still, he managed to assure his wife that the children would be fine and not to worry, the most important thing now was for her to get well.

After the hospital admissions process was started on Sarah, the doctor explained more of the unpleasant details to Daniel. Such a huge percentage of Sarah's lungs was filled with fluid that he was concerned that the baby was not getting enough oxygen. This could mean there was a danger to the life of the unborn baby—as well as to Sarah. Confirming the term of Sarah's pregnancy, Dr. Zachariah added, "We'll do the best we can, now try not to worry too much, and get some rest yourself. You look like you could use some rest, too."

Daniel never remembered a time in his life when he felt such despair. He could barely stammer out the confession to Dr. Zachariah of the other bad news he had received earlier that day. He explained his uncertainty of the insurance coverage as he pleaded that it would not be a factor in getting the best care for his wife and baby.

As compassionate as he could be, Dr. Zachariah pledged that Sarah would be in the finest of care—no matter what the insurance status. "I so hate to bring this up, but no matter how unpleasant, I think it would be advisable that you have a serious talk with your children. As I said before and emphasize again, Sarah

is in grave condition and the children need to understand why she isn't coming home now . . . and even be
prepared if. . . ."

The doctor found it unnecessary to say the rest of
the words, as Daniel's tear-stained face reflected the
anguish of the worst-case scenario as a potential reality.

Daniel took the children home after explaining as
best he could about their mother. As he tucked them
into bed after they were bathed and had eaten an evening snack, he said prayers with them, and then they
all prayed a very special prayer for their mama.

"Daddy, I know God will help mama get better. I
know it, because he told me so when I was saying a prayer
at the hospital," little Jonathan blurted out with complete confidence, as he hugged his daddy goodnight.

"Don't worry, Daddy, she will get all better and be
home for Christmas," he said again, as Daniel turned
off the lights and clicked on the night-light.

Early in the morning, Daniel called the priest at their
church. The whole family was very active in St. Mary's
Parish, and had been for most of the years they had lived
in the Chicago area. He could not keep himself from crying over the phone as he told Father Cassidy about Sarah
and also of being laid off permanently from work.

"Please, Father, will you put Sarah on the prayer
list and do you have time to go see her in the hospital?"
Daniel pleaded.

Father Cassidy prayed with Daniel over the telephone and said he would come to the house right after he visited Sarah in the hospital.

Daniel had already called the hospital to check on Sarah's condition and was attempting to locate a baby-sitter to be with the children while he went to see her. By the time the priest arrived at the house, Daniel had not found anyone, so he was just going to take the children with him and stay as long as he could while they waited in the reception area.

Father Cassidy was very calming and just his presence in the house gave Daniel the courage to face his fears with faith. Telling the priest that he thought he would take the children with him as he was rounding up some books and toys that might occupy them at the hospital, Daniel thanked him profusely for his time and prayers.

Father Cassidy responded by saying there were "things in the works" and soon there might be some more helpful things rounded up as well . . . from the parish. "By tomorrow, I think the good Lord and the good people of St. Mary's will be able to help the Gomez family out just a bit," the father added with a twinkle in his eye and love in his heart.

For nearly two weeks, Sarah remained in very serious condition. She was on a respirator and powerful antibiotics. From all indications, the baby—if it made it—could be brain damaged from the lack of oxygen. The priest had arranged for several ladies of the church to come help with the Gomez children and with chores such as cooking and cleaning, to free Daniel up to be at Sarah's side. The prayer groups at the church were all praying for Sarah and family, even putting them on an international prayer list with a special request for prayer of the pope.

Father Cassidy conducted a special anointing ceremony at Sarah's hospital bedside. A group of dedicated people through the church decided it was important to do a more intensive prayer vigil, and they maintained a "prayer chain" with a volunteer taking an hour at a time, until all twenty-four hours of each and every day were covered with healing and prayer for Sarah, Daniel, and the children. Although there was little or no change in Sarah's health, or that of the unborn baby, during the two weeks, many other miracles began occurring.

Literally, Daniel had gone through what little savings and money he had to buy groceries and pay the bills for that immediate period . . . leaving no money from that point on for any necessities. They were down to the last bar of soap, the cupboards were growing quite bare, and there was not even laundry soap left to wash clothes with. The volunteers grew in number, and many people brought food already prepared in casserole dishes, cookies, and snacks. As the word spread that the shelves in the Gomez family home were about empty, bags of groceries would appear on the doorstep, with nothing but an anonymous note and the ringing of the doorbell to indicate something was there. Money was received in the mail, some checks, some cash—and some anonymous.

This overflow of love and generosity deeply touched Daniel's spirit. He found the weight of the burdens he was carrying get lighter and lighter, until he felt more strength and courage than he ever thought he could have in a whole lifetime. His trust and belief that whatever God had in store for him and for his family would ultimately be for the best to make them stronger, grew.

Faithfully, Daniel spent every moment possible at his wife's side in the hospital. One day, as he went home to shower, grab a bite to eat, and kiss the children, he was greeted by a huge surprise when he returned to the hospital.

He had been gone for only two hours—two hours that showered healing on his beloved wife! Sarah's fever broke like magic, and there she was, sitting up in bed, slightly complaining about how hungry she was and questioning why she was in the hospital.

The entire two, almost three, weeks seemed not to have even occurred. She didn't even know she had been sick! The doctors, nurses, friends, family, and

Father Cassidy were all claiming her sudden healing was absolutely nothing short of a miracle.

Several days later, Sarah was discharged from the hospital, returning to her very ecstatic children and husband. It was still not certain what the outcome would be for the unborn child, but all were hopeful. When first arriving home, Sarah was so amazed that the house was spotless and things were in order that she could hardly contain her excitement. There were more groceries in the pantry and refrigerator than she had ever seen, the children had not even a single toy out of place and had clean clothes in their drawers, there were no piles of dirty clothes in the laundry room, and there were even fresh towels in the bathroom! "How could you possibly do all this while you were working?" she asked in amazement. "I can hardly believe my eyes! Did you get a raise and an early Christmas bonus?

"Oh, shopping for Christmas presents is going to be so much fun! I almost feel good enough to go out right now so we can pick out a real tree and get some more lights so we can decorate inside and out!" Sarah gleefully said, not giving Daniel a chance to respond.

Then suddenly she realized he wasn't responding. Looking into his eyes she could tell something wasn't right.

"Oh, did I spoil the surprise? Wasn't I supposed to know about the raise and the Christmas bonus yet? I'm sorry, sweetie, I am just so happy!" she said while hugging him with a near smothering grip.

Daniel didn't have the heart to tell her. He rationalized that it was more important to keep her in good spirits—which he believed to be an immune-boosting strategy. He would at least give her a few days to get stronger and then he would tell her. Now, he just had to pray the kids didn't say something first. He knew if he told the kids not to . . . that's just when they would slip and say something. He managed to give her a strong hug back and a broad enough smile—along with a twinkle in his eye and a wink that seemed to avert any further questions—and said nothing more, at least, not immediately.

"Oh Mommy, I told Daddy not to worry, that God told me you would get all better. I am sooo happy you are home for Christmas!" Jonathan squealed as he went to hug her around the waist, stopping when he remembered how big she was with child. Then he gently kissed her tummy and said, "I'm happy you are here too, little brother or sister."

Sarah acknowledged his joy while patting him on the head and rubbing his back, then suddenly grabbing his hand and putting it on her tummy. "See, he or she heard you, Jonathan. The baby is kicking, feel."

Sarah turned to Daniel and said, "I really think everything is going to be just wonderful. The baby seems fine!"

Katie's motherly instinct had her fluffing up the pillows as she had just retrieved a blanket and was making a cozy place for Mom to sit on the couch in front of the television. "Can I feel too, Mom?" she gingerly asked, feeling like she might be too big for such things. "Of course, darling, let me just sit down in the perfect little place you have readied for me, and I think you will feel the baby still kicking," Sarah said as she stroked Katie's long pony tail that was topped by a big, fancy red-lace bow. "My, don't you look pretty, Katie! Did you wash and brush your hair all by yourself?"

Daniel balked. "Ummm, well, we had a little help. . . ." he began to stutter, as Sarah quickly caught on and coyly smiled her unspoken acknowledgment that help was okay, too. Daniel held his breath and hoped that the kids wouldn't pick up on that and spill the real extent of it. They didn't. The baby kicking again saved the day, as that became the talk of the eve until bedtime. Katie and Jonathan were guessing and bantering back and forth if it was going to be a girl or a boy and what they wanted as names for either. Sarah and Daniel made the decision to not find out the gender, but looked forward to the surprise.

Soon it was time to tuck the kids into bed, say prayers with them, and then get ready for bed themselves. Both husband and wife decided that it would be wise to go to bed early, as they were both exhausted and the reality about how long Sarah had been gone had finally sunk in.

Daniel was up early the next day, and had the table set for breakfast with pancakes, freshly made and keeping warm in the oven. The smell of hot coffee and sausage and bacon sizzling on the stove, awakened the rest of the family in a hurry.

As Sarah shuffled out to kitchen with her wooly slippers dragging and wrapped in her thick winter robe, she kissed her husband good morning, and said, "Wow, how long do I get to be pampered like this? Did they give you the week off, too?"

Daniel kissed her back as he motioned for her to go ahead and sit down, while he pulled out her chair and asked Katie to pour the orange juice.

Feeling very guilty that all the insinuations were bordering now on lies, he didn't think he was going to be able to wait to tell her the truth. Christmas was only four more days away, and he knew she would want to go right out and do shopping and decorating—even though she realized she was supposed to be taking it easy.

"Honey, there is something I really need to talk with you about," he murmured in a low voice, feeling that all-too-familiar queasy feeling in his stomach again.

Once again, he was saved by a child, this time it wasn't the unborn child's kicks, but little Jonathan knocking over his glass of orange juice. Juice ran all over the table, onto Katie, and spilled down onto Mom's robe. The panic of the cold juice everywhere interrupted the continuing glum thoughts in Daniel's head, and he was most grateful. Something he never thought would happen. He was actually happy that one of the kids had spilled something at the table! He knew he would have to face the truth-telling soon, but for now . . . saved by the mess!

Many hours later, when all were dressed and settled into the newness and excitement of Mom being home and Christmas around the corner, Santa's impending visit was brought up.

"Well, ah . . . Sarah, I really do have some things I have to say to you, and I guess I'd better do it now," Daniel said.

Sensing it wasn't good news by the look on her husband's face, Sarah suggested to Katie that she take Jonathan and go watch television for a little bit while she and Daddy talked—then they would go shopping. Katie took Jonathan by the hand and went into the family room, wanting to please her Mother.

Daniel said a silent prayer as he sat Sarah down on the couch, cushioning her back against several pillows, which he fluffed to support her head and neck. Then, taking her legs, he stretched them out, seated himself at the edge of the couch, and started to remove a slipper and give her a foot rub. "Ooooh, that is just what I need." Sarah groaned with pleasure.

The words came more easily to Daniel after he prayed. It was as though the faith that pulled him through the whole ordeal was stronger than ever now, and he believed that God would give Sarah the strength as well, to face their uncertain future together. At least they had each other, their health back, and two wonderful children and all indications of a third coming soon.

Tears streamed down Sarah's cheeks as Daniel told her the scenario as it unfolded from the beginning; about his job loss, sense of despair, turning to Father Cassidy, and then the miracles that came from God through the church. He told of all the help and gifts they had received, from food to groceries left on the steps to money in the mail to volunteers too numerous to mention, who babysat, cleaned, cooked, and did the laundry.

"I didn't want you to worry and I knew you would, so I thought it would be best not to say anything at all until you were stronger, but . . . well, I just don't feel right with you thinking the opposite . . . a raise, Christmas bonus, and all," he said.

Sarah wiggled her toes out from under Daniel's loving massage and reached over to give him a hug. "Oh, you poor darling," she said softly as tears continued to flow.

No more words were spoken as they remained in the embrace for what seemed an eternity—until the baby kicked and they both laughed out loud.

At that moment the phone rang. Daniel got up to answer it, as the phone was in the other room.

When he returned to the living room, his ear-to-ear smile revealed the call to have been a good one. It was Father Cassidy asking Daniel's permission to give his phone number to a parishioner fairly new to the church. The man had called Father Cassidy because he had heard that Mr. Gomez was highly skilled in a particular area, and he was looking for someone to manage a division of the company he was transferred to the area to oversee. Later that day, more was learned about the potential job, but the interview would not be until the first of the New Year.

The Divine love and mercy they had received through Sarah's miracle healing, and the overflow of love and generosity of the church, overwhelmingly touched them both—at the same instant—as they sat together holding hands. Daniel explained the phone conversation regarding the possible future employment to Sarah. "God has truly blessed us with so much," he said, "let's give a prayer of thanks."

Bowing their heads and still holding hands, they each prayed out loud, then hugged and cried again.

"Surely there are no gifts greater than those we have already received that we could have for Christmas," Sarah said. "But what will we do about gifts for the children?"

"Don't worry about us," Katie shouted, betraying her peeking and listening from just around the corner. "We'll be okay, Mama, we'll still have presents under the tree, you'll see!"

Katie's words were barely out when Jonathan beat her to the couch. "Yeah, you'll see," he added, not really knowing with certainty what was meant by that.

"Come on, kids," Daniel blurted out with an exultant tone in his voice, indicating his inner feeling that things truly would be okay, and happy for the way his family was responding to this crisis now nearly passed. "Come sit down by Mommy and Daddy. Let's have a little family talk," he said as he scooted over, making room on the couch.

He then proceeded to explain the situation in more detail, as much as he felt they were capable of understanding, as Sarah chimed in now and then with an affirmative "We'll get by with God's help."

After another group hug, Katie took Jonathan by the hand as she told Mom and Dad they had some secret things to do for Christmas. Off they went, asking to have, "No peeking."

To this, Daniel and Sarah laughed with the sense that they had done all right so far in raising their kids, if they could be that loving when they were just told there wasn't any money for Christmas gifts. Maybe, though, just maybe, there might be a little after Christmas.

Sarah resisted her motherly concern and instinct to check in on what the kids were up to as she could hear things falling in first one room and then in another, and she knew they were going from room to room and even to the garage, rummaging and getting into who knew what kind of mischief. Knowing their little hearts were filled with good intentions, Sarah controlled the urge to check in on them.

She curled up on the couch with the blanket Katie had brought for her the night before to warm her and fell into a sleepy nap, while Daniel "took care of some things" in another part of the house.

Several hours later, Katie emerged with Jonathan following her, helping to drag and push a large box. They had filled an empty box she found in the garage with "secret" gifts to put under the tree—if and when they had one. Carefully "hiding" the box of goodies in the front hall coat closet, she decreed that it should stay there "until the right time" and requested that nobody peek under the blanket she had spread over the treasures.

Daniel had been in the attic and outside in a storage shed he built to hold the kids' bikes and some yard tools. He came into the living room just after Katie and Jonathan managed to get their Christmas goodies into the closet. Seeing their dad with his arms full of boxes and strands of Christmas lights dangling from his neck and hanging off both his arms, the kids let out a shriek that would have awakened the neighbors, had they been deaf!

"Daddy, Daddy, Daddy!" they squealed. "Yaaaaay . . . Yaaaay . . . can we help?" They all pitched in and strung the lights around the windows, hung decorations, and put up their artificial Christmas tree.

Sarah felt so good that she said if the kids wanted to, maybe the next day they could do some Christmas cookie baking—even as she said it she was hoping they had enough ingredients on hand.

"It would be wonderful if we could say thank you to all the wonderful people who gave so much to our family," she added. "I have an idea of how we can make little gift bags by coloring and decorating paper lunch bags. We'll fill each one with our family Christmas baked goods and tie a big bow on each one. How does that sound?"

Jonathan and Katie were so excited about the prospect of making gifts, they wanted to start right in on decorating the bags, which they did.

For the next two days, the entire family baked special Christmas cookies and decorated gift bags. Never had all four of them enjoyed such closeness and quality time together. They had good talks about many things that deepened the bond between them. Soon they had the most amazing lineup of colorful Christmas bags filled with goodies—each with a special note of thanks and giving off the most divine fragrances of cinnamon, peppermint, and vanilla.

Since it was Christmas Eve, Daniel said he would bring the gifts to the church, where Father Cassidy would make arrangements for delivering them. Sarah was advised not to risk exposing her still sensitive immune system to crowds, so the Gomez family planned their own private Christmas service at home.

When Daniel arrived back home, the family read the Christmas story from the Bible and recounted the supernatural miracle of Sarah's healing and being home for Christmas. Katie pulled out the mystery box from the closet, which was full of the things she and Jonathan had found around the house and wrapped with pictures they had colored so they would have some gifts to put under their tree.

Sarah and Daniel were astonished that not a single word was mentioned about Santa Claus coming that night when the kids were tucked into bed.

Several hours later, as they were brushing their teeth and getting ready for bed themselves, they thought they heard bells ringing outside.

"Did you hear that?" Sarah asked. They listened very intently and all was quiet.

"We must be hearing things," Daniel said, then added, "but I sure thought—"

He hadn't even finished his sentence when they distinctly heard what sounded like loud sleigh bells, and then the doorbell rang. They both ran to the front room and peeked out the window. Not seeing anything, but just to be sure, Daniel opened the front door to behold a huge plastic bag with red and green and stars all over it.

"What in the world is this?" they both said in harmony. Daniel noticed a tag reading: "From Santa to the Gomez family"—so he carried the bag into the living room. It was completely filled with beautifully wrapped gifts, mostly for the kids, but there were several for Sarah and Daniel, too.

As they put the presents under the tree, tears of joy streamed down both their faces. This would be a Christmas they would never forget; one that through the caring and selfless giving of others had enriched their lives and deepened their bonds. They also knew that even if there had not been any gifts at all, the true treasures were found in faith, prayer, and each other. The miracles of this Christmas would last them a lifetime.

*P*rayer can heal and transform a person's life any time of the year, but Delores Baca is convinced that prayers for mercy on the behalf of people in trouble have extra power during the Christmas season—and such prayers might even produce a special Christmas angel that can work a miracle, just as it happened for her.

A mother of three daughters who lives near Anaheim, California, Mrs. Baca had become a faithful member of the church prayer group that had been established by their priest.

"Father Gomez instituted a wonderful home enrichment program," she said. "Those of us who wished could gather in one another's homes in groups and join with like-minded people who felt strength and unity in prayer. I will be forever grateful to God that I was a member of such a group, for just before Christmas in 1994, our prayers miraculously helped to save the life of my oldest daughter, Linda."

One night in December when it was her turn to host and to conduct the prayer circle, Delores had a sudden frightening vision of Linda, who was driving home from college for Christmas vacation.

"Since I knew she would be leaving for home that day from Sacramento, I had been concerned all afternoon about her safety," Delores said. "When the terrible images first appeared in my thoughts, I was fearful that my own anxiety was just creating negative pictures in my mind. But then, I reasoned, I surely did not have to be embarrassed to ask my prayer partners to pray with me for my daughter's safety."

Before she could make the request, however, she received a terrible mental picture of Linda approaching a very dangerous stretch of highway.

"My inner vision seemed to take on a life of its own," Delores said. "It was as if I was watching a motion picture beyond my control."

Then, she remembers, she gasped aloud, hoping with all her mother's love that she was not seeing a true image of what was happening to Linda.

"I saw her car being struck by a large truck at a desolate intersection," she said. "I felt as though I would faint when I saw in my mind's eye Linda's car being nearly demolished by the violent impact."

Several of Delores Baca's prayer partners had noticed her anxious behavior, and they asked what was so troubling to her. Delores rose unsteadily to her feet and in a voice trembling with concern, she asked each of the twelve women assembled in her living room that evening to pray for Linda's safety.

"It was at the very moment that I declared my heartfelt plea for their prayers that the miracle occurred," Delores said. "As I spoke the last word of my request for prayers for Linda, an overpowering spiritual presence seemed to enter the room and envelop everyone in it. I beheld a beautiful angelic figure clothed in gold-and-white light walk through the very midst of our prayer group and command, pray!

"Later, at least eight of the women said that they had also seen the beautiful angel of light, and everyone in the group had heard and heeded the command to pray for Linda as she traveled on the highway," Delores said. "Each of us bowed our head in prayer, and we continued our supplication for about thirty minutes. At that time, we all heard the angel's voice say, 'It is past.'"

Late that evening when Linda arrived home, she told her parents and sisters of the harrowing experience that she had undergone while on the road. She had been crossing an intersection in a rather desolate area of highway when the brakes of a heavily loaded truck failed and sent it speeding unchecked directly at her car.

"It would have struck me broadside," Linda said, shaking her head in bewildered memory of the near-fatal experience. "I should have been history. But somehow my car gave a sudden lurch and literally propelled me out of the truck's path. It almost felt as if my car were some kind of living thing that had the power to jump out of the truck's path. Or, even weirder, it kind of felt as though something just lifted my car out of harm's way."

When Delores informed Linda of her vision of the accident, the combined power of the prayer group, and the manifestation of the angel of light, she was extremely moved.

"That would have been at exactly the time that I was approaching the intersection," Linda verified. She sat for a few moments in complete silence, then she crossed herself and said that she must set out at once for church to light candles and to offer prayers of thanksgiving.

Delores said that the entire family accompanied Linda to the church that night.

"We all felt the need to kneel and give thanks for Linda's deliverance," she said. "I cannot explain why the beautiful heavenly being of light chose to answer my pleas and lend its mighty energy and divine power to our prayer group that night. I have not always lived an exemplary life, but I shall be everlastingly grateful that the angel of the Lord had mercy and overlooked my trespasses and saved my daughter's life. Such a miracle was the most wonderful Christmas gift I have ever received."

On Christmas morning, 1957, Mrs. Oleta A. Martin was straightening up the house for her children, who had arrived the night before with their families for a holiday dinner with all the trimmings. Then, suddenly, a pain near her heart made breathing so difficult that she could not even form words to call for help.

Her youngest daughter saw her agony and ran upstairs to awaken the rest of the late-sleeping family.

Oleta's husband moved her to a sofa, and the entire family stood by, helplessly watching the woman in her excruciating pain. Someone went to call for an ambulance.

Oleta Martin's eyes closed and she said later ("My Proof of Survival," *Fate* magazine, June 1969) that she thought she was dying. She seemed to be floating away, and she lost all sensation of pain and all awareness of her surroundings.

When she stopped floating, she found herself at the edge of a wide chasm. It was so dark beneath her that she could not see the bottom. At first she experienced great fear, then calm, when a bright "spiritual" light appeared on the other side of the abyss.

She could make out the general form of a manlike being in the midst of the light, but the illumination was so brilliant that she couldn't distinguish any part of him from his shoulders up.

To the entity's left stood a dozen or so other beings in long, white garments. They seemed to be telling her not to be afraid, that she could cross the chasm without danger and that they would be waiting for her on the other side.

Oleta Martin remembered that she was eager to join them, but the awareness was heavy upon her that once she crossed that wide chasm she would never return. She thought of how greatly her youngest daughter still needed her and how much she would miss being a part of the rest of the family's individual lives.

The pressure on her chest returned. She gasped for breath and again became aware of the room around her. She opened her eyes wider to see her family's tears of worry and grief change to shouts of joyful surprise when they saw that she had smiled weakly.

Her assembled family members cried out "Mother!" in unison and moved toward her as one, but the paramedics who had arrived with the ambulance held them back with a warning that she had just had a very close call and must not become excited.

After a checkup at the clinic, Mrs. Martin gradually improved her heart condition with rest, medication, and a change of diet. Because of her Christmas miracle, she was given another chance to prepare for a more timely opportunity to cross the great chasm to the other side where the heavenly beings await her.

$\mathcal{M}$ ike McGuire had a wife and six kids to support. He worked as a welder on a city maintenance crew in a large New England city from 6:30 A.M. to 3:30 A.M. and had a part-time job as an attendant at a self-serve gas station from 7:00 P.M. until midnight three nights a week. With six children, ages ranging from two to seventeen, eagerly counting the nights until Christmas Eve, Mike was trying to get as much overtime pay as he could so he could really pile up the presents under the tree. Everyone who knew Mike knew how crazy he was about his kids.

By 3:15 that afternoon, two days before Christmas Eve in 1991, the power-shovel crew had laid the last pipe in place for the day. At 3:30 sharp, the rest of the crew knocked off work for the day, but McGuire did not have to report for work at the gas station that night, so he decided to pick up some overtime by finishing the welding on the seam between the last two pipes in the trench.

"Mike, I'll buy you a beer, man," his best friend Jimmy Wissler told him. "C'mon, it's cold out here. Let's warm up before we head for home."

McGuire grinned at his buddy, Jimmy the bachelor, who never understood about paying dentist bills for braces and buying shoes for six pairs of feet that never seemed to stop outgrowing the new ones you'd bought just three months before.

"I'll take a raincheck, Jimmy," McGuire told him. "This is my last chance for overtime before Christmas. Got to take it, man."

Jimmy shrugged, waved a goodnight, and walked away to leave McGuire to crawl back down into the fourteen-foot trench that housed the new water pipes for a soon-to-open housing district.

"I had just finished my work on the inside seam and was about to begin on the outside of the joint when tons of earth, clay, and stones caved in around and upon me," Mike McGuire said. "I had absolutely no warning of any kind. The damn trench had caved in on me silently and suddenly, as if it had just been waiting to trap me."

McGuire was knocked down in a kneeling position against the big pipe. His nose was crunched up against the plate of his welding mask. For a few moments, he was conscious of searing pain as his right shoulder was pressed against the hot weld he had been making on the pipes. In agony, he tried desperately to squirm away from the burning pipe, but the press of the cave-in held his shoulder fast against the red-hot weld.

"The fact that I had been wearing my welding mask saved my life," he said. "Without the pocket that the mask made around my face, the loose dirt would have covered my nose and mouth—and I would soon have suffocated."

He lay very still, taking stock of his situation.

"I had been covered by a cave-in in a trench in a new housing district where there would probably be little if any traffic. That was definitely a negative," he reasoned in his interior monologue.

"The rest of the crew had gone home—and I was all alone. That was a really big negative.

"My nose hurt like blazes and it was bleeding. I figured it was broken. That was a pretty big negative.

"I had no idea how long I could continue to breathe in this air pocket before I would suffocate. Another negative. A really big negative. There really didn't seem to be any positives at all."

McGuire tried hard not to slip into complete despair, but it seemed that his only chance was that some passersby might have occasion to walk by the trench and notice the cave-in.

But why would they think there was anyone buried in the cave-in? How would they be able to see him?

The terrible realization that there would be no one to come to his rescue began to slice away at the thin mental barrier that had saved him from immediate panic.

"Sure, I knew that my wife Megan would start missing me if I was late for supper," he reasoned, "but it would be hours before she would want to trouble my boss or Jimmy and ask about me. And by then, I could be long suffocated."

Then McGuire realized that his right hand was sticking up through the dirt!

"I could feel the cold air against my open palm and fingers," he said. "Somehow, when the force of the cave-in had struck me, my right shoulder had been pressed against the hot weld and my right arm had been straightened back and above my body, thus allowing my hand to remain above the surface, free to wave like a lonely five-fingered flag. That hand could be my salvation. And the fact that my hand was above the dirt also told me that the cave-in had been very uneven and there wasn't fourteen feet of earth, clay, and stones above me, but only a few feet."

But those were feet of earth heavy enough to prevent McGuire from rising from his kneeling position against the big pipe.

"I had hoped to be able to push the dirt away from my shoulders and stand up," he said. "But there were hundreds of pounds of clay and stones on top of me."

The muscles in his legs were cramping from being forced into a kneeling position, and it was becoming difficult to breathe.

He had been fortunate in having been forced up against the large pipe, thereby creating air pockets near him. But the blood from his broken nose kept dripping into his throat, and he feared that he would soon choke and strangle on it. He was sickened by the thought of drowning in his own blood.

McGuire thought of his wife and his children, and he was startled by the vividness of their images on his mental viewing screen. It truly seemed as if each member of his family had suddenly entered the terrible trench to be with him in his anguish.

"The more I thought about my family, the more I wanted to be with them," he said. "And when I remembered that it was soon Christmas Eve, I was nearly overcome with despair. What a miserable, hellish Christmas present I would be giving my family if I didn't somehow get out of this damn trench. But how was I going to accomplish that miracle?"

Each breath that Mike McGuire took was beginning to feel like molten lava being forced into his nostrils.

Then, the next thing he knew, he seemed to be floating above the trench.

"I figure now that I must have passed out and left my body, but then I thought for certain that I had died," he said. "I could see my hand kind of drooping down over a bit of my wrist sticking out above the dirt. I didn't really seem to care about what had happened to me. That's the way it goes. Tough. Too bad.

"But then I thought of my family—and just like that, I was there in the kitchen of my home and feeling terrible sadness and longing," McGuire continued. "My wife Megan was there peeling potatoes for the evening meal. Katie, my oldest girl, was helping her. I went through the rest of the house and saw each one of the kids. Some were watching television. Others were doing their homework. I wanted to hug them one last time. I wanted them to see me. That's when I felt really sad. I didn't want to leave Megan and the kids. I wanted to live."

McGuire remembered that he seemed to float into the kitchen and that he got right up next to his wife's shoulder. "I tried to scream in her ear that I needed help, but she couldn't hear me. Next, I reached out to touch her—and whether or not it was coincidence, she jerked around with a surprised look on her face. I tried screaming again, 'Call the boss. Call Jimmy Wissler!' But I just couldn't get through to her."

Then McGuire found himself back in his pain-cramped body, gasping for the last breaths of air in the pocket around the pipe. "I knew then that I wasn't dead—yet," he said. "But there was some inner voice that told me that I really had been floating out of my physical body and having a last look at my wife and kids. And that same inner voice was telling me that I could do it again."

But this time, McGuire thought he would try to travel to Jimmy and somehow get his best friend to see or hear him. "Old Bachelor Jimmy would be having a cool one at our buddy Squint's bar. He would be sitting there without a care in the world. I just prayed that he wouldn't be shooting pool or something with the boys and hooting and hollering."

McGuire recalled that he only had to think of his friend and he was there beside him. "I gave thanks to the Almighty that Jimmy was just sitting quietly all alone at a table in the corner. I could see his wrist-watch because he had slipped out of his heavy coat and rolled up the sleeves on his sweatshirt. It was 4:35. I had probably been trapped in the cave-in for about forty-five minutes! I could be taking my last breath any minute."

Mike McGuire said later that as he seemed to float above his friend, he could actually see certain things that he was thinking. "Jimmy's thoughts were kind of all jumbled up, like in a dream. I suppose it was because he was just sitting there relaxing, daydreaming—and maybe that's how I got through to him. It wasn't like Megan, peeling potatoes, concentrating on her cooking . . . listening to Katie tell about her new boyfriend . . . hearing the roar of laughter, shouting, and arguing from the other kids in the other rooms . . . trying to mute out the blare of television commercials and the latest hits on the DJ radio show. When I concentrated on Jimmy and said, 'Hey, man, it's Mike. I need you, buddy. I'm trapped in a cave-in at the trench,' he set down his beer bottle and his eyes opened wide."

Jimmy frowned, then said Mike's name aloud. He got up from the table, walked to the bar, and stared hard at himself in the mirror behind the pyramids of bottles and glasses.

Squint asked him what was wrong. "You look like you're looking at a ghost, man."

"You believe in ESP? Telepathy, that sort of thing?" Jimmy asked the bartender.

"Sure," Squint laughed. "I'm Irish, ain't I? And speaking of the Irish, where's your buddy, McGuire?"

McGuire remembered that he prayed that Jimmy and Squint wouldn't get into any philosophical discussion.

"Oh, dear God," Mike thought with all his mind and spirit, "Forgive me my sins. Send your angels to watch over Megan and the kids if I don't make it. But please get Jimmy over here fast. Dear lord, I'm fading away."

The next thing Mike McGuire knew, strong hands were pulling at him, and as if from very far away, he could hear a lot of excited voices. Above all the noise and confusion, he could hear Jimmy telling everyone to take it easy with him.

"For quite a while there, I was still confused," McGuire said. "I really didn't know if I was still floating around like some ghost, or if I was really back in my physical body. Right away, I was frightened, because I thought that my mind was just playing tricks on me and that I was really dead. Then a wonderful kind of peace came over me, and when I opened my eyes again, I was in the hospital and Megan and all the kids were crowded around the bed."

Jimmy Wissler was there, too. And later, when Mike felt better, his friend told him how he had at first heard Mike's voice inside his head, crying out for help.

"I had really been nervous about leaving you there alone, man, you worrying about getting your overtime pay in time for Christmas," Jimmy said. "And I guess you were really on my mind. For a minute there, I thought it was just my worries playing tricks with me, but then, Mike, I swear I saw a vision of you all covered up with clay and stones in that trench. And then I heard your voice again, asking me to come quick and help you. I'm glad I believe in these kinds of things, because the paramedics and the doctors said that we didn't have a whole lot of time to spare. You were sucking the last drops of air from the pocket around you, buddy."

Megan was extremely upset when she learned of the risk in which her husband had placed himself in order to gain some extra money for Christmas presents.

"You are more important to us than any gift you might put under the Christmas tree could ever be," she told him. "You should know by now that Christmas is about far more than presents. The love you give us is what matters to us."

Mike felt the tears come when all the kids chimed in and thanked God for the Christmas miracle that had saved their father's life.

"And Jimmy was our Christmas angel," Katie McGuire said, giving her father's friend a warm hug. "We'll never forget what you did for us tonight, Jimmy."

Jimmy the Bachelor had to excuse himself to get a tissue to remove the "something" that had gotten into his eye and made it tear up all of a sudden.

*D*uring the mid- to-late 1960s, through an innovative Graduate School Professor Exchange Program offered by the Lutheran School of Theology at Chicago, Sherry Hansen Steiger considered herself fortunate to have taken courses from Dr. Elisabeth Kubler-Ross, who was soon to become internationally famous for her pioneering work with dying patients. While attending Dr. Ross's courses, such as "Church History in Psychoanalytic Perspective" and "On Death and Dying," Sherry quite frequently brought her infant son, Erik, bedding him down on a blanket in the back of the classroom.

Sherry was immediately taken with her professor's research into the death process, for even during her undergraduate work in nursing, she had had the first-hand opportunity to observe that dying patients often experienced an encounter with the supernatural. On those occasions when one of her patients had miraculously "come back to life" after a near-death experience, Sherry had witnessed that their lives seemed transformed by what they had seen on the other side.

During one of her lectures, Dr. Kubler-Ross remarked that in her experiences working with dying children, it seemed as if they always knew in advance when they were going to die. Regretfully, she commented, not many doctors or nurses—or even parents—would pay adequate attention to the messages that dying children gave of their awareness of what was imminent in their lives. Understandably, Dr. Kubler-Ross stated, most of the time everyone involved with the child preferred to think only positively and to focus on the prospect that the child would survive the crisis and live.

Perhaps because in Dr. Kubler-Ross Sherry had an extraordinary teacher—who in later years would become a dear personal friend—she was more attuned to the messages that her son Erik would one day attempt to convey regarding his approaching death. Of course, accepting the reality of existence without her dear son would be an entirely different matter.

The 60s were a time of great personal and social upheaval. A time when religious, moral, political, and individual values and belief systems were torn apart, questioned, and often re-evaluated beyond recognition.

We were a nation in crisis and Chicago was at the very heart of the turmoil. The Lutheran School of Theology was a new multimillion-dollar building, located on the south side of Chicago, and on a street declared the "neutral" zone between two very active rival and warring gangs: the Blackstone Rangers and the Devil's Disciples. LSTC was itself in crisis with unrest and dissention from some of the students regarding more relevant curriculum in dealing with the moral issues of the day, of anti-war protesting and security issues in living in such a dangerous area. LSTC was quite literally under attack, and was considered an ostentatious threat and an affront to most of the surrounding ghetto community.

A myriad of experts, special-task forces, various committees, and cadres who had been called in for problem solving and negotiating failed at their attempts to address the various situations threatening the school, staff, and students. Sherry found she could no longer hold back. Presenting what she considered to be very simple, obvious, and apparently overlooked solutions with her own thoughts and ideas to Seminary officials, Sherry was soon asked to repeat her "plan" to the Graduate School's Board of Directors. Following several additional meetings where she was queried regarding the specifics of how she envisioned such a plan implemented, Sherry was offered a position on the staff of LSTC, where she was asked to carry out the job description she had inadvertently created!

Dealing with such intense social issues and "helping others"—whether it is through the ministry or any other service-oriented job—does not provide in exchange immunity to one's own problems, but in fact can often serve to mask them. Perhaps especially during the tumultuous times in the '60s and '70s, many couples who were so immersed in helping others through the times of crisis would find little time to realize they were in crisis themselves, and Sherry and Paul were one such couple. It is never a planned or desired thing when families drift apart, but after considerable effort at attempting to resurrect a failing marriage, Sherry and Paul agreed to divorce in the mid-'70s.

In 1973, the family had embarked on a new venture to the rocky-mountain-high state of Colorado. An idea they had been working on for a creative "seed ministry" together had been planted and risks were taken to tend to the newly sprouted seeds, but the vision wasn't yet rooted in deep enough to weather the many obstacles and unforeseen storms.

Following a period of separation, it was decided that Sherry and daughter Melissa would remain in Colorado while Paul would eventually accept a call from a small rural church in Ohio. It was Paul's conviction that Erik should be with his father and Melissa with her mother, so after much consideration and debate it was decided how to go about the daunting task of telling the children. They took great care in making certain that both Erik and Melissa knew how much they were both loved by both parents and that this was in no way a result of anything they did, as children so often feel in such situations.

Sherry would decide to relocate to Virginia Beach, Virginia, as it would only be a day's drive back and forth to Ohio, enabling easier and more frequent trips for the kids to stay in close contact. So, Melissa and Mom moved to Virginia Beach, and Erik went with Dad to Ohio.

After only several days, Erik was "acting out" and Paul was calling daily to report problems that Erik was having adjusting to the situation and to seek counsel as to how best to deal with it. Paul thought it best not to let Erik talk to his mom until a little more time passed, in hopes that things might balance out and Erik get more accustomed to a new regiment. But nothing seemed to help and the situation escalated with Erik's distress growing. It was later that month that Erik's mounting trauma would result in hospitalization, where tests would reveal a minor heart problem and stress and anxiety, most likely caused by the separation.

Because of her son's intensely traumatic response to the situation, Sherry cancelled the divorce proceedings on December 1. Although her decision to live separate from her husband remained firm, she agreed to travel to Ohio during the Christmas season to reunite the family for the holiday. Paul had come to realize, albeit painfully, that Erik wanted to be with Sherry, but the burden of losing his entire family during the pressures of Christmas, the busiest season of the year for pastors, was more than he felt capable of managing at that time. Sherry and Melissa left their home in Virginia Beach and drove to the parish in Ohio, where they even became somewhat involved in the church functions, as Sherry loved the warm, friendly country spirit of the parishioners.

Sherry later remembered that it was at Erik's school Christmas pageant that she received an almost unbearable glimpse into the future. As she proudly watched her son singing Christmas carols on the auditorium stage, Erik's red hair appeared to have an extra-shiny gleam and the stage lights seemed to capture every freckle on the face that she loved so much. His whole manner seemed to exude an extra-joyful spirit, and he appeared to be ablaze with the excitement of Christmas and the knowledge that his mommy and little sister were back in his life again.

Although Sherry sat with Melissa on her lap in seats that were midway toward the back of the large auditorium, she sensed a strange feeling of oneness with her son. While the class was singing "The Little Drummer Boy," Erik's favorite Christmas carol, a terrible uneasiness crept up to seize her solar plexus and her throat. The next selection of the children's chorus, "Away in a Manger," forced her eyes to well up with tears.

As the children sang the words "no crib for his bed," a surreal scene was frozen in a stopgap of time in Sherry's mind. She will remember it always as if a camera lens had focused in for a close-up, and then captured the image in a freeze-frame. And then a voice from out of nowhere said ever so clearly to Sherry: "This is the last Christmas you'll see your son."

"It was as though I had been struck a cruel and vicious blow to my stomach," Sherry said. "The psychic pain was so overwhelming that it was little Melissa who jolted me back into reality."

Melissa was actually shaking her and asking if she was all right. "Why are you crying, Mommy?" she wanted to know. "Isn't this a happy time?"

Suddenly aware that she was weeping, Sherry wiped her tears away and tried to regain her composure. "Yes, sweetie, yes, it is a time to be happy," she told Melissa. "I guess Mommy was just crying tears of joy."

Although the terrifying freeze-frame image of Erik and the awful message still pierced her heart, Sherry saw that Melissa was comforted by her explanation.

The remainder of that evening proceeded as normal—except for the memory of the troubling vision that haunted Sherry and forced her again and again to attempt to understand its exact meaning.

Then came the special midweek children's Christmas service at the church where Paul served as pastor.

"The church was packed," Sherry recalled. "It was customary for all the children of the congregation to gather at the steps near the altar, while the pastor gave a sermon just for them."

Children from under two years to ten were all excitedly sitting on the steps, listening to the pastor deliver a Christmas message structured to teach them the true meaning of the holiday. It was baby Jesus' birthday, and the pastor pointed to the manger scene under the decorated tree.

After the brief sermon, Pastor Paul posed a question for the gathered children. "What gift would you give the baby Jesus?" he asked, going on to create a colorful scenario. "Since it is baby Jesus' birthday, let's pretend that you are invited to his birthday party and you can take him any gift you wanted to. What gift would you bring him?"

Pausing to emphasize the seriousness of the query, the pastor said, "I want you to really think about it. Then, when you are ready, I want you to tell everyone here tonight what your gift would be."

It took only a few seconds for the children, one by one, to seem satisfied that they had selected the perfect gift for the baby Jesus. A little boy offered his toy fire engine. A girl was willing to give up her favorite doll. Another little girl said that she would give baby Jesus her very favorite cuddly teddy bear, the one that went with her everywhere.

Sherry could almost hear the wheels turning in Melissa's head as she thought about her own birthday, which was just days away. Melissa was nearly born on Christmas Day herself. She would be four years old on the day after Christmas, December 26. "I'd give baby Jesus my love," she said emphatically.

"I was very touched by Melissa's response," Sherry said, "and I smiled back at those members of the congregation who turned to me with warm smiles, silently bespeaking, 'Oh, how sweet, how precious.' "

Then came Erik's turn. "He was not a shy boy," Sherry said, recalling the scene of that long-ago Christmas service. "Erik had something of an impish element to him. He liked to tease and play. In a situation such as this, he might be embarrassed and say something cute or silly to make people laugh."

But Sherry noticed how serious Erik was as his father, Pastor Paul, prompted him, "Erik, what would you give baby Jesus?"

Looking directly at the image of the baby Jesus in the manger, Erik turned and spoke boldly and with conviction: "I'd give him my soul!"

"The tears in my eyes welled instantly to overflowing," Sherry said. "I choked back a gasp as I could not help being reminded of the 'freeze-frame' incident days earlier and the horrible message that had come with it that this would be the last Christmas that I would see my son. No! rang through my head so loudly that I was certain others could hear it."

Sherry stated that she has no memory of what took place between Erik's declaring the gift of his very soul to baby Jesus and the final blessing of the pastor at the end of the service.

"I stood there, shaking hands with members of the congregation in an altered state of consciousness," she said. "I was stuck somewhere among my thoughts and the terrible confusion that I felt."

So many strange little things occurred in the days that followed. And some of them were harbingers of the awful events that lay ahead.

"Paul took the kids in his van to pick up a baby-sitter and the driver's door kept flying open as he drove down the snow-and-ice packed country road," Sherry said. "When they returned, Erik came bolting in the front door, laughing and declaring how much fun it had been to be in the van when it spun around and around on the ice. To his child's mind, to spin on the ice wasn't dangerous; it was like an amusement park ride. As he described the door opening and the van spinning in circles on the ice-packed road, I felt my face go white."

On the next two mornings, totally out of character, Erik arose first and knelt at his mommy's bedside. "Erik was one who didn't like to get up in the morning," Sherry said, "so I was shocked to see him kneeling there and staring at me. When I asked him if something was wrong, he answered, 'Nothing's wrong, Mommy. I just love you so very much, that's all.'"

Sherry awakened to see Erik kneeling at her bedside for the third morning in a row. Once again, he assured her that nothing was wrong. She slipped back asleep, but a little while later, Erik once again came back into the room and told her that he had a present for her.

"He took me by the hand and led me into the playroom where he had assembled a puzzle that pictured a single white horse grazing in a beautiful green meadow," Sherry said. "I hugged him and gave him a kiss, and he solemnly informed me that the puzzle could not be disassembled and put away. It was a present for me."

With so many other things on her mind, Sherry agreed to Erik's request. It seemed very strange to her that he had taken such great pride in the accomplishment of having pieced this particular puzzle together.

From the time he was very small, he had always been the greatest of puzzle solvers and assemblers. This was a very simple fifty-or-so piece puzzle, the kind that he had put together effortlessly when he was three or four years old.

But she had more pressing matters to consider. It was now time to get ready for church on Christmas Sunday—and the weather was formidable. It was sleeting, snowing, and blowing, and extremely cold.

Paul had left for church quite some time earlier, and there had already been three or four phone calls from concerned parishioners warning Sherry not to venture out on such bad roads. Pastor Hansen's house was out in the country, and it was about a twenty-minute drive to church.

"Don't you feel that you have to come out because it's Christmas Sunday or because of Pastor Paul or any other reason," one earnest lady had told her over the telephone. "The roads are terrible and dangerous. There are warnings for folks to stay inside. All of the other churches in the entire surrounding area are closed. Pastor insists that he will hold services for whoever wants to make it out since he's already there. But we don't want anything to happen to you and the kids. Just stay in and be safe."

Sherry felt pleased with the sincere expressions of concern, but since she and the kids were all ready, she decided that they might as well go—carefully—to church.

"Not until I was in the garage trying to open the door to my Fiat convertible did I realize how really bad the weather was," Sherry said. "My car had been in the shop getting a new top, and this was the first time I had gone out to drive since I brought it back from the garage. The doors wouldn't open. They were frozen shut."

Sherry tried a hammer and boiling water. Nothing would budge those doors.

After about twenty minutes of failed efforts, Erik said, "Good, Mom. Let's just go in and build a fire and you can read us a story."

That sounded like the perfect plan to Sherry. But Melissa wasn't satisfied with it. "No, let's go to church," she yelled. "We can take the jeep."

Sherry walked over to the jeep that had been loaned to Pastor Paul by some parishioners. She said that she had never driven such a vehicle, and she would have no idea where the keys were kept.

"Daddy always leaves the keys in the ignition," Melissa said.

Sure enough, they were there.

Sherry turned the keys in the ignition but got no response from the engine. After a second and third attempt, she concluded that trying to start the jeep was a waste of time. "Okay, kids," she said, "let's go into the house and build a fire."

For some reason, such a pronouncement made Melissa start to cry and insist that she wanted to go to church.

"I suspected that the reason behind Melissa's youthful dedication to church was a normal desire to play with other children her own age in the nursery," Sherry said, "but I gave the jeep one more try. This time it started."

As she looked over at her two children, half-crouched and half-standing on the passenger side's bucket seat, for the first time the flimsy structure of the loaned jeep became apparent to her. It was really more or less a customized vehicle that had been hand-built from an army surplus kit. And it didn't even have seatbelts.

"After all the attempts to open my car door and to start the homemade jeep, it occurred to me that we would end up being late for services anyway," Sherry said, "but I started out very carefully on the hazardous country road. The maximum speed that I would dare drive was about fifteen to twenty-five miles an hour. But I thought that even if we arrived for only the last fifteen minutes of church, at least we would have been there."

When they were about halfway to the church, the passenger door of the jeep flew open. Since they were traveling at a slow speed, Sherry came to a near stop and Erik pulled the door shut. But it came open again and again.

"That does it," Sherry exclaimed. "We are definitely not taking this back home."

When they finally arrived at the church, they went to one of the back pews and quietly sat down. The service had been late to start, granting a little extra time for those who chose to brave the bad weather.

"Erik and Melissa seemed amazingly loving with one another during the service," Sherry remembered. "Once I turned just in time to watch Erik remove his cherished Native American Star necklace and silently place it around his sister's neck. He was never without that necklace. It was his most treasured possession. And now, with a kiss on her cheek, he had bestowed it upon Melissa. In turn, Melissa removed her beloved linked chain with the 'fish that wiggled' and placed it around Erik's neck, positioning the little fish just so."

Sherry felt a strange reaction to the sweet scene of sibling affection. "My kids had performed what seemed to be a sacred act, vowing to one another their love," she said, "yet I felt a rush of panic similar to the ones that I had felt at the school auditorium, at the children's Sunday school Christmas service, upon hearing about the van spinning on the ice, and upon viewing Erik's gift of the white horse puzzle."

She had always been one to pay heed to signs seemingly sent by a higher power to communicate assistance and to ward off danger. Many times her premonitions had saved the very lives of her family and friends. She suddenly felt guilty, wondering if she had acted irresponsibly by not staying home in the safety of a warm farmhouse.

Sherry was mouthing the final liturgy of the service when she received a strong mental and physical picture of the jeep's door flying open on its own. A firm conviction took hold of her. She would not drive the jeep home.

During the customary shaking of hands with the congregants at the door, Sherry made her appeal to Paul. She told him that she had to take the jeep since the doors on her car were frozen shut. The jeep had no seatbelts, and its passenger door had kept flying open all the way to church, endangering the lives of the kids, who had to sit huddled next to her to keep from falling out.

"I am not taking it home," Sherry said firmly. "I have a bad feeling about it. I'll leave it in the church parking lot and someone can pick it up later."

Paul seemed to ignore her, concentrating on greeting the parishioners. When he did answer her, he completely astonished her by stating that she would have to get permission from the family who owned the jeep to leave it in the church parking lot.

As if trapped in some incredible drama of the absurd, Sherry spent the next ten minutes pleading with the individual members of the "jeep family" for permission to leave their makeshift vehicle in the parking lot so she and her children could ride home with Pastor Paul. Incredibly, they were all unwilling to grant her this favor. They had plans so none of them could drive their vehicle to their home, and they adamantly refused to allow it to sit unattended in the parking lot.

Then Paul told her that he could not take her and the kids with him in the van, because he had promised to take some of the elderly home, and then he had to return to the church for those who wished to sing Christmas carols.

With a growing sense of mounting doom, Sherry could no longer hold back tears of frustration. Speaking as firmly as her ebbing strength permitted, she said to Paul, "I feel so strongly about this. I insist that the children go with you. If I have to take the jeep without any seatbelts and a door that won't stay shut, fine. But Melissa and Erik are not going to be in it with me."

At last, with obvious irritation, Pastor Paul agreed. He locked the church doors as Sherry made certain that Erik and Melissa were in the van.

As Paul hurriedly raced toward the van, Sherry rolled down the window of the jeep and asked that they stay close together because the weather was so bad. "I'll follow you," she said. "Keep watching for me out your back window."

He nodded agreement and climbed into the van, slamming the door behind him.

Sherry saw that the weather had become even worse. Visibility seemed zero as it continued to snow.

The van pulled to the edge of the parking lot, then suddenly and abruptly came to a halt. Shocked, Sherry saw Erik getting out. Then he was crying and running toward her.

"Erik!" she screamed, rolling down the window once again. "Get back in the van. What on earth are you doing?"

As she watched in disbelief, she saw the van pull out of the parking lot and turn right, leaving Erik behind with her. "No, no, no!" she screamed again and again.

When Erik crawled into the jeep, he was still crying. "What happened, honey?" Sherry asked. "Don't you know that you were supposed to ride with Dad?"

Erik shook his head. "I want to be with you, Mom. I want to be with you."

It was now more than apparent that Paul was not returning with the van to pick up Erik. Sherry got out to check the doors of the church, hoping to find one unlocked. If need be, she and Erik would stay there until Paul returned for the caroling. But no doors had been left open and there was no one in sight.

As Sherry surveyed the grim situation, she came to the inevitable realization that she had no choice other than to embark in the makeshift jeep with Erik.

"Sweetie," she told him, "sit as close to Mommy as possible. Hold on to the back of my seat or to me, just in case the door opens up again. And push down on the lock. Maybe that will help keep the door closed."

The road was slicker than ever and the visibility was almost zero. Sherry could drive only about ten to fifteen miles per hour.

The silence of her concentration on her driving was suddenly broken by what seemed to be a strong mental message coming from Erik: "It's okay, Mom. I love you." She wasn't sure if he didn't actually say it out loud.

At that very instant the jeep hit a bump and began to skid. First they slid to one side of the road, then back to the other. Then something seemed to catch at the right side of the jeep—and it flipped over in the snow.

"I was unable to open the door on the driver's side, so I rolled down the window and climbed out," Sherry said. "I called out Erik's name as I brushed the snow from my long skirt and sweater. Because we had been going so slow, it never dawned on me that he could be injured."

When she received no response from her son, she looked around and saw only the spinning wheels of the jeep, the snow, and the empty fields.

As she walked around to the other side of the vehicle, Sherry half-expected her pixie son to be playing a trick on her. Maybe he was hiding, and he was about to jump out and say, "Boo!"

But still there was no Erik. "I called out his name several times, but heard no answer," Sherry said. "By now I was becoming worried that something must be very wrong."

Then she saw Erik's little feet trapped under the mass of steel. "No!" she cried in a mother's deepest anguish.

Desperately she tried to lift the jeep while trying at the same time to call to her son. "Erik, can you hear me?" she screamed as she tried to move the jeep. Erik made no reply.

Again and again she attempted to lift the jeep off her beloved only son. For years she had read stories in which people under duress had accomplished such a miraculous feat, regardless of how impossible it may have seemed. For even more years, Sherry had worked at her faith. The words of Jesus raced through her mind and mouth: "If you just believe, you shall be healed . . . Nothing is impossible unto you if you so believe!"

She directed every exertion of life energy from every cell of her body and mind into each attempt to lift the jeep and free Erik. She knew that her faith was strong and she did believe.

But no matter how much she strained and pushed and tried, she could budge the jeep by only a few inches. She needed somehow to roll the vehicle over and off her son in order to pull him out. She tried desperately again and again. But she could not do it.

At last a truck that was passing by stopped to assist her. Inside the cab were three stocky men, one of whom was a member of Pastor Paul's church and an off-duty ambulance driver. The men had a CB unit in the truck, so they radioed for an ambulance, then proceeded to set about righting the jeep, shouting at Sherry to pull her son out from under the vehicle as they held it off his body.

In horror Sherry looked at Erik, who appeared not to be breathing. Her nurse's training told her that he should not be moved. "Just roll the jeep off him," she shouted at the men. "He shouldn't be moved until medical help arrives."

Although she shouted the same demand over and over, each time the men retorted, "Just do it! Pull him out, for God's sake!"

Mired once again in a feeling of helplessness, Sherry did as they ordered and pulled Erik out from under the jeep. As soon as he was free, she knelt beside him and placed her coat around his body. She cradled his head in her lap. When she saw the bubbles coming out of his nose, she knew his lungs were damaged.

Completely immersed in grief and despair, Sherry hardly noticed that the ambulance had finally arrived—forty-five minutes after it had been called. The drivers had gotten lost.

Once the paramedics were on the scene, though, they sprang into action. Sherry was dimly aware of shouts of confusion all around her, and she barely perceived that Paul's van was now present. Then she realized that the paramedics had put her on a stretcher and were monitoring her because they had been informed that she had a hole in her heart from a prior condition, and they feared the effects of the stress of the accident could provoke a cardiac incident. Erik was on the stretcher beside her in the ambulance.

Sherry remembered that she kept telling the personnel in the hospital emergency room to leave her alone and to give all their attention to Erik. "I was hooked up to all kinds of equipment, and I prayed aloud, 'Oh, God, please take me and spare my son. Please, please, please! Take me, not Erik!' "

A Catholic priest, a friend of Pastor Paul's, tried to calm her. "You don't know what you're saying," he said. "You can't bargain with God. Only God knows if it is Erik's time and He is calling him home. That is not your decision. It is the Lord's."

Sherry recalled that at that moment she felt very much betrayed by any higher power. "I was suffused only with the desire to sacrifice my life for that of my only son," she said. "I continued to wail in anguish, and I didn't care who heard me."

And then all at once, Sherry was completely silent. There was Erik standing at her bedside. She reached out and took his hand, and her cries of grief gave way to a smile. "Erik," she asked him, "what are you doing up? Are you all right?"

Erik smiled and squeezed her hand. "I'm all right, Mommy. I'm okay. I love you very much, Mommy."

Sherry was distracted by the priest at her side asking her what she was seeing.

"It's Erik," she laughed. "He's all right."

And then the image of her son was gone, and Sherry shrunk back in terror as she saw several doctors and a nurse trailed by Paul burst into the room. She saw the nurse fill another hypodermic needle, and she screamed out, "I don't want another shot! I don't want another—"

Sherry's trailing protest was met with the most dreaded words a mother can ever hear: "I'm sorry. We tried everything. We lost him. He's gone."

The physician had said the awful words as tenderly and as gently as possible, but Sherry would not accept the pronouncement. "No, it can't be. Erik was just here. He told me that he was all right . . . and that he loved me," she told the doctor and the others in the room.

The priest finally broke the silence that had fallen on the hospital room. He squeezed both of Sherry's hands, even more firmly than before. "You are truly blessed to have had Erik appear to you so vividly with such a confirmation," he said. "Erik came to tell you that he is all right. He's with the Lord now, and he is truly at peace. God's will be done."

Since that Christmas Day many years ago, Sherry has often reflected upon the sorrowful episode. "Why, during that last week of his life, did I not take to heart the omens that Erik had been giving me?" she has wondered. "Why could I not perceive the clues that he had been offering, that his time with me, as well as his gift of life, were coming to a close? Was Dr. Kubler-Ross correct about children knowing that they were about to die and that God was calling them home? I can see clearly now that Erik's soul was aware of another calling, one with which he seemed to be at peace."

Sherry has also pondered the meaning of the white horse in the puzzle that Erik was so insistent should have meaning for her. Because she is of Chippewa heritage, as well as French and Swedish, and because she has spent a good deal of time with Native American shamans, Sherry was aware that for many Native American tribes, a vision of a white horse represents Death coming to accompany the spirit to the land of the grandparents. Since his earliest childhood, Erik was enthralled with so many of the mythological aspects of the native tribes, and he was buried with his cherished star necklace, put back on his chest by his sister and his mom. A white horse may also symbolize magic powers, and the enchanted animal may serve as a warrior's ally in transcending the trials and tribulations of Earth.

It is said that the most grievous loss to endure is that of losing a child. "Although the pain never entirely goes away, it brings with it a sort of mystical link to every mother or father who has ever lost a child—under any circumstances—to unfair and untimely death. Since it was Christmas Eve when Erik was buried, how could I not think of the meaning of Christmas of Jesus' birth, and the suffering that not only he would go through, but the suffering and agony of his mother, the Blessed Mother. She too, long before I would lose Erik, would have to endure and accept the death of her beloved son. And so too have many, many mothers and fathers lost their young ones at an all-too-early age, throughout the history of life on earth," Sherry said.

Sherry Hansen Steiger has long been at peace with her son's death, and she has come to realize that she gained a much deeper meaning, design, and purpose to life because of the pain of her loss. She holds dear a poem that Erik gave her just before he died, and she regards it as her son's awareness of the transitory nature of life and his ability to see the act of physical death as being merely the changing of one life form to another. Here is that poem:

> The caterpillar, brown and furry,
> Caterpillar, in a hurry,
> Take your walk
> To the shady leaf or stalk.
> May no toad spy you.
> May the little birds pass you by . . .
> To live again . . .
> a Butterfly.
>   Love, Erik

The biggest lesson that Sherry learned to pass on to others and to apply in her own life is that at any given instant of any given day, our loved ones may be taken from us—or we from them. Knowing this, it seems that the most important thing we could ever do in life would be to live each moment completely with love and fullness, as if it were our very last to be with our loved ones.

If each morning when we awakened we considered the possibility that this might be the last day that we would see our husband or wife, our son or daughter, our mother or father, our sister or brother, how completely that would change how we would respond to them or interact with them. And that, Sherry believes, is the real message of Jesus and the most important message of all faiths and religions: To live each moment in love and caring, selflessly and unconditionally.

What greater Christmas miracle could a mother receive from her son?

On the one hand this Christmas miracle may not seem like a miracle at all, with the death of a very young, vital, and loving boy who will never again see another first snowfall, another tree being trimmed with sparkling, magical lights of another Christmas. Yet on the other hand, in reality not every miracle brings with it what we call a "happy ending."

We include this story not to make you sad, but to remind you that while we rejoice in relating those miracles that accomplish acts of healing, happiness, and wholeness of body, mind, and spirit, in our other stories there is a deeper point we wish to make. Perhaps those miracles that often serve to bring about greater awareness, understanding, insight, and compassion, may not always have warm fuzzy endings. Often we can see the furthest at night. When it is dark and we look into the heavens above us, we can see millions and billions of miles away. On the clearest of days, however, we cannot see further than one mile, if we stand on the ground. So too, it is often through the most painful experiences in life that we are drawn closer to God.

The process of sorting through the pain and breaking free into a greater understanding and spiritual depth necessitates a vulnerability to experience the pain and the grace to know there may be a higher purpose and much more—a divine plan of God's Wisdom at work. It might not be our desired plan—it might not be what we would wish for. It might not have the kind of ending that we ourselves would write—if we could—or plan—if we could. But God is a far better author than we could ever hope to be. It only takes looking at the beauty and rhythm of nature surrounding us on earth, and then viewing the vast, complex infinite beauty, order, and design in the heavens above to realize that The Master of Miracles, our Creator, has done an awesome job in creating the universe and is so much more than a genie in a magic lamp, ready to obey our every wish and command for our human, earthly desires. It might be that we don't know best after all. While we may never completely grasp the greater purpose or divine plan for the way things sometimes unfold and turn out in our individual "life dramas," by having faith and trusting that God does we might draw to ourselves an even greater miracle!

About the Authors

BRAD STEIGER is the author/coauthor of over 100 books with millions of copies in print, covering such diverse subject matter as biographies, true crime, and the paranormal. A former high school/college English and creative writing teacher, Brad's early success as a published author launched him into writing full-time and professionally since 1963. In 1978, Brad's book *Valentino* was made into a motion picture by British film director Ken Russell, starring Rudolf Nureyev. Later that same year, Brad co-scripted the documentary film *Unknown Powers*, winner of the Film Advisory Board's *Award of Excellence* in 1978. Brad is considered one of the leading experts in the field of metaphysics and the paranormal. Among Brad's honors: Metaphysical Writer of the Year, Hypnosis Hall of Fame and Lifetime Achievement Award.

SHERRY HANSEN STEIGER, author/coauthor of twenty-nine books has an extensive background as diverse and varied as a writer, creative director for national advertising agencies, magazine editor, producer, model, and actress to studying the healing arts and theology—traditional and alternative. A former teacher, counselor, and an ordained minister, Sherry co-created and produced the highly acclaimed

Celebrate Life multi-awareness program performed around the country for colleges, businesses, and churches, from the mid-1960s on, and established one of the earliest non-profit schools with new approaches to healing body, mind and spirit—*The Butterfly Center for Transformation*.   Among her honors: International Woman of the Year from Cambridge, and Five Hundred Leaders of Influence-Twentieth Century Achievement Award, on permanent display in the U.S. Library of Congress.

Brad and Sherry have been featured in twenty-two episodes of the popular television series, *Could It Be A Miracle*.   Together their television appearances and specials include: *The Joan Rivers Show, Entertainment Tonight,* HBO, *Inside Edition, Hard Copy, Hollywood Insider,* USA network, The Arts and Entertainment (A & E) Channel, and The Learning Channel, among others. The Steigers write a monthly angel column for Beliefnet.com and are frequent guests on international radio talk shows.

Visit the Steigers' Web site at
www.bradandsherry.com.